Jesus and the Future

Jesus and the Future

Unresolved Questions for Understanding and Faith

Richard H. Hiers

John Knox Press
ATLANTA

Acknowledgment is made for permission to quote from the following copyrighted sources:

Abingdon Press, for *The Principles of Christian Ethics* by A. C. Knudson, © 1943.

E.P. Dutton Co. for *The Mission and Message of Jesus* by H.D.A. Major, T.W. Manson, and C.J. Wright, © 1938.

Fortress Press for *Jesus in Contemporary Research* by Gustav Aulén, © 1976; and *Jesus and the Language of the Kingdom* by Norman Perrin, © 1976.

Harper & Row, Publishers, for *Rediscovering the Teaching of Jesus* by Norman & Perrin, © 1967; *The Ethic of Jesus in the Teaching of the Church* by John Knox, © 1961; and *Jesus and the Origins of Christianity* by Maurice Goguel, © 1960.

Journal of Biblical Literature for "Not the Season for Figs" by R.H. Hiers, *JBL* 87 (1968) 394–400; used by permission.

The Lutterworth Press, Guildford and London, for *The Kingdom of God and the Son of Man* by Rudolf Otto, © 1951.

Macmillan Publishing Co. for *The Historian and the Believer* by Van A. Harvey, copyright © 1966 by Van A. Harvey; *The Ethical Teaching of Jesus* by E.F. Scott, copyright 1924 by Macmillan Publishing Co., Inc., renewed 1952 by Ernest F. Scott; and *The Mystery of the Kingdom of God* by Albert Schweitzer, copyright Macmillan, 1950 (English language rights exclusive of the U.S.A. by permission of Adam and Charles Black, Ltd., London).

J.C.B. Mohr, Tübingen, for *Geschichte der Leben-Jesu-Forschung* by Albert Schweitzer, copyright 1906, 1913, 1929, 1951.

Oxford University Press for *The Apocrypha and Pseudepigrapha* by R.H. Charles, copyright 1913.

Charles Scribner's Sons for *Jesus Christ and Mythology* by Rudolf Bultmann, © 1958; *The Irony of American History* by Reinhold Niebuhr, © 1952; *The Parables of the Kingdom* by C.H. Dodd, © 1961; and *Christian Ethics and Moral Philosophy* by George F. Thomas, © 1955.

Sheed & Ward for *The Church* by Hans Küng, copyright 1967.

Walter de Gruyter & Co., Berlin, for "Zum Verständnis der Gottesherrschaft" in *Zeitschrift für die neutestamentliche Wissenschaft* by Erich Grässer, vol. 65 (1974), pages 3–26.

The Westminster Press for *Eating and Drinking with Jesus: An Ethical and Biblical Inquiry* by Arthur C. Cochrane. Copyright © 1974 The Westminster Press. Used by permission. And for *Early Christian Fathers*, Volume I, The Library of Christian Classics, newly translated and edited by Cyril C. Richardson. Published in the United States by The Westminster Press, 1953. Used by permission.

Acknowledgment is also made to *Dialog, Theology and Life,* and the *Scottish Journal of Theology,* respectively, for articles which appeared in earlier form in these publications and are the basis of Chapters I, III, and IV in this volume: "Interim Ethics, An Essay in Tribute to Albert Schweitzer," *Theology and Life* 9 (1966): 220–33; "The Historical Jesus and the Historians," *Dialog* 11 (1972): 95–100; "Satan, Demons and the Kingdom of God," *Scottish Journal of Theology* 27 (1974): 35–47.

Library of Congress Cataloging in Publication Data

Hiers, Richard H
  Jesus and the future.

  Includes bibliographical references and indexes.
    1.   Kingdom of God—Biblical teaching.   2.   Jesus
Christ—Teachings.   3.   Jesus Christ—Person and
offices.   I.   Title.
BS2417.K5H49   236   80-82189
ISBN 0-8042-0341-5

© copyright 1981 John Knox Press
10 9 8 7 6 5 4 3 2 1
Printed in the United States of America
John Knox Press
Atlanta, Georgia 30365

Preface

Modern Fascination with Jesus—But Which Jesus?

Even in such a supposedly secular period as the last quarter of the twentieth century, the figure of Jesus continues to fascinate modern thought and imagination. Stage and film spectaculars[1] augment the continual outpouring of popular and scholarly writings about Jesus. Viewers and readers often find the situation bewildering, for these portrayals present many different images of Jesus. Jesus has always been depicted in accordance with the fashions of particular times and locales. For instance, artists through the centuries have represented him as both bearded and shaven, ascetic and corpulent, Western and Oriental.[2]

Both the modern fascination with Jesus and the wide variety of representations may be understandable in connection with certain developments in the course of Western civilization. Since the time of the emperor Constantine, Christianity has played a number of central roles in the development and direction of this civilization.[3] Jesus, of course, has always been the central figure in Christianity. Until modern times, scarcely anyone questioned the conception of Jesus that had emerged in traditional theology and piety, as One with God and the Saviour of souls. But with the Renaissance, the Protestant Reformation, and the eighteenth century Enlightenment, there developed not only a variety of Christian theologies, but also various humanistic movements. These movements often declined to accept theological tradition without question, and generally were inclined to look for the mind of man in the formation of religious truth. Thus the beginnings of biblical textual research can be traced to the Renaissance, while the first effort to treat Jesus' intent and activity from a historical standpoint appeared in the milieu of the Enlightenment.[4] Ever since the last quarter of the eighteenth century, there has been a steady stream of writings about Jesus. Most of the writers wished to claim Jesus' support for their particular conceptions of Christianity, but there were also those who wished to discredit Christianity by discrediting its founder.

Jesus' prestige is still so great that even the recent radical branches of Christian theology have sought him as prophet and more than prophet for their respective movements. Jesus has been hailed as sponsor or spokesman for "death of God," "revolution," and "liberation" theologies. He also has been presented as proponent or exemplar of more moderate positions, such as the liberal and kerygmatic-existentialist schools represented, respectively, by Harnack and the "post-Bultmannians." Conversely, some of the cultured among the despisers of Christianity have endeavored to demolish traditional Christianity's portrait of Jesus. Typically, they have tried to represent him as a pathetic, absurd, or offensive figure of some sort. Some of these writers appear to hold Christianity responsible for everything that has gone wrong in the modern world, in much the same way that adolescents sometimes blame the ills of the world on their parents or their parents' generation. Perhaps Western civilization is going through an adolescent phase. The meanings and directions for faith and life once supplied by "Christendom" are widely believed to have been discredited, and the authority of the older traditions has been rejected in favor of various new "freedoms."[5] Those who propose to repudiate Christianity tend to represent Jesus in an unfavorable light.

Modern portrayals of Jesus have been influenced to a great extent by the interest or perspective of the writer. Even where interpreters have been primarily concerned to achieve a completely objective or historical understanding of Jesus, religious and other agendas often continue to shape the selection of sources or the resolution of problematic issues without the interpreter's awareness. Furthermore, some of the beliefs and expectations attributed to Jesus in the gospels are quite difficult to understand in terms of modern presuppositions and ideas. Interpreters of many schools tend to assume that Jesus' ideas were really not so different from their own. This assumption can be very attractive. It enables the interpreter to avoid the complex and uncertain tasks of sifting sources and endeavoring to understand the alien thought-world of first century Judaism and Christianity. Best of all, this assumption assures the interpreter that his or her search for the historical Jesus will result in the discovery of a Jesus sufficiently suitable to the interpreter's purpose. Sometimes this assumption is elevated into the hermeneutical proposition that, since complete objectivity in historical research is impossible anyway, the interpreter might as well abandon the quest for objectivity in research and be content to follow the path of least theological resistance. This assumption or proposition has some drawbacks. In particular, it opens the way to the interpreter's exercise of unrestrained subjectivity and closes off the possibility of learning anything from history.

The Historical, Eschatological Jesus: A "Stranger and Enigma" to Modern Thought

At the beginning of the present century, in his classic study of historical Jesus research,[6] Albert Schweitzer demonstrated that nineteenth century authors had found it very difficult to recognize the character and significance of certain beliefs and expectations held by the Jesus described in the earliest gospels. These beliefs and expectations are now commonly designated "eschatological,"[7] a technical term derived from the Greek noun, *to eschaton*, meaning "the last." Foremost among these is Jesus' reported proclamation that the Kingdom or rule of God was near and would soon be established on earth. Closely related is Jesus' declaration that the time of Judgment was near. Then those still alive, together with the resurrected dead of previous generations, would learn whether they were to enter the Kingdom of God or be consigned, perhaps forever, to the fires of gehenna. Such eschatological expectations pose some serious problems for Christian interpreters. If Jesus expected that the Kingdom of God would come and the Judgment take place within the lifespan of at least some of his contemporaries, it would appear that he was mistaken. But the Jesus of traditional doctrine was supposed to be omniscient and infallible. Surely Jesus could not have been mistaken. Moreover, if Jesus was looking for the eschatological fulfillment in the form of the coming of God's Kingdom, what can this hope mean in the twentieth century, where kingdoms of all sorts are out of style, and the fulfillment of human life is expected to result from science and technology? Few people today seriously anticipate that they will stand before the Son of man at the last Judgment, much less face punishment in a fiery gehenna. The eschatological Jesus depicted in the historical tradition is not the Jesus of any modern church or school of theology. It is understandable, therefore, that the eschatological features of Jesus' outlook and message have often been ignored, or else construed to mean something else by interpreters who find them something of an embarrassment. Even interpreters hostile to Christianity usually appear to be unaware of the eschatological aspects of Jesus' reported attitude and activity.

In biblical, as in other types of historical research, nothing can ever be considered finally proven. But we shall see that a substantial body of evidence indicates that Jesus really did hold the eschatological beliefs attributed to him in the first three gospels. If so, he is indeed, as

Schweitzer put it, a stranger and an enigma to modern thought. It is understandable that a great deal of twentieth century N.T. research has been prompted by the desire to show that the historical Jesus did not hold such strange, and presumably irrelevant, eschatological beliefs after all.

The Present Study: A Preliminary Overview

Interpreters' Quest for a Non-eschatological, Unenigmatic Jesus

In the following chapters we shall observe that interpreters tend either to avoid or to interpret away any evidence suggesting that Jesus actually held or conducted himself in accordance with the eschatological ideas attributed to him in the synoptic gospels. Moreover, we shall see that as interpreters ignore or re-interpret the eschatological traditions, they leave the way clear to "discover" in Jesus whatever figure is most congenial to their particular doctrines, ideologies, or programs. This pattern appears not only in the more obvious and extreme instances, but also in the rather awkward combinations and accomodations by interpreters who are, to some extent, prepared to acknowledge certain eschatological elements in Jesus' world-view, yet are anxious to limit or redefine Jesus' basic eschatological perspective in order to portray a Jesus who is not so problematic to modern faith after all. The result, frequently, is a Jesus who is intelligible neither in his own time nor to modern understanding.

We have examined elsewhere a number of synoptic passages that commonly are said to support the view that Jesus regarded the Kingdom of God somehow as present.[8] We found that although a few sayings can be interpreted plausibly to mean that Jesus thought the Kingdom in some way present, none requires such a reading. Even these sayings more probably indicate, as do numerous unambiguous ones,[9] that he looked for the advent of the Kingdom of God in the near future. Even if Jesus did regard the Kingdom as present somehow, it is clear that he considered its future coming to be the decisive eschatological event for which his contemporaries should prepare themselves.

We have not found sufficient evidence to sustain the customary hypothesis that Jesus believed the Kingdom to have been in some way present. This possibility is not entirely excluded. However, it is significant that interpreters who maintain that Jesus believed the Kingdom both present and future typically accentuate its purported presence, while de-emphasizing the more substantial indications of his futuristic and apocalyptic expectations.[10] For example, it is often urged that the synoptic passages indicative of futuristic beliefs are to be assigned to the churches, while anything that can be read to mean that Jesus believed the Kingdom present is taken to be authentic. Thus it is often proposed that the meaning of "Kingdom of God" should be understood in the context of the psalms (which antedate Jewish apocalypticism), or of rabbinic Judaism represented by the Talmud (which had virtually abandoned apocalyptic ideas). Interpreters then urge that God's Kingdom really means his "kingship" or "reign" which is "always present." Surely, such interpreters conclude, Jesus must have understood the Kingdom in this way as well. Frequently interpreters invent a variety of terms and concepts which, in common, are calculated to convey the impression that the Kingdom was at least partially actualized or present in Jesus' time. Without apparent misgiving, such interpreters proceed to attribute these expressions and ideas to Jesus himself. Subsequent interpreters then repeat the expressions as if they represented the assured results of historical Jesus research. Thus perhaps a majority of modern N.T. scholars are likely to state flatly that Jesus proclaimed the Kingdom to be "dawning," "breaking in," or "manifested." The fact that such expressions are not to be found in the gospels gives no pause to interpreters who have already decided what Jesus should have believed.

Basic Features of Jesus' Eschatological Message and Activity

A great many commentators today have been preoccupied with concern to show that Jesus thought the Kingdom of God somehow present. This preoccupation may account for the fact that interpreters have generally paid at most scant attention to several other basic features of his reported message, expectation, and activity that are likewise eschatological in character. The greater part of the present study is devoted to examining these neglected topics: Jesus' message of impending Judgment, his summons to an "ethic for the interim," his exorcism of demons, and his assurance that his followers would eat and drink in the Kingdom of God.

We begin with a brief resumé of recent treatments of the historical Jesus, noting the persistence of doctrinal or ideological interests on the part of interpreters who usually endeavor to de-emphasize or reinterpret his proclamation of the coming eschatological Kingdom of God. Next we consider Jesus' reported proclamation of coming Judgment. The first three or "synoptic" gospels report numerous sayings in which Jesus warned that only those found fit for the Kingdom of God at the Judgment would be allowed to enter it. Because the coming Judgment is such an important aspect of Jesus' reported message and expectation, and because it has been so largely neglected, we consider at some length a number of relevant primary sources. We then take up the closely related matter which Schweitzer referred to as Jesus' "interim ethics." Schweitzer observed that Jesus' message was intended for those living in the brief interim before the coming of the Kingdom. Most interpreters misconstrue what Schweitzer meant by "interim ethics" and ignore the synoptic evidence that gave rise to and clearly justifies this description. That Jesus should have gone about exorcising demons is, likewise, out of tune with modern assumptions. Nevertheless, as described in the synoptic gospels, exorcism was a basic feature of both Jesus' activity and that of his disciples. This activity, we suggest, presupposes and exemplifies the dualistic perspective characteristic of Jewish and early Christian apocalypticism. It is, moreover, entirely consistent with Jesus' recognition that the Kingdom of God had not yet come. A fourth important but commonly ignored feature of Jesus' outlook and message is his expectation and assurance that his followers would, perhaps soon, join together at table in the Kingdom of God. Perhaps modern interpreters find the idea of eating and drinking in the messianic age too materialistic or otherwise incongruous. At any rate, the subject is hardly ever mentioned in studies of Jesus and his message. Here again, we see considerable similarity between the beliefs and expectations of Jesus as reported in the gospels and those of apocalyptic Judaism.

Summary of Findings

Our studies here confirm the central place of Jesus' futuristic and apocalyptic orientation in the synoptic representation of his beliefs and message. They also demonstrate that interpreters still experience a great deal of difficulty in acknowledging the reality and importance of this orientation for the Jesus portrayed in the first three gospels. Many interpreters evidently take the position that if the eschatological features of Jesus' message and outlook were allowed to stand, he would appear too much out of step with modern thought and belief. Consequently, often perhaps unconsciously, interpreters attempt in one way and another to avoid, counter, or explain away much or all of these troublesome eschatological features. We shall see that interpreters also tend to ignore or disparage apocalyptic sources and ideas generally, and to dissociate Jesus from both Jewish and early Christian apocalypticism.[11] In the course of our studies, we examine a number of apocalyptic writings, and find that there is less basis than commonly supposed or claimed for differentiating Jesus' outlook from that of apocalypticism.

To some degree, the conclusions reached here accord with those reported by Johannes Weiss and Albert Schweitzer many years ago.[12] Their proposals are more correct and important than recent writers usually have been willing to admit. Christian interpreters typically misunderstand and reject Schweitzer's findings, perhaps because they are unwilling to confront the implications of such findings for faith and ethics. Their hesitancy is understandable. I am personally sympathetic with several of the theological and ethical viewpoints which some of Schweitzer's critics share. After first experiencing the disparity between modern Christian faith and the eschatological world-view of the synoptic Jesus, I found C. H. Dodd's program of "realized eschatology" very appealing.[13] Later, for a while, I was persuaded that Rudolf Bultmann's demythologizing method, together with his concept of "radical obedience," resolved important problems, particularly with respect to the relevance of Jesus and his "word" for Christian ethics. I do still find Dodd and Bultmann helpful interpreters in this connection.[14] Nevertheless, these and other interpreters generally have failed to do justice to Jesus' futuristic eschatological orientation and the problems this raises for faith and ethics. I do not think it helpful for either understanding or faith to gloss over the eschatological character of the synoptic evidence.

Those interpreters who are unwilling to suspend their theological or ethical concerns until they have completed their historical-critical analysis seem to fear that Christianity as they know it might collapse if historical research is allowed to proceed unmonitored. This kind of fear has surfaced again recently in the Roman Catholic hierarchy's concern over studies by Hans Küng and Edward Schillebeeckx. My conviction, however, is that faith can only gain by our seeking to know, as best we can, what Jesus himself intended and proclaimed.[15] Even if historical inquiry should call into question basic Christian beliefs, such inquiry ought not on that account be suspended. I am sure that many other interpreters also are convinced that faith need not be sheltered from any truth.

The eschatological interpretation of the historical Jesus is no longer new. But many of its insights have not yet fully been brought to bear upon the task of understanding and describing the traditions about Jesus found in the synoptic gospels.[16] At all events, what we attempt here is to take serious account of the eschatological outlook reported in the synoptic traditions. The eschatological aspects of Jesus' preaching and teaching are not merely incidental or peripheral, but form the substance or core of his message as recounted in the synoptic gospels, which are the earliest, best, and virtually only sources we have for information about the historical Jesus.[17]

Often it is impossible to determine with any assurance whether a particular saying can be considered a reasonably accurate recollection and rendition of Jesus' own words. There sometimes is cause to suspect that a passage probably was shaped or created by a Christian community or editor. We cannot claim to know *a priori* what sorts of things Jesus could or would not have said. Often it is not possible to decide whether a report about Jesus' words or activity is based upon a core of historical tradition, or derives from the beliefs or concerns of the church. But we are seldom compelled to posit such a disjunction with regard to the basic features of Jesus' message and activity. The synoptic gospels give us little reason to suppose that the historical Jesus was significantly different from the Jesus whom these gospels portray. In this connection, we are particularly disinclined to credit the common wisdom which insists that Jesus' perspective was necessarily distinct from that of either the early Christian community or apocalyptic Judaism.

Contents

1 Jesus and His Message of the Coming Kingdom of God

Interpreters of Christian persuasion ordinarily have not been especially interested in what Jesus intended and did in his own time. Usually they have been concerned with the meaning of Jesus and his message for faith and life in their own times. Understandably, Christian interpreters tend to suppose that Jesus set out to establish the kind of Christianity they experience as familiar and meaningful. Even non-Christian writers ordinarily have tried to understand Jesus in terms of concepts familiar and intelligible in the modern world. It has been less than a century since a few biblical scholars first began to realize that the historical Jesus[1] proclaimed to his contemporaries as of the first importance something quite unfamiliar to either modern Christianity or modern thought: the Kingdom of God. The significance of that recognition has not yet been grasped by many who have written about Jesus and his message in the intervening years.

Until the last decade of the nineteenth century, liberal and traditionalist interpreters felt justified in claiming Jesus as the founder, respectively, of liberal and traditional Christianity. Liberal writers were more interested in Jesus' significance for ethics, and so focused on his "teaching." Traditionalists were more concerned to see him as the Christ of conventional Christian doctrine. Either way, interpreters could assume that "their" Jesus was essentially the same as the Jesus of history. The last great monuments to these assumptions were, respectively, those of H.H. Wendt and M. Kähler.[2] Neither apparently suspected any real trouble ahead.

But trouble began to appear as early as 1891, with the publication of two books on the Kingdom of God in the New Testament. Ernst Issel retained the liberal view of I. Kant, A. Ritschl, and J. Kaftan, to the effect that Jesus proclaimed the Kingdom of God as man's highest good and task. But Issel proposed that Jesus *also* looked for the coming of the Kingdom in the future, along with the Judgment.[3] Otto Schmoller went further: the Kingdom Jesus proclaimed was entirely future. By responding to his message, his hearers were not building the kingdom on earth but preparing themselves for admission to it when it comes.[4] These books themselves received little attention, but their publication prompted Johannes Weiss to release his own reflections on the subject.[5] Rudolf Bultmann later was to describe Weiss' book as "epochmaking."[6]

The Eschatological Interpretation: Johannes Weiss

Weiss pointed to such passages as Mark 1:15, and Luke 10:9, according to which Jesus proclaimed and instructed his disciples to proclaim that the Kingdom of God had come *near*. Jesus and his followers eagerly *awaited* its coming from first to last. That is why he taught them to pray for its *coming* (Matt. 6:10). Nothing was said here or elsewhere in the gospels about its further "consummation" or coming in some still more perfect way later on. From the standpoint of Jesus, the Kingdom was entirely future, but it might come at any time (Luke 17:22ff.; Mark 13:32). At the Last Supper, Jesus was still looking for it (Luke 22:18, 28ff.). *When* it came, all would be transformed into a new and splendid promised land, indeed, a new heaven and a new earth, in place of the old.[7] Thus Jesus' message was good news for those who would receive it and repent (Matt. 5:20; 6:19–33; 18:2f.); but those who failed to heed would face adverse judgment and forever be excluded from the joys of life in the Kingdom (Matt. 25:41, 46; Mark 9:47f.; Luke 16:23ff.). As Son of man, Jesus himself would preside at the Judgment over this generation and the resurrected dead of former times (Matt. 12:41f.; Luke 11:31f.). In the meantime, Jesus' work consisted partly of exorcising demons and thereby preparing for the coming of the Kingdom,[8] but mainly of proclaiming its nearness, along with the necessity of repentance as condition for entering it when it came. Repentance meant turning from everything that binds a person to this old world, and seeking first, before *all* else, God and his Kingdom. Weiss made use of both Jewish sources (which hitherto had usually been ignored except when their ideas might be shown inferior to those of Jesus), and eschatological passages in the synoptic gospels and other early Christian writings which had been equally neglected.

Though largely unnoticed by British and American scholars until recent years, Weiss' little book completely undermined the then prevalent liberal conception of Jesus as Founder and Teacher of the Kingdom understood as God's rule in the hearts of men or the structures of society.[9] At first, it seemed that a reasonable compromise might be worked out. Lecturing to a packed University of Berlin auditorium in 1899–1900 on "the essence of Christianity," Adolf von Harnack acknowledged that Jesus really had shared some apocalyptic ideas and expectations with his Jewish contemporaries. But Jesus *also* understood that the Kingdom of God meant his rule in men's hearts. What is *essential* is the latter, for it was the distinctive part of Jesus' understanding.[10] Harnack's proposal that the essential part of Jesus' outlook was the distinctive, i.e., non-Jewish, was picked up by later interpreters, some of whom, like Harnack, also urged that when Jesus spoke of the Kingdom of God he intended primarily to signify religious experience.[11]

Weiss himself continued to maintain a liberal theological position, but without the comfort of claiming the support of the historical Jesus for it. Thus a gap was opened between the Jesus of history on the one hand and the kind of Jesus desired by liberal theology on the other. One of the central preoccupations of N.T. research since the appearance of Weiss' book has been to bridge—or perhaps leap across—this gap.[12]

Consistent Eschatology: Albert Schweitzer's Position

Albert Schweitzer had not yet read Schmoller or Weiss when he wrote his *Sketch of the Life of Jesus*[13] in 1901, but his conclusions were very much like theirs. His famous *Quest of the Historical Jesus* (1906)[14] is sometimes said to be a "popularization" of Weiss' work. In fact it consists largely of a detailed description and critique of eighteenth and nineteenth century efforts to explain the historical Jesus, or at least to write about his "life." In it, Schweitzer also further elaborated his own interpretation, which he characterized as "consistently eschatological." By this, he meant that both Jesus' words and actions must be understood in connection with his eschatological beliefs. (In Schweitzer's view, Weiss had only considered the eschatological meaning of Jesus' message.) Strangely, a great many of Schweitzer's critics suppose that "consistent" or "thoroughgoing" eschatology meant something else.[15] A good many otherwise knowledgeable interpreters claim that Schweitzer portrayed Jesus as a "fanatic" or a man "deluded" or "wild."[16] In fact, Schweitzer showed that Jesus thought and acted quite reasonably and consistently on the basis of his beliefs and expectations which were, in turn, coherent with those of apocalyptic Judaism. The evidence from Qumran has since confirmed Schweitzer's appreciation of the importance of apocalyptic thought in first century Judaism. Interpreters also have had difficulty understanding what Schweitzer meant by the term "interim ethics." Some, for instance, supposed

Schweitzer to have meant that Jesus required adherence to certain "laws" or "rigid rules" as a precondition for entering the Kingdom. These and other misreadings serve, perhaps unintentionally, to discredit Schweitzer's position by caricaturing it, thereby enabling the mis-reader more confidently to maintain his own opinions. [17]

Schweitzer demonstrated that the Jesus depicted in the eighteenth and nineteenth century "lives of Jesus" was a fiction, invented by the authors of these "lives" in accordance with their own interests. He noted that with few exceptions these authors persistently ignored or interpreted away the main features of Jesus' eschatological orientation evidenced in the gospels. Also writing in 1901, William Wrede proposed that the eschatological and messianic beliefs attributed to Jesus by the evangelists were not his own, but those of the church or the evangelists. The particular issue between Wrede and Schweitzer was the historical value of the synoptic, especially Marcan, tradition. Wrede held to what Schweitzer called the "literary solution," or that of "skepticism" as to the historical worth of Mark. [18] Wrede's theory was that Mark had authored substantial portions of the gospel pursuant to his point of view, so that modern interpreters should be skeptical as to its historical value. Schweitzer, on the other hand, felt justified in preferring the historical, eschatological interpretation. He considered it unlikely that the church would have invented and attributed to Jesus sayings and expectations which had already failed to be fulfilled. [19] Schweitzer did not insist upon the absolute chronology or accuracy of Mark, much less upon any "bruta facta," [20] but he held that Mark and Matthew did incorporate essentially accurate recollections of much that Jesus had said and done. Contrary to assertions by some of his critics, Schweitzer's theory does not stand or fall with the historicity of the mission of the Twelve in Matthew 10 or any other particular unit of tradition such as Mark 13. Some features of Schweitzer's interpretation are questionable; but on the whole, it has survived as a coherent and cogent account of the basic synoptic evidence regarding Jesus' message and activity. We suggest that Schweitzer's position has been more misunderstood and misrepresented than refuted by subsequent scholars.

The Twentieth Century Quest for an Uneschatological Jesus

After Weiss and Schweitzer, the eschatological interpretation had to be reckoned with. [21] Several subsequent scholars have accepted its basic thesis, which is that for Jesus, the coming of the Kingdom was the future, imminent, and decisive event for which his hearers should prepare.[22] In 1958 Bultmann could state, "Today nobody doubts that Jesus' conception of the Kingdom of God is an eschatological one—at least in European theology."[23] But not all scholars agreed that Jesus regarded the coming of the Kingdom primarily as a future event.

Liberal writers preferred a Jesus whose ethical teachings could be taken over directly as relevant and normative for modern life. E.F. Scott, Hans Windisch, Amos N. Wilder, C.H. Dodd, T.W. Manson, and J.A.T. Robinson might be mentioned here. The first three tried in different ways to untangle Jesus' ever-valid teachings from his time-conditioned eschatological beliefs. In order to affirm the relevance of Jesus' "ethics," they assumed that it was necessary to discount his "eschatology." The latter three, especially Dodd, wished to challenge the eschatological interpretation at its root. In their view, the historical Jesus had not proclaimed the imminence of the Kingdom at all; instead, they urged, the Kingdom was already present, somehow, in connection with his person or ministry.[24] This theory of "realized eschatology," as it has been called, was especially popular in British and American liberal circles. There, however, it usually was combined with somewhat grudging recognition that Jesus also thought the coming of the Kingdom a future event.

Traditionalist theologians and pastors who took cognizance of it generally found the eschatological interpretation incompatible with the doctrine of Jesus' divinity. In traditionalist theology, Jesus was supposed to have been incapable of error. The eschatological interpretation was also contrary to the traditional picture of Jesus as the Christ or Son of God who proclaimed first and foremost the necessity of believing in himself. Such a Christology, necessarily, has little room for Jesus' proclamation of the coming Kingdom of God. In the Fourth Gospel, of course, Jesus does not proclaim the nearness or coming of the Kingdom of God. Instead, he proclaims that those who believe in him already have, or will have, eternal life. Traditionalist theologians and laymen have generally viewed the Fourth Gospel not only as the gospel of choice, but as a reliable historical record.[25]

Neither Bultmann nor his pupils fit nicely into a "liberal/conservative" typology. They are "liberal" in the sense that they are willing to utilize historical-critical methods of research. Bultmann was also "liberal" in his interest in the relevance of Jesus' message for the moral life.[26] Most are Lutheran ministers, as well as academicians, and, understandably, wished to find something in the Bible on which to ground Christian faith or doctrine. For Bultmann, it was enough, theologically, *that* Jesus came; the *"kerygma"* (or Bultmann's reading of

Pauline-Johannine theology) is sufficient basis for the faith of later believers. The "essence of Christianity" is not Jesus' message, but the church's. Functionally, the *kerygma* replaces the historical Jesus.[27] Bultmann thus visualized a gap between the historical, eschatological, Jewish Jesus of the synoptic tradition, and the Jesus who is relevant for faith, but only through the "kerygma." For Bultmann it was also a matter of theological importance that the historical Jesus should be wholly other than the "Christ event" proclaimed by the church, lest the church's faith somehow be "legitimated" or proven by historical research.[28]

Interpreters of various theological schools turned hopefully to *form criticism*, a type of literary analysis developed in the 1920s by (among others) Rudolf Bultmann. Proponents of form criticism (also sometimes referred to as tradition history) tried to infer the types of settings in which certain kinds of traditions may have been used in the life of the early Christian communities. Form critics conjectured, often with good reasons, that given units of tradition were used in the early community's liturgy, preaching, or teaching. Form critics tended to assume that such traditions not only were utilized by early communities, but in large measure had been created by them. This assumption led to the view that traditions purporting to represent Jesus' sayings and deeds were primarily the product of the churches and, consequently, contain little that might be considered historically reliable. Such a view had already been suggested at the turn of the century by M. Kähler and W. Wrede. Kähler thereby hoped to defend the traditionalist image of the "biblical Christ" against liberal criticism.[29] Wrede, on the other hand, meant to free the liberal conception of Jesus as teacher of timeless truths from the messianic doctrines attributed to him by the gospel accounts.[30] Form critics commonly assume as a matter of principle that any traditions preserved from early times first existed only in the form of separate units ("pericopes") which the evangelists then assembled, like beads on a string, according to their own particular theological designs or preferences. This assumption, together with the fact that the evangelists evidently did modify some earlier traditions on the basis of their interests or concerns, led to a still further subdivision of literary analysis known as *redaction criticism*. Redaction critics attempt to identify the theological and other concerns of the gospels' editors.[31]

Form and redaction criticism undoubtedly have contributed much to scholarly understanding with respect to the formation of the gospel tradition. These methods of analysis have not, however, shown that historical Jesus research is impossible. Van Harvey discerned the interest underlying this sort of proposition.

> Consider . . . the oft-repeated claim that it is impossible to get behind
> the Biblical picture of Christ and to reconstruct the historical Jesus.
> The force of this claim is to set certain methodological limits upon his-
> torical inquiry, and once these limits have been set, faith feels itself
> liberated from any anxiety concerning the results of the inquiry, be-
> cause faith is said to have as its object the Christ of faith and not the
> Jesus of history.[32]

One is inclined to suspect an ideological element in such claims, especially when those making them go on to write an extensive characterization of Jesus' message and its meaning. The procedure is still more
suspicious when it is determined at the outset that authentic Jesus tradition, *by definition*, must exclude material that in any significant way
comports with the world-view of Judaism or early Christianity, and
must therefore be tested by the criteria of "distinctiveness" or "dissim-
ilarity."[33] Since both apocalyptic Judaism and early Christianity were
characterized by various eschatological beliefs and expectations, it then
is declared that the historical Jesus, by definition, could not have
shared such ideas or hopes.

Form and redaction criticism do provide insight into layers or
stages of developing tradition within the synoptic sources. Moreover,
it is often possible to recognize variant recensions and apparently editorial addenda and corrigenda. Some of these additions seem to have
been intended to explain "difficult" sayings or deal with questions that
had arisen in the course of the churches' efforts to live in accordance
with earlier norms of life and understanding. Taken with such other
criteria as persistence and consistency or coherence, it is possible to
achieve a general and sometimes fairly specific conception of the earliest tradition as to Jesus' sayings and actions.[34] We have shown elsewhere that this tradition cumulatively and regularly recalls a Jesus who
thought and also acted in accordance with certain eschatological understandings and beliefs.[35] Curiously, interpreters sometimes suggest that
many of the eschatological (or apocalyptic) sayings in the gospels derive from the interests of the later church, as if this would leave Jesus
innocent of such views. Yet these same interpreters concede that *some*
of the apocalyptic sayings are properly attributable to Jesus after all.[36]
The possibility that both Jesus and the church thought in terms of contemporary Jewish apocalyptic images and expectations does not seem
to have been seriously considered by many interpreters.

Several of Bultmann's former pupils, concerned over the gap in his
system between the historical Jesus and the church's *kerygma*, a generation ago undertook what J.M. Robinson designated the "new quest of

the historical Jesus." For the most part, these "new questers" shared Bultmann's existentialist presuppositions. Therefore the connection they sought was conceptualized mainly in terms of "the possibility of a new self-understanding" or "understanding of existence."[37] Their argument was that Jesus held and by his preaching prompted in others essentially the same "understanding of existence" as that later set forth or elicited by the *kerygma* or church's preaching. (Like Bultmann, the "new questers" tended to identify the *kerygma* with their own somewhat existentializing readings of Paul and John.) Consequently, it seemed important for them to insist that Jesus did not regard the coming of the Kingdom as wholly future, but instead to urge that he proclaimed that it had already "dawned" or "broken in," or that "the shift of aeons" had already occurred. Such phrases are repeated by one interpreter after another—in some cases attributed reverently to Bultmann—as if canonical.[38] The thought that the historical Jesus might really have expected the coming of the Kingdom in the future, particularly the near future, was as much a scandal to the "new questers" as it had been to the "old" authors of the "liberal lives" of Jesus. Even Käsemann, who takes eschatology more seriously than most of the other Bultmann pupils, spoke for all when he declared candidly, "I am unable to understand Jesus as an apocalyptic figure."[39] As theologian, Käsemann evidently would prefer to believe that Jesus had intended his call for us.[40] Such could not, of course, have been the case if Jesus expected the Kingdom to come within the lifetime of his own contemporaries.

Van Harvey has written an extensive analysis of the "new questers'" tendency to stack the deck in their definitions of historiography and faith. The so-called "new historiography," he suggests, is not so different from the "old" as its advocates pretend, and must work, after all, with the same kinds of data. Contrary to the claim of the new historiographers, such data does not provide access to a past person's "existential selfhood" apart from consideration of such mundane matters as the synoptic evidence and judgments as to the nature and reliability of its information, including chronology. Harvey suggests that in the final analysis, despite their protestations, the "new questers" wished to legitimate or secure faith by tying it to, or equating it with the historically dubious claim to have recovered Jesus' existential selfhood.[41] In any case, it is significant that the proponents of this "new quest," unlike Bultmann, argue that Jesus understood the Kingdom to be present as well as future, and moreover deny that Jesus thought in apocalyptic terms.[42] Here, as in other eras and schools of interpretation, theological and philosophical interests seem to shape the historical-critical results.

Not surprisingly, the Jesus "recovered" by proponents of the "new quest" is, in Klaus Koch's words, "practically indistinguishable from a German kerygmatic theologian of the twentieth century."[43] Koch also observes the tendency of modern commentators to equate "the 'situation' of each individual 'text' with the 'situation' of 'man today,' the two allegedly coinciding."[44] To the extent that such a coincidence is assumed, interpreters evidently feel relieved of the necessity of explaining the meaning and relevance of ancient and problematic beliefs for modern faith. It is understandable, then, that the "new questers," like their nineteenth century liberal predecessors, should look into the well of history and see there primarily a reflection of their own faces.

Jesus and his beliefs are also considered in wider circles of writings which report on the state of the old and/or new quests.[45] In the 1960s a number of books with similar titles but of more general character began to appear: e.g., the collections of essays by Harvey K. McArthur[46] and Hans J. Schultz,[47] and Howard Clark Kee's study of redaction criticism.[48] During this same period, several books focused on Jesus' conception of the Kingdom of God. Two appeared the same day in 1963, each with the title, *The Kingdom of God in the Teaching of Jesus.*[49] Other important studies were W.G. Kümmel, *Promise and Fulfillment* (1957), Herman Ridderbos, *The Coming of the Kingdom* (1962), Rudolph Schnackenburg, *God's Rule and Kingdom* (1963) and George Eldon Ladd, *Jesus and the Kingdom* (1964).[50] Generally these studies attend carefully to basic evidence; but in every case the authors finally reveal a desire to de-emphasize Jesus' futuristic beliefs. The writers then seize upon any texts that might possibly be read to show that somehow Jesus understood the Kingdom as a present reality, and assure their readers that this present Kingdom was what mattered most to him and should matter most to "us" today. This pattern of interpretation also appears in more recent studies, such as John Reumann, *Jesus in the Church's Gospels,*[51] and Gustaf Aulén, *Jesus in Contemporary Historical Research.*[52] Similarly, the annotator to Matt. 4:17 in *The New Oxford Annotated Bible* (1977) confidently explains: "Jesus taught both the present reality of God's rule . . . and its future realization." Typically these interpreters ignore the problem of logical consistency, namely, *how* Jesus could proclaim that the Kingdom was both present and coming, that it was already "dawning" or "breaking through" and also would do so in the future.[53]

In many different ways, writers assert either that Jesus believed the Kingdom present, or that it was present in or with him. They seem to mean that if the Kingdom was present in the days of Jesus, it can also be considered present in our own time as well.[54] *How* the Kingdom of God supposedly was present is a matter of some uncertainty. Several interpreters surreptitiously equate the Kingdom with God himself.[55] Others construe it to mean God's rule, reign, or kingship which was, *of course*, ever-present.[56] It became present in Jesus' words or message, so that those who accepted his words thereby participated in the Kingdom.[57] It was present or "manifested" in his "person and works" or "activity."[58] Jesus was the—albeit "enigmatic"—"representative of the Kingdom of God."[59] The Kingdom "is a matter of human experience" which is "to be found wherever God is active decisively within the experience of an individual."[60] It comes to those who attend to Jesus' parables and "when he sits with tax collectors and calls fishermen to be his disciples."[61]

Nearly all schools seem agreed that Jesus' futuristic expectations, if permitted to stand, would be an embarrassment, if not a disaster, for contemporary faith. Consequently, critics evidently are willing to read into Jesus' mind all sorts of modernizing reinterpretations.[62] Often interpreters suggest that Jesus spoke of the Kingdom of God *symbolically*; therefore no one need suppose that he really looked for it to come as eschatological event, unless perhaps in some psychological or "spiritual" sense.[63] Numerous interpreters, usually taking off from Matt. 12:28=Luke 11:20, describe Jesus' exorcisms as evidence for the presence of the Kingdom. The exorcisms are then said to have been "signs" of the "inbreaking power" of the Kingdom, or of "the powers of the Kingdom" that were "already operative."[64] Another explanation is that the Kingdom had "irrupted" in the person of Jesus.[65] Such expressions, though commonly repeated in the secondary literature, are not to be found in any of the synoptic accounts of exorcisms. We suggest that the exorcisms can be understood more plausibly in connection with Jesus' expectation that the Kingdom of God, not yet present, would soon come.[66]

Another procedure frequently used by interpreters who wish to disentangle Jesus from the complications of his eschatological perspective is to redefine "apocalypticism." These interpreters declare that to say that Jesus thought in terms of Jewish eschatological beliefs and expectations really means that he thought in apocalyptic terms. They then propose that apocalypticism is to be defined as a matter of "fanciful speculations" and "calculations" as to when the end will come. However, they urge, Jesus not only refrained from such speculations and calculations, he explicitly rejected all calculations.[67] Consequently, it is argued, the eschatological—which really means apocalyptic—interpretation is patently false, since Jesus was no apocalyptic.[68] The commonly asserted but mistaken notion that the apocalyptic viewpoint is characterized by interest in "calculating" the exact time of the end apparently originated with Maurice Goguel.[69] A related strategy is to interpret the historical Jesus in terms of a nonapocalyptic eschatology, that is, "eschatology" redefined in accordance with modern doctrinal or philosophical viewpoints. Thus, for Bultmann, eschatology actually meant the perennial existential crisis of decision; for Dodd, a remote "order beyond time and space"; and for Perrin, "human experience."[70] Modern scholars of nearly all schools tend to be out of sympathy with the apocalyptic perspective. In part, their distaste for apocalypticism may be in reaction to the fact that apocalyptic writings have been a happy hunting ground for millenial movements looking for signs that "Bible prophecies are being fulfilled before our very eyes." Such movements are generally held to be both theologically and intellectually unrespectable. Interpreters in the "mainstream" of Christianity and academe are disposed, therefore, to believe *a priori* that Jesus could not have shared such a bizarre world-view, and to discount all evidence to the contrary.

Jackson Lee Ice has called attention to the curious preoccupation with Jesus among the recent so-called "radical" theologians, particularly the proponents of the now defunct "death of God" school.[71] These writers had little or no interest in the historical, eschatological Jesus. Instead, they were looking for a figure abstracted from the world of apocalyptic expectation who could be transformed, one way or another, into a humanistic model for modern life, such as Bonhoeffer's portrayal of Jesus as "the man for others." The Jesus of the "radical" theologians is not far-removed from the rationalist and romantic Jesus of the "liberal lives," who was an exemplar and doer of good deeds. It is as if the historical research of the preceding hundred years had not occurred. In order to produce the desired humanistic Jesus, of course, the historical Jesus must be either ignored or radically re-fashioned.[72]

More recently, a quite different theological interest has appeared particularly in the writings of Jürgen Moltmann, Wolfhart Pannenberg, Johannes Metz, and Carl Braaten. Together with a few others, these authors have been labeled as proponents of the "theology of hope" or simply "the new theology." They have urged that the future is of fundamental theological importance after all, and that the Kingdom of God is the goal both of individual aspiration and for the church and the world. These theologians have been impressed by the significance of future hopes and expectations for the N.T. churches. Although mainly focusing upon the post-resurrection faith of the early Christian community, the "new" theologians have also shown an interest in the meaning of Jesus' proclamation of the coming Kingdom that has been lacking in critical theology this century. The new emphasis clearly results from dissatisfaction with the experiential and individualistic presentism of the Bultmannian and so-called "post-Bultmannian" positions which have, until recently, dominated European theology. This dissatisfaction is based partly upon the results of critical N.T. research, but also upon recognition of the desperate character of the human condition in the closing decades of the twentieth century. It also results from a renewed (and neo-Protestant) awareness that individuals and human society alike are in no position to deliver themselves from evil, even by achieving a new "self-understanding." In this respect, proponents of the "new theology" of hope differ significantly from the "radical" theologians who wished to affirm the essential goodness of humanity (if not its deity), and the capacity of such humanity to work out its own benign if not glorious destiny.

There is some danger that this "new theology" will use the historical Jesus ideologically to sanction its own affirmation of hope for the future, in the same way that liberal theology used him to sanction its optimism about the immanence of God's rule in men's hearts and social progress. Theologians of hope do sometimes tend to bypass Jesus' proclamation of the *imminent* Kingdom and the prospect of Judgment and to repeat some of the shibboleths of liberalism.[73] Nevertheless, a theology that values the future is more likely to provide a milieu conducive to appreciation of the meaning of Jesus' futuristic beliefs and message than was the case under the aegis of theologies which regarded Jesus' futuristic orientation as problematic and therefore expendable.[74] The writings and lectures of Wolfhart Pannenberg and the work of Carl Braaten have shown that the "new theology" is also interested in understanding the significance of the eschatological perspective of Jesus and early Christianity for some of the basic problems of ethics and public policy confronting the modern world.[75]

The Historical Jesus and the Historian: The Perils of Co-mingling Historical with Theological Interests

Before Weiss, Kähler, Schweitzer, and Wrede, it could be assumed that the first three gospels represented more or less objective accounts of Jesus' ministry and message. Their work, and that of J. Wellhausen, M. Dibelius, R. Bultmann, and others, has made it clear that all of the gospels are products of the believing churches.[76] Subsequently, redaction critics have attempted (with peculiar lack of consensus) to identify each evangelist's special theological interests and other concerns. It now seems probable that both Jesus and the early churches looked for the coming of the Kingdom of God and/or Son of man or Messiah in the near future.[77] It is impossible to say with absolute certainty which traditions go back to the historical Jesus and which were shaped significantly or created by the churches and the evangelists. But the main problem in interpreting the historical Jesus is not so much the character of the source. It is instead the fact that the Jesus depicted in the sources is and remains the Jewish, eschatological, apocalyptic Jesus. As Schweitzer observed some eighty years ago, the historical Jesus is a stranger and an enigma to modern thought. Despite the best efforts of the "new quest," the "new historiography," and the "new hermeneutic," the historical, eschatological Jesus was not the founder of any school of modern theology.

Nevertheless, the historical Jesus may be regarded as a proper subject for historical inquiry. Those who deny the *legitimacy* of such inquiry only reveal their over-commitment to doctrinal considerations, and their unwillingness to deal with the historical question. It is often objected that the historian can never hope to achieve a state of complete objectivity. This is doubtless correct. But this insight does not justify the harnessing of exegetical and historical investigation to dogmatic interest. It is important *what* the interpreter's concern is. Interest in understanding what others actually believed and hoped for is less likely to distort the findings of historical research than interest in protecting or justifying the beliefs and ideas the researcher considers meaningful.

Regarding the process of historical inquiry, Reinhold Niebuhr has stated:

> One must admit the subjective element in historical judgments, but also insist upon the distinction between purely arbitrary judgments and those which throw real light upon the variegated events of history. Patterns of meaning are arbitrary if they do violence to the facts, or single out correlations or sequences of events, which are so fortuitous that only some special interest or passion could persuade the observer of the significance of the correlation.[78]

Viewing the process of exegesis and historical research from the perspective of the "sociology of knowledge," one is not surprised to find that commentators or exegetes "socially located" within the Christian community are influenced and reinforced by the "knowledge" shared in that community.[79] Interpreters of Jesus ordinarily are both churchmen and scholars. We can better understand the wide divergences in the methods and conclusions of modern interpreters if we recognize that each may be influenced by different, and often conflicting, perspectives. It is important to ask, what is the interpreter's "social location"? Is his primary devotion to the scholarly community and its quest for truth, or to the church and its doctrines—or to some other "cause"?

If the interpreter's basic concern is to determine, within the limits posed by the nature of the sources, what the historical Jesus said, did, and intended, he will proceed differently than if his principal interest is to find a Jesus who will endorse or sponsor his own and his fellow-believers' preferred doctrines or programs. In the first instance, the interpreter will attend to the text and try to reconstruct the intentions and understandings evidenced in it, taking into account other relevant data from the period.[80] In the latter instance, nearly anything goes; at any rate, the great temptation is to read into the "historical" Jesus what one intends to read out. To illustrate, mention could be made of claims to the effect that Jesus was sponsor if not founder of "situation ethics," of the death of God theology, and the secular city=Kingdom of God equation.[81] He has been presented as exemplar of marriage, a fanatical, calculating manipulator, and an almost-if-not-quite Zealot revolutionary.[82] And, especially in certain socially concerned German circles, he has recently been represented as a proponent of thoroughgoing social and political reform.[83]

For various reasons interpreters may also be prompted by hostility to Christianity. Such hostility is obvious, for example, in Rudolf Augstein's *Jesus Son of Man* (Urizen Books, 1977). The author's furious rhetorical style leaves the reader in doubt as to whether he wishes to object that Jesus "never existed" (p. 9), that he was a revolutionary (p. 59), "raving mad" (p. 69), or a "runaway Essene" (p. 129). His main complaint against Christianity, he says, is that churches take positions—evidently the wrong ones—on social-political questions. Consequently, he finds "no choice" but to go forward with his effort to unmask Christianity's claims about Jesus (p. 10). Morton Smith's *Jesus the Magician* (Harper & Row, 1978) may be prompted merely by a desire to discredit Christianity, or as he puts it, to correct the bias of Christians who, from early times, have refused to recognize that Jesus thought himself a god by virtue of his magical powers (pp. vii, 149–50). Smith readily explains the lack of evidence for his claim that Jesus came forward as a magician: Later Christianity *suppressed* this evidence. Here we see the argument from silence with a vengeance! Joseph Klausner's *Jesus of Nazareth* (Macmillan, 1925) faulted Jesus for being too "otherworldly" in his thinking about the Kingdom of God. As a Zionist, Klausner held that the coming of the Kingdom of God was to be "the fruit of long and hard work," in short, "Jewish socialism" (p. 406). Two recent studies of Jesus by Jewish scholars show little animus toward Jesus. David Flusser pictures Jesus as a preacher of realized eschatology in the context of rabbinic Judaism (*Jesus* [Herder & Herder, 1969]). Geza Vermes' *Jesus the Jew* (London: Collins, 1973) represents Jesus as a Jewish miracle-worker and healer. Neither Flusser nor Vermes propose to understand Jesus in connection with his reported proclamation of the coming Kingdom of God or any other apocalyptical beliefs and expectations. J.M. Allegro has persisted in his determination to discredit Jesus. In *The Sacred Mushroom and the Cross* (Doubleday, 1970), Allegro urged that the N.T. stories about Jesus were fictions invented by leaders of a mushroom-eating sex-drug cult in order to perpetuate their secrets. Earlier, Allegro had undertaken to portray Jesus as a mere imitation of the Qumran "teacher of righteousness." Allegro based that claim on his own revisions of certain texts in the Dead Sea Scrolls, augmented by imaginative interpolations.

It is not surprising that these otherwise diverse representations of Jesus generally ignore or minimize his reported declarations concerning the future coming of the Kingdom and related events. In order to produce the Jesus desired by modern interests, the eschatological Jesus of the synoptic tradition must somehow be set to one side. Those interpreters who know beforehand what Jesus really should have meant do not hesitate to proceed accordingly.

The more difficult and more typical situation is that of the interpreter who is seriously committed *both* to historical research and to a Christian faith-understanding with respect to Jesus. The fact that he perceives that the results of historical research may well imply complications for faith—his own and his community's—may then tempt him to reach conclusions that minimize such complications. We have already noted the pattern that appears in some of the excellent scholarly studies published in the late 1950s and 1960s: the writer candidly acknowledges and reviews synoptic traditions indicating Jesus' futuristic eschatological beliefs, but then turns to the few passages that can be construed to mean that he thought the Kingdom somehow present, and finally concludes by suggesting that only this latter belief is important for modern faith.[84] Here we see one strategy for avoiding the dilemma faced by the interpreter who wishes both to pursue critical historical inquiry and to maintain and express a theological position that might otherwise be questionable in the light of the historical-critical findings.[85] Another strategy is that of construing eschatological expressions in the gospels in terms of concepts derived from modern theology.[86] The late Norman Perrin left us a particularly lucid and penetrating critique of the "new hermeneutic." Perrin demonstrated that the central interest of Fuchs and his pupils, Linnemann and Jungel, was to show that Jesus' own faith and message not only offered his own contemporaries the possibility of achieving a new existence, but also can do so for modern listeners or readers, through the interpreter's "sermons" (as Perrin characterizes them) which are supposedly based on Jesus' sermons.[87] These writers generally use presentist and existentialist terms, dispensing more or less completely with the eschatological Kingdom of God which, if referred to at all, is reinterpreted vaguely as "the future" or a "language event."

A closely related strategy that persists, indeed, flourishes among contemporary writers, is to devise or utilize various modernizing terms which are purported to express the meaning of Jesus' eschatological understanding or proclamation. These terms invariably point away from the eschatological and therefore theologically problematic beliefs and expectations indicated in the synoptic tradition. Instead, they convey, if rather obscurely, the idea that Jesus really had in mind the presence or immanence of the Kingdom of God. Several writers suggest that the eschatological events referred to in the gospels are to be understood primarily as subjective occurrences in the realm of individual consciousness.[88] Robert W. Funk, Dan O. Via, Jr., and John D. Crossan, for example, use such amorphous existentializing expressions as "the parabolic world," "the future of every hearer," "opportunity for meaningful existence," and "breaking open the hearer's world."[89] Even L.E. Keck wrote that the Kingdom was present in or with Jesus, who "set in motion the Kingdom's impact," "effectuating" it "in advance," as its "irruption," "vanguard," or "prolepsis," and that it was present as "parabolic event."[90] Other writers beyond the circle of the post-Bultmannians or "new questers" have commonly adopted that school's practice of asserting that in Jesus or his actions the Kingdom was "breaking in" or "dawning."[91] Such expressions, however, do not occur in the gospels, and it is doubtful that they aptly express the understanding of any of the synoptic evangelists. In order to differentiate the asserted presence of the Kingdom from the coming of the Kingdom which the synoptic gospels regularly describe as a future occurrence, scholars proceed to infer or invent further special terms or distinctions. Paul Achtemeier, for example, proposes that Mark meant his readers to understand that when Christ comes again, he will "*consummate* the age and inaugurate *visibly* God's rule on earth." Likewise, he distinguishes between the previous "dawning" of the Kingdom and its "final" coming at the parousia.[92] Similarly, Kee approves Kümmel's view that a distinction may be found in the tradition between the Kingdom "inau-

gurated" in Jesus' words and actions, and the "fulfillment" or "consummation" of the Kingdom in the future.[93] But as J. Weiss observed
in 1892, there is no basis in the synoptic gospels for the view that Jesus
contemplated the arrival of the Kingdom in stages or by degrees, and
there is no reason to suppose that the evangelists had such a process in
view either.[94] These interpreters, who are among the most capable
scholars in the field of N.T. research, are not to be faulted for developing these terms and distinctions. The difficulty appears inherent in the
dual task and responsibility they undertake: on the one hand, that of
historical research, and on the other, that of theological reflection in
the Christian community.[95]

Such contemporary interpreters are aware of the foibles of earlier
generations of critics who freely read their own theological and moral
concepts and distinctions into the words and intentions of Jesus. But
because the modern categories are relatively new, and also, perhaps,
because they are commonly repeated in congenial circles of able fellow
scholars who find them meaningful, it may not be so obvious to those
who use them that these expressions likewise have been imposed upon
the evidence. Numerous interpretive categories have been coined and
widely circulated in the last several years, typically, it seems, in an effort to disengage the meaning of Jesus and his message from the unfortunate concepts which—it would otherwise appear—he shared with
apocalyptic Judaism. In the process, necessarily, the terms and concepts appearing in the synoptic sources themselves have been rather
neglected.

In consequence, historical Jesus research has not advanced significantly in recent years. Theological and ethical interests are now somewhat different than in the days before Weiss and Schweitzer. More is
known now about apocalyptic Judaism. Literary criticism has yielded
further information and theories about the development of the N.T.
tradition. Yet the fact that the eschatological Jesus is the only Jesus
about whom we can learn anything from the sources has not yet been
recognized widely. Accordingly, efforts to describe some other Jesus
go on apace. It is not our view that modern interpreters deliberately set
out to distort the evidence. Rather, their procedure is probably, on the
whole, intended to be straightforward. And yet, as Marc Bloch has
stated concerning historical research generally, "in the criticism of evidence, almost all the dice are loaded. For extremely delicate human elements constantly intervene to tip the balance toward a preferred
possibility."[96] Such elements likewise prompt interpreters to avoid un-
desired possibilities. These "elements" are likely to be even more operative when the matter investigated affects, or is thought to affect the

interpreter's own basic sense of ultimate meaning and hope together with that of his or her community of faith. As studies in "cognitive dissonance" have shown, consistency, if not necessarily a virtue, is easier to live with than open or unresolved questions.[97] Thus, without consciously intending to do so, the interpreter may resolve dissonance by emphasizing the presence of the Kingdom, while down-playing the more theologically troublesome evidence that Jesus expected it to come in the lifetime of his own contemporaries.

At the beginning of the twentieth century, Adolf von Harnack conceded that Jesus did think and speak of the coming eschatological Kingdom of God, but argued that he *also* understood it to mean God's rule, "a still and mighty power in the hearts of men."[98] The former was traditional, nonessential, the "husk"; the latter was distinctive and essential, the "kernel" which is meaningful to modern man. Harnack was not the first, nor would he be the last analyzer of Christianity to believe that the interpretation which he found profoundly meaningful was *the* true interpretation for all times, past, present, or future. The difficulty arises when the historian takes his own theological position as the ultimate criterion by means of which past affirmations and understandings can be sorted out into valid "kernels" and insignificant "husks." Subjectivity is thereby given free rein. Subsequent interpreters of the historical Jesus have tended to repeat Harnack's basic procedure by regarding what they construed to be relevant for modern faith as the basis for identifying the *historically* distinctive in Jesus' outlook and message. The eschatological and particularly the apocalyptic interpretation of Jesus is still viewed as strange and irrelevant to modern faith. Consequently it is regarded—by definition—as mistaken, or at best, "one-sided" or "extreme." As was true in the late nineteenth century, mediating solutions are still generally preferred. Klaus Koch has said of twentieth century interpretations what Schweitzer found with respect to eighteenth and nineteenth century "life-of-Jesus" research: "Apocalyptic serves as a touchstone for the extent to which exegetes work consistently historically, i.e., how far they really transpose themselves into the spirit of the age which they profess to be talking about."[99] Further historical Jesus research then must confront this basic question: should interpretation begin with modern faith and then look for a Jesus who can give it support? Or should such inquiry begin with the traditions in the gospels, apocalyptic, dualistic, or otherwise strange as they may seem to modern faith, and then try to recognize the Jesus who is described in that historical milieu?

II The Judgment in Jesus' Proclamation and Apocalyptic Judaism

One of the central elements in the message of Jesus according to the synoptic gospels is his proclamation of the impending Judgment. At that time, men and nations will be judged according to their deeds, and either be invited to inherit the Kingdom of God or consigned to gehenna. In the meantime, Jesus warned his hearers, they must repent. Moreover, the synoptic gospels all report that Jesus commissioned his followers and sent them out through all the towns of Israel or Galilee so that their inhabitants, too, might hear the message of repentance in the face of the coming day of Judgment. Recent years have seen numerous books and articles on the Kingdom of God and Son of man in the teaching of Jesus or the gospels. Yet, despite its important place in Jesus' preaching and the great mass of related synoptic passages, the Judgment generally has been mentioned only incidentally in studies of Jesus' message and the gospels.

In view of its optimistic appraisal of God and man, it is not surprising that Protestant liberalism showed little interest in the final Judgment. For Harnack, the gospel of Jesus was basically "a glad message assuring us of life eternal" and of God's Fatherhood.[1] There was no room for any act of divine judgment against sinful man.[2] It was left to the eschatological school to bring Jesus' sayings about the Judgment forward as a topic for scholarly comment. Even here, comment is nearly all there was: Weiss gave less than six pages to the subject,[3] and Schweitzer hardly more.[4] The school of "realized eschatology," of course, found no warning of future Judgment in Jesus' message. Since the Kingdom had already come in Jesus' own person and message, so had the Judgment. Jewish leaders and the multitudes alike already "passed judgment upon themselves" by their "reactions to the developing situation."[5] The topic is examined seriously, however, by J. Jeremias,[6] T.W. Manson,[7] and W.G. Kümmel[8] who acknowledge, if not always consistently, that there was indeed a significant future element in Jesus' eschatological orientation. Such discussions, however, are exceptional.[9] Most British and American commentators have little or nothing to say about the Judgment.[10] Their predominant tendency is to read any Judgment sayings which the commentator cannot avoid attributing to Jesus in a vague or generalizing way, accentuating only the positive.[11]

Bultmann says little about Jesus' expectation of impending Judgment, but is bothered theologically by the apparent conflict between the radical obedience Jesus calls for, and the promises of rewards and threats of "hell fire" which sometimes are associated with this summons to obedience.[12] Surprisingly, Bultmann does not propose to demythologize the message of impending Judgment, other than by implying that its meaning is to be found in the summons to decision or repentance and to doing the will of God.[13] In Bultmann's interpretation, focus is upon the present, the existential "Now" of decision. The future Judgment is collapsed into an ever-recurring crisis of decision before God "who is always the coming God."[14] Bultmann, like most other modern commentators, prefers to discuss Jesus' message of the Kingdom rather than his warnings of impending Judgment, and to emphasize the prospect or presence of redemption rather than the fate of the condemned. This tendency is even more pronounced in Bultmann's pupils, who wish to ascribe to Jesus the claim that the Kingdom was already in some way present,[15] and to subsume Jesus' message (or "self-understanding") into the "kerygma" or theology of the early church.

It might be expected that the "new theology" of hope, which proceeds from an appreciation of both the biblical and existential importance of the future, would recover some of the gospels' expectancy of coming Judgment. To date, however, proponents of this theology have been emphasizing the aspect of hope (in particular, resurrection), to the virtual exclusion of any sense of adverse judgment or condemnation. Thus Jesus is represented as savior but not as judge; the subject of Judgment does not come up for discussion in the *magna opera* of Moltmann and Pannenberg.[16] Even Braaten, who keenly appreciates the potentially catastrophic character of many of the bio-social-political crises of our time, does not bring into focus the warning of divine Judgment which, as we shall see, was central to the message of the Jesus of synoptic tradition.[17]

Some critics may be reluctant to acknowledge that Jesus had been mistaken in his expectation that the Judgment, like the coming of the Kingdom of God and Son of man, would occur within the lifetime of the generation of his own contemporaries. Neither traditionalist nor liberal theology is easy about the idea of Jesus' being mistaken. Moreover, except for some "fundamentalist" or "literalist" circles where few scholarly interpretations of the historical Jesus are attempted, hardly anyone in the twentieth century is looking for the fulfillment, either soon or later, of an apocalyptic vision of Judgment where men and nations will stand before the throne of divine judgment. Interpreters also may find the prospect of Judgment objectionable on ethical or theological grounds. Most modern theologians, including the late Karl Barth, prefer to think of man's destiny in terms of a universal salvation. The synoptic scenes and statements concerning the final condemnation of the unrighteous accord neither with the humanistic idealism of liberal thought nor with the emphasis on the grace of God in traditionalist theology.[18] Proponents of the latter in fact can point to several non-synoptic biblical texts in support of the hope for the redemption of all mankind.[19] Modern theories of corrections emphasize the "rehabilitation" or restoration of "the criminal" to society, rather than punishment or retribution in the name of "justice." Moreover, Bultmann was especially concerned that the response of radical obedience or love would be degraded if Jesus were thought to have summoned his hearers to act with a view to eschatological "reward" or "punishment."[20]

For these and perhaps other reasons N.T. scholars have generally avoided the subject of Jesus' proclamation and warnings of coming Judgment. Scholarly discussions commonly repeat stock assertions intended to relieve Jesus of the onus of apocalyptic error. Thus it is said that even if some Judgment sayings must be assigned to Jesus (instead of the early Church), at least he did not go in for the vivid descriptions supposedly typical of Jewish apocalypticism, or that Jesus opposed Jewish apocalypticism's alleged enthusiasm for "calculating" when that day would come.[21] In this connection, it frequently is suggested that Jesus' own beliefs and expectations were in no significant way related to those of the Judaism of his day, and that with only moderate ingenuity he and his message can be abstracted entirely from that unfortunate milieu. Our finding, however, is that the conceptions of Judgment which are assigned to Jesus in the synoptic gospels are consistent, for the most part, with other features of his eschatological outlook and activity as evidenced in these sources, as well as with many features of apocalyptic Judaism dating from the late-biblical, inter-testamental, and early Christian period.

The Synoptic Evidence: The Beliefs of Jesus and the Early Church

As with every other question relating to the historical Jesus, consideration of this matter runs directly into the kind of antithesis posed by Schweitzer in his controversy with Wrede as to the historical value of the Marcan traditions. Here the issue is whether the sayings concerning the impending Judgment derive from and accurately report the words and outlook of Jesus. Or should the interpreter attribute them to the literary activity of the early Church or the evangelists? There are reasons to be skeptical about the skeptical position. Several of its latter-day advocates invoke the magic name of form criticism as justification for disregarding sayings found objectionable on theological or moral grounds. This strategy has been utilized widely in the interpretation of Jesus' apocalyptic sayings.[22] On the other hand, one cannot assume that every saying assigned to Jesus, apocalyptic or otherwise, was handed on and copied down verbatim into our gospels. It is a question of probability: in the first place, in the analysis of each pericope or unit of tradition; and then, overall, as to the preponderance of evidence. There are a great many sayings which present no special cause to be treated as secondary, in which Jesus speaks of the coming Judgment.

We do not wish to attribute undue merit to the four-source theory. However, as a convenience, we shall first review the more obviously relevant passages found in Mark (if also in one or both of the other synoptics); then in "Q", i.e., in Matthew and Luke, but not in Mark; in "M" (Matthew's gospel only); and finally, in "L", the sayings peculiar to Luke. It will become apparent that impending Judgment was a basic feature of Jesus' message and outlook from the beginning until the end of his public activity as presented in all four of these gospel "sources." At the least, it can be demonstrated that the attribution of such beliefs to Jesus is not confined to only one or two of the gospels or their sources.

Mark

Mark 6:7–11 (cf. Matt. 10:1, 9–14; Luke 9:1–6). Jesus sends out the Twelve, two by two, intending them to preach that men should repent (6:12). The instructions suggest a mission of some urgency. The Twelve are to travel light. If any place will not receive them, as they leave, they are to shake off the dust from their feet "for a testimony *against*" such places (6:11). The gesture implies condemnation, both then and at some decisive time yet to come.

Mark 8:35–38 (=Matt. 16:25–27 = Luke 9:23–27). The prospect of Judgment is implied in the distinction between saving one's present life or gaining the whole world, and saving one's life—eternal life—in the coming age. This prospect is made more explicit in the saying about the Son of man coming in the glory of God with the holy angels. Mark does not here identify the coming Son of man as Judge, though this may be hinted at in the word of warning: "Of him will the Son of man also be ashamed" (8:38). Matthew includes a more emphatic admonition: "And then he will repay every man for what he has done" (16:27b).

We may have two or possibly three separate sayings here: 8:35; 8:36f.; and 8:38. The first and third of these indicate a definite relation between a person's response to Jesus and his ultimate fate, while the second (8:36f.) in effect is a parable, comparing the value of life in this world with that of eternal life in the Age to come or Kingdom of God.[23] Each of these sayings, and all of them together, suggest that each man will be judged and his final destiny determined on the basis of what he does now, in this life, in response to Jesus and his words.[24] Appropriately, Mark concludes this little collection of sayings to the disciples and "the multitude" with Jesus' promise and warning that some of them would live to see the potent coming of the Kingdom (9:1).

Mark 9:43–48 (cf. Matt. 18:8f., and Matt. 5:29f.). This is probably the most vivid description of the fate of the condemned in the entire biblical tradition—apart from Rev. 19 and 21. The radical advice to dismember oneself now, rather than face eternal torment in the unquenchable fire of hell, whether construed literally or as "oriental hyperbole," unmistakably and seriously summons the hearer-reader to do all now he can to prepare for Judgment, lest he experience such a horrible fate.[25] The frightful quality of the saying may have been what prompted Luke to omit it entirely, though he does give the unreassuring vision of Dives in Hades (Luke 16:23–28). Even Matthew condenses and omits portions of Mark's report: notably, 9:45 and 48, if not also vv. 44 and 46.[26] The idea of eternal torment expressed in 9:44 and 48 may be particularly offensive. Although the latter verse evidently derives from Isa. 66:24,[27] we cannot simply assume that it was the early church or the Marcan redactor who inserted it in response to some post-resurrection *Sitz-im-Leben* or theological interest.[28] We shall see that there are other explicit references both to hell fire and eternal punishment in the synoptic sources.

Mark 10:17–31 (=Matt. 19:16–28, 30 = Luke 18:19–31). The rich man (called "young" only by Matthew) is confronted by Jesus with a decision. He must choose between the good life associated with his great possessions "now in this time," and the hope of inheriting eternal life in the Kingdom of God or age to come. This is the basic kind of decision Jesus' parables and sayings ordinarily present. The fate of those excluded from the Kingdom of God is not described, but it is said simply that "many that are first will be last, and the last first" (10:31). The evident point of these several sayings is that men will be judged and their final destiny determined on the basis of their decisions and actions—or indecision and inaction—now in this life.

Mark 13:24–29 (=Matt. 24:29–33; cf. Luke 21:25–31). It seems likely that the schematic arrangement of the sayings of Mark 13 into a series of sequential periods and events is based on the church's and/or Mark's interests. Mark may well have been concerned to account for the fact that nearly a generation after the time of Jesus, the Kingdom of God and Son of man had not yet come. Some of the sayings incorporated here may derive from other experiences, needs and concerns of the Church. The third person plural at 13:26 suggests that Mark understood the saying to have been meant for others than those whom Jesus had addressed during his lifetime.[29] But the assurance of the coming of the Son of man in power and glory (v. 26) comports entirely with other Marcan sayings of Jesus, particularly those at 8:38–9:1, and 14:62. The Son of man will come "to gather his elect," evidently in order to vindicate and induct them into their final state of blessedness.

Mark 13:33–37 (cf. parallels). Here the emphasis is on watching, being ready for the arrival of "the time" and "the master of the house." The saying clearly has to do with the decisive importance of being found faithful and responsible at the critical time when the master returns. Judgment is implicit here, although there is no direct reference to the Son of man, trial, or the fate of either the righteous or the condemned. That Mark understood the saying to refer to the coming of the Son of man is apparent from the context. The train of thought beginning at v. 26, concludes in v. 37 with the final admonition, "And what I say to you I say to all: Watch." Mark evidently considered that Jesus' message was intended not only for those to whom he had spoken directly, but also or especially for those who would be alive—including some of the generation of Jesus' contemporaries—at the time of the parousia. They would live to experience "all these things."[30]

Mark 14:62 (=Matt. 26:64; cf. Luke 22:69). Here Jesus warns his accusers, the high priest and the council, that *they* would see the Son of man "coming with the clouds of heaven." The context makes it plain that Jesus expected to be vindicated, while his accusers would soon be on trial before the Son of man. It is uncertain whether the saying goes back to Jesus, himself. How could his followers, who stood off at a safe distance, have heard what he said? Nevertheless, the saying reports what the Marcan church (and, perhaps earlier bearers of tradition) believed Jesus had said. It is not inconsistent with other early traditions and recollections as to his expectations.

"Q"

More references to the Judgment are found in "Q" than in any of the other synoptic "sources."[31] Since "Q" by definition comprises those traditions, mainly sayings, found in both Matthew and Luke but not Mark, this tells us that both Matthew and Luke considered the Judgment to be an important part of Jesus' message for their readers. We shall later see that this inference is substantiated by numerous additional sayings on the subject reported by Matthew and Luke separately. Moreover, if "Q" was an early sayings source, this emphasis would suggest the importance of Judgment in the early tradition. In reviewing the "Q" sayings, as a convenience, we shall follow the order in which Matthew gives them.

Matt. 3:7–12 = Luke 3:7–9, 16f. Here we find a summary of the Baptist's warning of impending judgment ("the wrath to come") and his proclamation of the urgency of repentance. There is no time to lose: "Even now the ax is laid to the root of the tree; every tree therefore that does not bear good fruit is cut down and thrown into the fire." The one the Baptist proclaims as coming, presumably Elijah,[32] will "gather the wheat into the granary, but the chaff he will burn with unquenchable fire." Luke's characterization of this message as "good news" (3:18) suggests that he was thinking mainly of the fate of the "wheat": those who heard, believed, and acted in accordance with the message of repentance. For such as these, the message was good news indeed, for at or after the Judgment, they would, presumably, enter into the Kingdom of God. If Judgment was near, then the time for entering could not be far away. Nothing in the synoptic tradition indicates that Jesus repudiated the Baptist's message.[33]

Matt. 5:3–12 = Luke 6:20–23. Luke's version of the Beatitudes is more abbreviated than Matthew's; or perhaps Matthew has added other sayings to give an expanded account. In any case, both versions report that Jesus promised those who now suffer privation (if not also persecution) that they would experience vindication and blessing in the Kingdom of God which would be theirs.

Matt. 5:25f. = Luke 12:57–59. The setting is secular: a man is on the way to court with his accuser who will certainly win his case and then the judge will put the man in (debtors') prison. To avoid this fate, the hearer (who is identified with the accused) is advised, "Make friends quickly with your accuser"; "Settle with him on the way." As in the case of the Parable of the Unjust Steward (Luke 16:1–9),[34] we clearly have a parable of the Judgment, not a piece of moral wisdom for all times. It is not too late to act now, but soon it will be. Do what you can, while you can.

Matt. 6:19f. = Luke 12:33. The same idea is expressed here as in the Beatitudes, though here it is less a matter of privation than renunciation. Those whose conduct is righteous lay up for themselves "treasures in heaven" (cf. Matt. 5:12 = Luke 6:23). As with the Beatitudes, the meaning is that their conduct is known to God, who will see to their ultimate vindication and inclusion in the blessed life of the Kingdom of God.[35]

Matt. 7:1f. = Luke 6:37f. This gnomic saying is not expressly eschatological. One could treat it as a wisdom saying, meaning simply that the righteous will be rewarded in this life, while, conversely, those who judge others harshly will experience condemnation. Such also could be the meaning of the Parable of the Unmerciful Servant (Matt. 18:23–35) and the Matthean supplement to the Lord's Prayer (6:14f.). However, in view of the predominantly eschatological orientation of the gospels, and particularly, of the "Q" material, it seems more likely that reference here is to final eschatological judgment and recompense.

Matt. 7:13f. = Luke 13:23f. Where does the narrow gate or door lead? To life, according to Matthew. "Life" often means eternal life, which is to be experienced in the Kingdom of God. Here again we see the basic decision Jesus regularly set before his hearers: either seek the blessings of the present life, or give these up for the sake of eternal life in the Kingdom of God. It is a question of either/or. Did Matthew add the antithesis, "the gate is wide and the way easy that leads to destruction"? Or was this part of the "Q" saying which Luke omitted? In any case, it only makes explicit the alternate fate that awaits the many who do not "strive to enter by the narrow door." There is no judgment scene; but there can be little doubt that the saying refers to the final Judgment and the destinies of those who hear the word of Jesus and either respond seriously, or fail to do so.[36]

Matt. 7:24–27 = Luke 6:47–49. This parable or similitude of the two houses (or foundations) is a parable of Judgment. Those who hear the words of Jesus and do them "will be like a wise man who built his house upon the rock." Those who hear but do not do, can only look forward to ruin. Responsiveness to Jesus' words determines one's destiny. All depends on doing the words of Jesus in the interim, before it is too late and the flood waters come.[37]

Matt. 8:11f. = Luke 13:28f. Here is a statement about what is to occur at—or perhaps after—the Judgment. As in Mark 13:27, the elect (Matthew, "many"; Luke, "men") will come from the extremities of the earth to enjoy the blessings of life in the Kingdom of God with the fathers, while those found unworthy will be excluded from the Kingdom and, in Matthew's phrase, "thrown into outer darkness," there to weep and gnash their teeth.

Matt. 9:37f.; 10:5–8, 15 = Luke 10:2, 9, 11b, 12. The image of the harvest perhaps was meant to suggest the gathering of men into the Kingdom of God which was to take place in conjunction with the Judgment. At all events, Jesus sends out his followers, as in Mark, to cast out demons, heal, and preach repentance. In these accounts, the missionaries are also to proclaim that the Kingdom of God has come near (*engiken*). The last verse leaves no doubt that this mission was understood (by Matthew and Luke, at any rate) as a summons to repentance and action before "that day," the "day of Judgment." On that day the men of Sodom, raised from the death and rubble of that ancient city, would hear a more favorable verdict than the citizens of the towns and villages of Israel in the present generation who had failed to heed the words of Jesus' messengers. All this seems in accordance with the ominous gesture the missionaries are told to make as testimony against such places in Mark 6:11.

Matt. 10:32 = Luke 12:8f. Here a direct relationship is shown between men's present response to Jesus and their being acknowledged before God (or His angels) in the future.[38] Luke's version refers to the Son of man, apparently as Judge, or possibly as prosecutor, at the great assize. Matthew's account uses the first person singular, attributing to Jesus the role of the one who acknowledges or denies those who will come before God. This could be one of those places where "Son of man" is confused with the first person singular, or vice versa.[39] We suspect that the reference to the Son of man and the passive form of Luke 12:8f. represent the earlier reading, since these features correspond to the Marcan tradition at 8:38 = Luke 9:26. Matthew's version may be influenced by his desire, as at 7:22f., to express a higher christology or, at all events, to resolve any doubts as to whether the eschatological judge would be Jesus himself.

Matt. 11:21–24 = Luke 10:13–15. This saying in effect parallels and may be related to the earlier sayings about Sodom. In Luke, these several sayings are combined into a single collection (10:12–15), while Matthew gives them separately at 10:15 and here, adding also another saying about Sodom after that addressed to Capernaum (11:23b–24). Possibly the "Q" version followed here originally contained the saying(s) about Sodom which Luke then reduced and rearranged. In any case, the saying here refers to Chorazin, Bethsaida, and Capernaum, where Jesus and/or his disciples had preached repentance and exorcised demons. The people of these cities failed to repent. Therefore the punishment in store for them on the day of Judgment will be worse than that which awaits the pagan (Phoenician) cities of Tyre and Sidon.[40] The latter, it is asserted, would have repented if they had seen the mighty works done in Chorazin and Bethsaida. Even the proverbially wicked land of Sodom will have less to fear on the day of Judgment. Capernaum "shall be brought down to Hades." In short, the cities of Israel which had opportunity to repent but failed to do so will experience a terrible fate in the coming (day of) Judgment. The inference lies at hand that those who heard the message and saw the "mighty words"—namely, the generation contemporary with Jesus and his disciples—would experience this verdict.[41]

Matt. 12:38–42 = Luke 11:29–32. Here again, Jesus contrasts the lack of repentance on the part of his Jewish contemporaries with the repentance and responsiveness of pagans, this time, the ancients of Nineveh who repented at the preaching of Jonah, and the Queen of Sheba, who came to hear Solomon's wisdom. These old pagans "will arise at the Judgment" and join in condemning "this generation" which failed to repent even though "something greater" than either Jonah or Solomon was there.[42] Again, the implication is that the Judgment was expected to take place within the lifetime of the generation then alive.[43] Instead of witnessing God's judgment against the foreign nations, this generation of Israelites would find themselves judged and condemned by these foreigners.

Matt. 19:28 = Luke 22:28–30. Luke's version is reported in the context of the Last Supper, Matthew's in the course of Jesus' journey to Jerusalem. Matthew's visualizes the Son of man seated on his glorious throne in the *Palingenesia* or "New Age"; Luke's refers to the Kingdom (or reign) that has been appointed for Jesus, where his followers are promised the blessing of eating and drinking at Jesus' table in his kingdom.[44] In both Matthew's and Luke's versions, the disciples are assured that they will sit on thrones, judging the twelve tribes of Israel. The Son of man (Matthew) or Jesus himself (Luke), it seems, would superintend the process of judging the tribes of Israel; but in the first instance, that task would be carried out by Jesus' followers, those who have continued with him in his trials (Luke), identified in Matthew as the "Twelve."[45] Nothing is said about their first needing to die and be raised before the time of judging. As reported, it appears that this task of judging was expected to take place within their lifetime.

Matt. 23:34–36 = Luke 11:49–51. The saying[46] indicts the entire Jewish people for the persecution of the prophets and warns that retribution for all this persecution and killing will "come upon you" or "be required of this generation." There can be no doubt that this means the generation of Jesus' contemporaries.[47] The form of Judgment is not specified, and there is no suggestion either of the historical catastrophes of 66–70 A.D. or the coming of the apocalyptic Son of man. Evidently Luke's reference to apostles (11:49) was meant to extend the indictment to include those who had persecuted Christians.[48]

Matt. 24:37–41 = Luke 17:26f., 30. Just as people were caught unaware by the catastrophe that befell the world in the days of Noah, so also those who now go about their affairs as usual will be surprised by the sudden and catastrophic coming or revelation of the Son of man. The implication is that those who are not ready for this great impending day will likewise be "swept away" or destroyed. The earlier saying about the Son of man at Matt. 24:26f. = Luke 17:23f. also makes clear that the "day" or coming of the Son of man will be unheralded, but more to the point, universally and unmistakably obvious when it occurs.[49]

Matt. 24:43f. = Luke 12:39f. We have here the Parable of the Householder and the Thief.[50] The householder does not know when the thief is coming. Like the householder, Jesus' hearers must be ready all the time, "for the Son of man is coming at an hour you do not expect." The thrust of the saying is that those who are not ready will have occasion to regret it. It is not said here directly that the Son of man will come as Judge at the great Judgment; but this seems implicit. The saying corresponds to several others in the synoptic sources which urge constant faithfulness in preparation for the decisive time when the Son of man (or in some of the parables, "the master") comes.

Matt. 24:45–51 = Luke 12:42–46. In this parable, everything hinges on the conduct of the servant or "steward" while the master is away. If he does as he should, "blessed is that servant whom his master when he comes will find so doing." If not, the master who "will come on a day and an hour when he does not expect him and at an hour he does not know, will punish him and put him with the unfaithful." [51] One could construe this and other such sayings as "anti-apocalyptic," in the sense that the point is made that the exact time of the master's return (or the parousia) is unknowable. But the main point of the parable, clearly, was to urge the importance of faithful conduct in constant readiness for the decisive time when the Son of man would come, *which might be any time now.*

Matt. 25:14–30 = Luke 19:12–26. The versions here are so divergent that we cannot be certain that they are recensions of the same parable. Luke's shows Jesus' attempting to correct his followers' mistaken expectation that the Kingdom of God was about to come then and there as they drew near to Jerusalem (19:11). Probably Luke added references to a *"far* country," receiving "kingly power" (or simply, a kingdom), and the nobleman's citizen-enemies who did not want him to reign, in order to show that Jesus (unlike his prematurely enthusiastic followers) knew very well that the Kingdom of God would not come then, or until after the historical destruction of Jerusalem.[52] Matthew adds his characteristic description of the fate of the condemned: "and cast the worthless servant into outer darkness; there men will weep and gnash their teeth." This addition, of course, rather forces the point of the story, since the man or master in the parable is not represented as the eschatological Judge. Nevertheless, the point is clear enough: Jesus tells of persons who will be judged on the basis of their responsiveness to their master's wishes and expectations. Then those who have been faithful will receive more; those who have not been, will lose what they have.[53] Security is not to be achieved by holding on to what one has, but through risks attendant upon the venture of believing and doing the will of God.

Sayings Found Only in Matthew or Luke

If there once was a "Q" source, it is likely that some of the "M" sayings, as we know them, actually derived from "Q", having been, for some reason, omitted by Luke. Similarly, some sayings found only in Luke may actually have been drawn from "Q". Matthew was more conservative than Luke in reproducing Marcan material, and perhaps also included more from "Q" than Luke did. Matthew and Luke were free to include or omit the items of tradition they had before them. Consequently, critics should not exaggerate differences between "Q" and "M" or "L" material as the basis either for claims as to authenticity, or for identifying the distinctive viewpoint, of the evangelists. An "M" or "L" saying could be just as authentic as a "Q" saying—it could even *be* a "Q" saying. Moreover, a "Q" or Marcan saying included by Matthew or Luke might give as much insight into the special viewpoint or concerns of the later evangelists as, respectively, their inclusion of an "M" or "L" tradition. In fact, the sayings about the Judgment found only in Matthew or Luke correspond quite closely to those given in Mark and "Q". The differences are minor, or matters of emphasis.

"M"

The so-called "M" sayings are those found in Matthew's gospel that do not appear also in Mark or Luke.

Matt. 5:5, 7–10. These beatitudes are given only by Matthew, but they fit in with the others included by both Matthew and Luke. Jesus promises those who now are "meek,"[54] merciful, pure in heart, peacemakers, and persecuted for their pursuit of righteousness, that they shall inherit the earth, receive the Kingdom of Heaven, obtain mercy there, see God and be called sons of God. There is no scene of Judgment; but the recompense of the righteous in the Kingdom of God is assured.[55]

Matt. 7:21–23 (cf. Luke 6:46; 13:26f.). It may be that these sayings should be assigned to "Q" since they have somewhat similar Lucan counterparts. In any event, the sayings urge obedience to the words of Jesus, which are understood in Matthew to call for doing the will of God. It will not have been enough simply to have associated oneself with Jesus' name or even person. In Matthew's version, it is definitely a question of eschatological Judgment. Clearly many will be judged adversely: "Not everyone . . . shall enter the Kingdom of God . . ."; "On that day many will say. . . ." Jesus himself expects to be the eschatological Judge: "And then I will declare to them, '. . . depart from me, you evildoers.' "

Matt. 10:23. Matt. 10:17–22 appears to draw on Mark 13:9–13, and describes the conditions Jesus' followers may look for in the time of testimony and trials before "the end" (Mark 13:13). Much if not all of this may reflect the experience of early Christian missionaries. Verse 23, however, seems to refer back to the earlier part of Matthew 10, which consists of the instructions Jesus gave the Twelve for the urgent mission on which he reportedly sent them during his lifetime, through the towns and villages of Israel. It is understandable that Luke would have omitted a saying that ascribed to Jesus belief that the Son of man would have come before the Twelve had completed this mission. But there is no reason to suppose that Matthew would have invented the saying—which already had failed to be fulfilled during the lifetime of Jesus, and still remained unfulfilled at the time Matthew was writing.[56] While it is not said here that the Son of man would come as Judge, clearly his coming would be the decisive event, associated with the coming of the Kingdom of God and the day of Judgment mentioned earlier in the instructions to the Twelve, at 10:5–7, 15.

Matt. 11:23b–24. These verses might have been in "Q", but, perhaps because of their redundancy, were omitted by Luke in his report at 10:13–15. Or it may be that Matthew simply repeated for emphasis, with slight adaptation, a saying he had given already at 10:15 (=Luke 10:12) and 11:21b. At all events, Matthew here reports that Jesus declared that a severely negative judgment was in store for those cities which had opportunity to repent, but failed to do so.[57]

Matt. 12:36f. Possibly Matthew understood the saying as a final comment on the matter of blasphemy against the Holy Spirit (v. 32). There also might be some relation with the admonition at 5:21f. against calling one's brother "fool." In any case, the saying contemplates that "on the day of judgment" men will be judged not only for their deeds but also for their words. Or, more precisely stated, the deeds for which men are to be judged will include their words.

Matt. 13:24–30. The Parable of the Weeds, though captioned by

Matthew as a parable about "the Kingdom of heaven," obviously refers
to the final judgment. In its present form, it seems intended to instruct
the church to defer judgment against the "tares" or "weeds" in its
midst, presumably unrighteous church members, and the parable as a
whole may plausibly be seen to reflect the interests of the early church.
Harvest and harvest time seem to refer to that time of gathering both
the wheat and the weeds, in effect, the time of Judgment.[58] The reap-
ers, we infer, are not the church and its leaders (who correspond rather
to the "field" and "the servants"), but the angels who will gather the
elect into the Kingdom. Then the weeds are to be bound into bundles
and burned. As in the case of the unfruitful tree (7:19), the interpreter
need not identify this burning or fire with the fate of the wicked in
gehenna, since such burning probably would have been common agri-
cultural practice. Still, even if the parables are not to be construed alle-
gorically, the implicit analogy to the fate of the unrighteous is
suggestive.

Matt. 13:36–43. Matthew's account of Jesus' explanation of the Parable of the Weeds is certainly allegorical. It corroborates most of our
conjectures as to the significance of various components, except that
here the field is represented alternately as "the world" (v. 38) and the
Kingdom of the Son of man (v. 41). The "weeds" are described as the
"sons of the evil one," meaning, perhaps, both demons ("all causes of
sin," v. 41) and the unrighteous ("all evil doers"). They will be thrown
by the angels of the Son of man into "the furnace of fire," there to
"weep and gnash their teeth," while the righteous take part in the
transcendent glories of life in the Kingdom of God. This is one of the
more vivid descriptions of Judgment.

Matt. 13:47–50. Again contrary to its Matthean title, we have here a
parable or similitude about the Judgment. The analogy is to a fish net,
thrown into the sea, and the later process of sorting out the fish. Verses
49 and 50 explain the parable: "So it will be at the close of the age."
These verses are not part of the parable, but like Matt. 25:31–46, describe how things will be when the Judgment takes place. The expression, "the close of the age," is Matthean[59] as is the idea of throwing the
unrighteous "into the furnace of fire." However, "gehenna" and "Hades" are mentioned as the place(s) of punishment for the wicked in
Luke as well, and the unquenchable fire of gehenna is a prominent
feature of Mark 9:43–48.[60] That angels would function to gather the
righteous and eject the wicked, who would then weep and gnash their
teeth, is also stated in other synoptic sources. Neither the Son of man
nor God is named as the eschatological Judge.

Matt. 16:27f. These verses present only slight variations upon the traditions given at Mark 8:38–9:1. Matthew refers to the angels who will accompany the Son of man at his coming as *his* angels,[61] and to the Kingdom as the Kingdom of the Son of man. That the Son of man is to be Judge is stated explicitly in v. 27b: "And then he will repay every man for what he has done."

Matt. 18:23–35. Though described as a parable of "the Kingdom of heaven," the Parable of the Unmerciful Servant is more a parable about the coming Judgment. The servant who had been forgiven much was willing to forgive his fellow servant but little. The "king" then turned him over to "the torturers" or jailers until he should pay his debt. "So," Jesus explains to Peter (18:21f.) and perhaps all the disciples (18:1), and through Matthew to the whole church, "my heavenly Father will do to every one of you if you do not forgive your brother from your heart" (v. 35). Here the Judge is God himself,[62] though the judgment is not explicitly described in eschatological terms.

Matt. 22:13. This verse is part of the sub-parable of the man without a wedding garment, which Matthew connects (through v. 10) to the Parable of the Marriage Feast or Great Banquet.[63] The fate of the unfortunate man seems incommensurate to his offense: "the King" orders him bound hand and foot, and cast into outer darkness where "men will weep and gnash their teeth."Perhaps the wedding (or wedding reception), as in the Parable of the Ten Bridesmaids, refers to the coming of the Kingdom of God and Son of man. Like most of the other parables, it had in view the all-surpassing importance of being ready for that great time. Those found unfit would experience adverse judgment. In its present form, however, this pericope seems somewhat garbled, in that we would not expect the human king of the parable to pronounce eschatological judgment. One suspects that the Matthean editorial hand may have been rather heavy here, as earlier in 22:6f.

Matt. 25:1–13. The Parable of the Ten Maidens or Bridesmaids is presented as a parable of the Kingdom of heaven, but it would be described more accurately as a parable of the time of Judgment. Those who were ready when the bridegroom returned "went on with him to the marriage feast." Those who were not ready were excluded with the devastating reproach: "Truly, I say to you, I do not know you."[64] Matthew concludes the parable with the unmistakable eschatological warning: "Watch therefore, for you know neither the day nor the hour." No doubt Matthew understood this as a warning to his readers, for Matthew, like Luke, did not contemplate the continuation of history for generations to come. It does not follow, however, that Matthew created the parable or the word of warning: both correspond to the viewpoint of Jesus as otherwise evidenced in the gospel sources.[65]

Matt. 25:31–46. From what has been seen so far, it should be obvious that the idea of judgment is not confined in the gospels to Matt. 25. Here, nevertheless, is the classic synoptic and New Testament description of the Judgment scene. It is not presented as a parable, but as Jesus' statement concerning how things will be. The Son of man will come in his glory, all the angels with him, and sit on his throne of judgment before which all the nations must pass. The "king" referred to in vv. 34 and 40 is apparently another designation for the Son of man as he sits in judgment. Perhaps the assembly over which he presides as Judge is the Kingdom of the Son of man to which Matthew elsewhere refers.[66] Though nations are assembled, individuals are to be judged. The great surprise is to be that they will be judged on the basis of their previous responsiveness to those in need, according to their several necessities,[67] with whom the King identifies himself: "I was hungry, and you gave me food. . . . As you did it to one of the least of these my brethren, you did it to me." The righteous—those who were responsive—will be invited to "inherit the Kingdom" (cf. Matt. 5:5). Those who had failed to respond with needed assistance will be condemned to the place of eternal punishment—the "eternal fire prepared for the devil and all his angels." It may be, of course, that the scene was entirely composed by Matthew. But those who wish to prove that this was the case would need to account for the presence of similar ideas in the other synoptic gospels. Those who propose the "literary solution" to the problematics of interpretation must be prepared to cut a wide swath through the synoptic tradition, one wider than generally thought necessary by interpreters accustomed to overlooking references to eschatological judgment in the gospels.

"L"

As with "M", some of the sayings assigned to "L" could well have come from "Q"; Matthew may have omitted some material from this "source" which Luke chose to include. At any rate, the "L" sayings about the Judgment do not differ significantly from those in the other synoptic sources, although there are a few special emphases and concepts. For instance, there is more emphasis on fire in connection with the punishment of the condemned. Also, in a few places, Luke reports sayings that seem to contemplate the idea that some of the righteous and unrighteous might enter into their final places of blessing or torment immediately at death, even though the expectation of the coming day of Judgment generally is retained.

Luke 12:47f. Perhaps this is only a final comment upon the Parable of the Faithful and Wise Servant (Matt. 24:45–51 = Luke 12:41–46); or it may have been a separate parable. Its central idea is similar to that in the Parable of the Talents or Pounds: "Everyone to whom much is given, of him will much be required. . . ." The main thrust is to stress the importance of making ready by acting in accordance with the master's will. One suspects that v. 48a reflects Luke's concern for those gentiles to whom the *didachē* of the church may not yet have reached at the time of Judgment, who consequently "did not know, and did what deserved a beating." They would receive only "a light beating"; since less had been given to them, less would be required of them.

Luke 12:49. Jesus not only claims that he came to cast such fire upon the earth, but expresses his impatience that the time for kindling it has not yet arrived. Implicitly, this would be at the time of the coming eschatological Judgment. This does not seem to be the kind of saying that Luke would have invented.[68] It appears contrary to the intent of 9:54f., where Jesus reproaches his followers for thinking about calling down fire from heaven upon the unresponsive Samaritan village. It does accord, however, with the message of John the Baptist about the one who was coming who would baptize with fire, gathering the wheat into his granary, but burning the chaff with unquenchable fire.[69] It also corresponds, in substance, to the several "Q" sayings in Luke that warn of a fate worse than that of Sodom for the cities that fail to repent (Luke 12:12–15).

Luke 13:1–5. The sayings about the Galileans executed by Pilate and the victims of the tower in Siloam underscore the ultimate seriousness of failure to repent. Judgment as such is not mentioned, but as indicated in the caption to these verses (and to vv. 6–9) in the *Gospel Parallels,*[70] the choice confronting Jesus' hearers (and Luke's readers) is "repentance or destruction."

Luke 13:6–9. The Parable of the Fig Tree planted in a vineyard[71] represents a slightly extended version of the saying reported several times about good trees and bad trees and their respective fruits. Perhaps the saying here is related to Luke's concern to explain the delay of the parousia: the tree is given one more year in which to bear fruit. But *then* if it fails to do so, it will be cut down.[72] Whether the parable was meant to refer to individuals or to the community, the implication of prospective Judgment is obvious.

Luke 14:12–14. These verses follow the "parable" or proverbial advice about taking the lowest place.[73] Luke 14:11 seems to refer to the final judgment or determination as to his hearers' destiny. The point of contact between vv. 12–14 and the foregoing seems to be the mention of "banquet" in both sayings. Probably vv. 12–14 should be considered a separate pericope, which is not in the form of a parable, but rather is a direct admonition. Possibly we have here a reminiscence of Tobit 2:1f. The same kind of concern is indicated in Matt. 25:35ff. As in some other "L" traditions, the emphasis here is on the well-being of the poor and those otherwise in need. Here the reader's reward will be "at resurrection of the righteous." This particular expression of assurance may reflect Luke's recognition of the fact that some of Jesus' original hearers would not have lived to see the parousia. (Luke probably wrote the gospel after most of them had died.) In any case, the idea of eschatological Judgment is implicit in the prospect of repayment at the time when the righteous will be raised from the dead.

Luke 16:1–9. As with a great many of the other parables and sayings, the emphasis here is upon acting now in such a way as to assure oneself of being admitted into the place of final blessedness.[74] The prospect of Judgment is implicit in the summons to respond so that, when one's life or livelihood fails, one may be welcomed into "the eternal habitations." The implicit alternative is exclusion from this realm. Here evidently is another of the passages where Luke reports the possibility of each individual's entry into the place of final destiny immediately after death. By implication, judgment takes place at this time.

Luke 16:19–31. Here, though it is not so designated, we have another parable: the story of the rich man and Lazarus. It does not describe a Judgment scene, but simply states that when the poor man died he was carried "by the angels" to Abraham's bosom, a place of comfort and "good things." (In other synoptic sayings, angels were expected to accompany the Son of man at the Judgment, and serve to gather the elect.) Likewise, the rich man, on death and burial, passes directly to Hades, where he experiences anguish "in this flame." Perhaps Hades is named here, rather than gehenna, for the benefit of Luke's Greek readers; both evidently were thought of as places of fire and torment. The point of the story, like that of so many of the other sayings and parables in the several gospel sources, is that a person's final destiny will be determined by his responsiveness in this life to the will of God regarding the needs or well-being of others.[75] It is, in short, a parable about the judgment in store for those who do not repent and respond.

Luke 17:28–30. These verses about the days of Lot, the raining of fire upon Sodom, and the day when the Son of man is revealed are incorporated into the extended collection of eschatological sayings that Luke has assembled in 17:20–18:8. All have to do with the future, decisive, unheralded, and unmistakable coming of the Kingdom of God and Son of man.[76] Again, we see Lucan emphasis upon fire in connection with Judgment, though here Luke is interested mainly in stressing the importance of urgent and appropriate action in readiness for the parousia. This is also the evident sense of the "Q" verses preceding (Matt. 24:37–39 = Luke 17:26f.).[77] It will not be enough to go about business-as-usual in the meantime. It is a time for emergency measures, interim ethics.

Luke 18:1–8. The Parable of the Unjust Judge reflects the same hope represented in the prayer Jesus gave his disciples as a model for their piety: that through their prayers they could move God at last to bring his Kingdom. Here they are advised "that they ought always to pray and not lose heart." Like the saying at Luke 12:32 where Jesus assures his followers that God will, indeed, give them the Kingdom, this parable also assures the hearer-reader that God will vindicate "his elect." The interpretation provided in vv. 6–8 corresponds to the main thrust of the parable. The interpretation is this: if even an unrighteous judge can be prevailed upon to vindicate the persistent petitioner, how much more can God be relied on to do so for those who look to him for help.[78] The interpretation further assures the hearer-reader that God will not delay long, that "he will vindicate them speedily." But the "elect" may not count on vindication simply because they have cried, "Lord, Lord!" As with many of the sayings and parables, the decisive matter will be how people have responded to God and his will in the meantime: "When the Son of man comes, will he find faith on earth?" Thus Luke ends his first collection of Jesus' parousia sayings with the reassurance and warning of impending action both by God and the Son of man: God will vindicate the faithful when the Son of man comes.

Luke 21:34–36. Much the same understanding as just noted is expressed in these verses with which Luke ends his second group of Jesus' sayings about the parousia.[79] Jesus' hearers (and Luke's readers) are to "watch at all times," taking care not to become weighted down with dissipation and the cares of this life. They must be ready at all times, lest "that day" come suddenly, finding them unprepared. "That day," the day of Judgment before the Son of man, can come at any time, and when it comes it will do so universally and unmistakably: "It will come upon all who dwell upon the face of the whole earth."[80] The admonition to "pray that you may have strength to escape all these things that will take place" refers to the *peirasmos* or tribulation expected in Jewish and other Christian sources before the coming of the new age.[81] Here, as in the Lord's Prayer, Jesus calls on his followers to pray that God bring his Kingdom and that they be spared the otherwise scripturally ordained tribulation.[82] Here, as in other passages, it is expected that the Son of man will come as Judge to decide the final fate of those who will appear before him on the basis of their conduct in the interim of history remaining until he comes.

Luke 23:27–31. Jesus is being led away to execution, followed by "a great multitude of the people" bewailing and lamenting. "Do not weep for me, but for yourselves and your children," Jesus warns, for "the days that are coming" will be a time of terrible tribulation. Whether the reference to green and dry wood points to the historical burning of Jerusalem, or to fire and brimstone, such as fell upon Sodom in the days of Lot, is uncertain. Verses 29 and 30 express the conviction that the time of final tribulation if not also judgment would come upon those then alive ("yourselves and your children").

The Judgment in the Synoptic Sources

These numerous Marcan, "Q", "M", and "L" traditions about the coming Judgment constitute a substantial portion of the synoptic material. They can scarcely be dismissed as of little consequence to the evangelists or the early church. Together, they present a fairly consistent pattern of understanding: the Judgment will take place soon, in the lifetime of at least some of those who themselves had heard Jesus' message. The Son of man will be the Judge and summon those who had done the will of God to eternal life in the Kingdom of God. But he will condemn those who have failed to repent and respond to Jesus, his message and the will of God, to exclusion from the Kingdom in a place of torment. Although some of the particular features that appear, for instance, only in "M" or "L" might be of questionable authenticity, there is no apparent reason to doubt that this basic understanding was shared by Jesus himself.

That Jesus expected these events to befall the generation of his contemporaries is attested in all three gospels and in all four of the "sources."[83] That the Son of man would appear as the Judge is not always indicated, though again, all of the gospels and sources present sayings to this effect.[84] A few "M" and "L" sayings attributed to Jesus refer to an anticipated reign or Kingdom of the Son of man, but in every case these passages seem to be honorific expressions for the role or function of the Son of man as Judge.[85] Similarly, the description of accompanying angels as belonging to the Son of man appears only in "M" material, and again represents only a minor variation, possibly in the direction of a higher "christology."[86] Two sayings indicate that Jesus expected that his followers would sit on thrones judging Israel, if not the whole world. In the more explicit saying, evidently "Q", Jesus assures his followers that they will "sit on twelve thrones judging the twelve tribes of Israel" (Matt. 19:28 = Luke 22:30). This expectation also is implicit in the request of the sons of Zebedee and Jesus' reply. They wish Jesus to promise them seats on either side of him in his "glory."Jesus does not deny that some will be so seated, but insists only that "it is for those for whom it has been prepared"(Mark 10:35–40 = Matt. 20:20–23.[87]

The expectation that the righteous will be invited to enter or inherit the Kingdom, while the wicked or unresponsive are to be condemned to a place of torment, also is attested in all synoptic sources. No "Q" traditions attribute to Jesus any sayings about fire in connection with this torment,[88] and only one Marcan passage does so, though it is both vivid and emphatic, warning that the fire is unquenchable and the torment interminable (9:43–47). Such an understanding is also indicated in certain earlier Jewish sources: Isa. 66:24; Judith 16:17. Jesus refers to fire in several "M" and "L" passages, either in connection with the impending tribulation or the final Judgment.[89]

"Weeping and gnashing of teeth" and "outer darkness" are expressions found most commonly in Matthean accounts of Jesus' sayings about the fate of the condemned.[90] The former expression also appears in Luke 13:28, which probably parallels Matt. 8:12, and may have been present in "Q". Matthew includes several references to gehenna which are not found elsewhere in Jesus' sayings,[91] but references to gehenna also are found in Mark.[92] Hades, understood as the place of final detention and torment, is mentioned in at least one "Q" pericope; Matt. 11:22f. = Luke 10:15, and in the "L" parable of Lazarus (Luke 16:23).

It is not certain, then, whether we should say that Matthew wished to emphasize, or that Luke wished to de-emphasize, the sayings regarding the punishment of the condemned. The fact that Luke chose to omit Mark 9:43–48 suggests that he might have intended to mitigate the severity of certain other sayings (e.g., about weeping and gnashing of teeth or gehenna) which may have been in "Q" and were reported by Matthew. On the other hand, the prospect of fire is not lacking in Luke's reports of Jesus' sayings about the destiny of the condemned, though it is missing from the "Q" sayings. Thus we could equally well conclude that such "Q" sayings as at Luke 10:15 and 13:28 and the Marcan pericope at 9:43–47 are exceptional, and that the earlier sources ("Q" and Mark) do not stress these more vivid features as much as the later ones do. But we are not in a position to determine whether these ideas may have been congenial or otherwise to Jesus himself. In any event, the prospect of final Judgment and the urgent importance of preparation for it now, while there is still time, runs like a scarlet thread through the whole of the sayings attributed to Jesus in the synoptic gospels and their "sources."

That Jesus proclaimed the Judgment as the decisive, future, and impending "moment of truth" for his generation—and for the resurrected dead of previous generations—can hardly be disputed. This aspect of his message and expectation, though related to various sayings about the coming or disclosure of the Son of man, is so solidly embedded in the synoptic tradition that even interpreters who find it theologically uncomfortable seldom venture to attribute it entirely to the later church. (Instead, they normally ignore it, or simply assert that Jesus meant something else.) The Judgment is also closely related to the proclamation of the coming Kingdom. But if a few synoptic passages can be read in such a way as to imply that Jesus or the evangelists believed that the Kingdom of God was somehow already present, there are none which suggest that the Judgment was thought to be in any way "actualized" or "realized."

Nevertheless, many sayings do imply that Jesus sometimes pronounced judgment upon those whose actions (or inaction, lack of repentance and response) showed them indifferent to his message of the will and coming Kingdom of God. Similarly, Jesus also pronounced a favorable verdict upon those whose present mode of being was as it should be. The "Beatitudes" illustrate both aspects. The poor, the meek, the merciful, and the like are already declared blessed, and are assured that they will enter the Kingdom of God, while—in Luke—those who are now rich, full, happy, and esteemed are condemned to experience a reversal of their fortunes in the coming dispensation.[93] Jesus already declares that those who are ashamed of him and his words will be condemned to shame by the Son of man when he comes.[94] In another Marcan saying, Jesus pronounces judgment against the "great buildings" of the Temple precincts: "There will not be left here one stone upon another, that will not be thrown down."[95] On the other hand, Jesus' declaration to the scribe who "answered wisely" to his summary of the two love commands, "You are not far from the Kingdom of God," evidently was a provisional commendation (Mark 12:28–34).

As is implicit in his instructions to the disciples to shake the dust of the unreceptive towns from their feet, Jesus explicitly pronounces doom in the day of Judgment against those cities that fail to receive these messengers or their message of the coming Kingdom: "It shall be more tolerable on that day for Sodom (and Gomorrah) than for that town."[96] Likewise, he declares to his contemporaries ("this generation") that the punishment for killing the righteous of all previous eras will come upon them.[97] In still another group of "Q" sayings, he decrees who will be forgiven and who will not be,[98] again implying a sense of authority such as might be expected of the one who would preside at the time of the Judgment. The Marcan story of the healing of the paralytic expresses this same sense of authority: "which is easier to say to the paralytic, 'Your sins are forgiven'; or to say 'Rise, take up your pallet and walk'?"[99] Another story in which Jesus pronounces forgiveness is Luke's account of the woman with the ointment (Luke 7:47–49). Whether Jesus also considered himself to be the Son of man who would pronounce Judgment from his glorious throne on "that day" we cannot tell, though some of the sayings definitely are to this effect.[100]

Many of these ideas seem strange to modern readers who are unfamiliar with the patterns of belief and expectation characteristic of apocalyptic Judaism. To be sure, Jesus' beliefs concerning the coming Judgment differ in some respects from those of apocalyptic Judaism as we know them from Jewish sources of the period. These sources themselves diverge considerably on many features concerning the anticipated Judgment. There are, however, a number of recurrent features that can be summarized fairly briefly.

Jewish Beliefs About the Judgment in the Inter-testamental Period

The idea of God's judgment was not new to Judaism in the intertestamental period. The history of man, of Israel, and of the nations had been understood as a series of acts of judgment by God against the cruelty and pretentions of men and nations, and in the case of Israel and the Jewish people, for idolatry, forgetting God, and violating the Covenant laws and ethics. Many of the prophets had looked for the day of Yahweh, that time of final judgment and redemption which would forever put an end to the ambiguities of human behavior, and transform history and the whole creation into a permanent era and realm of peace.[101] In the inter-testamental writings the emphasis shifts even more to the future period of judgment and redemption which will be both in and at the end of history. Here also attention is directed to the fate of individuals who will be judged according to their deeds. There is a tendency for both modern Jewish and Christian interpreters to ignore or bypass the inter-testamental writings in order more readily to leap directly from canonical Hebrew scriptures into "normative" Judaism or post-apostolic Christianity. However, it is important to observe that in many respects the "strange" world of apocalyptic Judaism is contiguous with the earlier prophetic tradition.[102] Our concern here, however, is simply to describe some of the main features of inter-testamental Jewish beliefs concerning the coming Judgment.

"The Day of Judgment." This term appears in several places, referring to a future "day" or period in which the final and decisive Judgment was expected to occur: e.g., Apoc. Moses 26:4; T. Levi 3:3; II Enoch 51:1–3; II Esdras 7:38, 104, 113; 12:34; Wisd. Sol. 3:18. Similar terms, "the great judgment," or "the great day of judgment" appear occasionally also, e.g., Enoch 22:4, 11; 65:6f.; 103:8. Most commonly, reference is simply to "Judgment" or "the Judgment" and related events.

The Judge. In a great many, possibly a majority of instances where the identity of the Judge is indicated, it is God himself who is expected to perform this role. Often a circumlocution is used, such as "the Lord of Spirits" or "the Most High." God is looked for as Judge in a wide variety of the sources, including some—most notably Enoch—which also refer to some other figure as the expected Judge: Vita Adae et Evae 29:10; Enoch 1:1–4, 9; 45:6; 53:2; 90:20–27; 91:7, 15; 100:4; T. Levi 4:1; T. Asher 7:3; Sib. Or. 3:659ff.; 741ff.; 4:41, 176f., 183f.; As. Moses 10:7; II Bar. 83:2f.; II Esdras 7:33; 9:2; Ps. of Sol. 15:12, 14; 17:51.

In Enoch, two different terms are used for a figure other than God, who was expected to appear or come as Judge: "Mine elect one," and "Son of man." In each case, it is expected that this figure will sit "on the throne of glory."[103] His function is to preside at the Judgment, punishing the wicked and vindicating the righteous.[104] Not surprisingly, it is "a new priest" who is expected as final Judge in the Testament of Levi (18:2–14). Though not so designated, his activity is clearly messianic, in the sense that he is to bring about both an end to sin and the power of Beliar, and the beginning of the final glorious era of light and peace. A "king" or "messiah" is referred to in Sib. Or. III:652–656. God will send him to "give my land relief from the bane of war," somewhat in the manner of the O.T. "judges." But a few verses later, it seems that God himself is the one who will act as Judge, overcoming the enemy nations and delivering his people: III:669–709, 741–761. The most explicit reference to the messiah as Judge is in II Bar. 72:2–73:7, a passage reminiscent in its latter verses of various Isaianic themes. Here the Messiah is to judge between the nations, sparing those which have not oppressed Israel, giving over to the sword those that have.[105]

The judged. In most places, it is clear that the Judgment will be universal: it will come upon "all men," or simply, "all."[106] Moreover, in some sources, it is clear that the judged will include the dead of previous generations: "the great judgment shall be for all generations of the world" (En. 103:8). The idea that all the dead will be raised and judged is indicated in T. Benj. 10:8: "Then also all men shall rise, some unto glory and some unto shame." Such, as we have seen, was the understanding attributed to Jesus in several passages. Something of the sort seems intended as well in Sib. Or. IV:176–183, where the destruction of the earth and the whole race of men is expected to precede the resurrection and judgment. Less dramatically, in En. 22:3f., the spirits of the souls of the dead await the great Judgment, presumably in Sheol. In some passages, the dead are thought already to be situated in their places of intermediate, if not final repose, as in the Lucan story of the rich man and Lazarus. The "treasuries of the souls" or of "the righteous" in II Baruch seem to be intermediate places where the righteous dead await resurrection and vindication at the Judgment.[107] It may be implicit that the souls of the wicked will not be raised or present at the Judgment, but they will experience only "the more" torment where they are (II Bar. 30:4f.). Enoch 103:2–8 offers assurance that the lot of the spirits of the righteous who have died "is abundantly beyond the lot of the living," while the souls of the wicked will experience judgment and tribulation in Sheol. It is not clear, however, whether these are to be their respective fates only after "the great Judgment" (103:8), or whether these will begin to be experienced also in the interval between death and the Judgment. The latter is indicated in II En. 7:1–5, in the case of certain apostate angels who experience torment in "the second heaven" while "awaiting the great and boundless Judgment." The most developed vision in regard to the fate of the spirits of the dead is in II Esdras 7:75–99. Here it is said that the spirits of the wicked shall "immediately wander about in torments, ever grieving and sad, in seven ways," the righteous experiencing "rest in seven orders" or groups. The medieval conception of seven levels of hell and seven heavens may derive from this passage.

As in prophetic thought, so in some of the inter-testamental visions, all nations or Gentiles will be judged by the messiah (II Bar. 72:2) or by God, himself (As. Mos. 10:7). Modern Christian interpreters commonly allege that Jewish apocalypticism was nationalistic if not chauvinistic, glorying in the impending destruction or subjugation of non-Jewish nations and peoples. A number of passages seem to justify this allegation: e.g., I En. 62:1–12, where the Son of man is to give the kings and the mighty and exalted over to the angels for punishment,[108] As. Mos. 10:7–10, where the Gentiles are to be punished, evidently in gehenna, and II Esdras 13:37–38, 49. On the other hand, as in the prophetic tradition,[109] there are several inter-testamental passages which anticipate a favorable verdict and a share in the new era of peace for at least some of the Gentile nations.[110] Testament of Levi 18:9 looks for the enlightenment of the Gentiles through the priestly Messiah-Judge, and

T. Benjamin contemplates the inclusion of at least some Gentiles in the future era.[111] Most references, however, as in the wisdom tradition, are to righteous and wicked individuals, mainly, we can assume, Jews. These are the ones whose judgment is generally looked for in the inter-testamental visions of the day of Judgment.

One other group is among the judged: the "watchers," fallen "stars," or apostate angels. Their situation is particularly emphasized in Enoch. Some of them have already been bound and put away until the time of Judgment.[112] Generally, they are expected to be condemned at the time of Judgment before the Son of man (En. 69:27-29) or God, himself (90:20-27; 91:15). This is also the understanding in a few other sources, e.g., T. Judah 25:3; II Enoch 7:1-2. Some of these passages, e.g., T. Judah 25:3 and En. 90:24-27, anticipate the expression found at Matt. 25:41, "the eternal fire prepared for the devil and his angels."

That "angels" would gather those who were to be judged, a common idea in the synoptic gospels, is suggested a few times in Enoch, e.g., 1:9; 100:4.

The basis for Judgment. Judgment would be based upon the attitudes and actions of each person. Commonly, as in the wisdom tradition, general categories are used, such as "the righteous," and "the wicked" or "sinners." Each would be judged accordingly.

> Blessed are you, you righteous and elect,
> For glorious shall be your lot.
> And the righteous shall be in the light of the sun,
> and the elect in the light of eternal life. . . .[113]

> Woe to you, you fools, for through your folly you shall perish. . . .
> And now, know that you are prepared for the day of destruction: wherefore do not hope to live, you sinners, but you shall depart and die; for you know no ransom; for you are prepared for the day of great judgment, for the day of tribulation and great shame for your spirits.[114]

Men would be judged for their secret thoughts, which would be made manifest: II Bar. 83:3. Moreover, they would be judged for their actions or deeds, notably for their responsiveness to others:

> Blessed is the man who does not direct his heart with malice against any man, and helps the injured and condemned, and raises the broken-down, and shall do charity to the needy, because on the day of the great judgment every weight, every measure and every makeweight (will be) as in the market, that is to say they are hung on scales and stand in the market, (and every one) shall learn his own measure, and according to his measure shall take his reward.[115]

In other sources too, it generally is expected that men will be judged for their deeds or misdeeds.[116]

The destiny of the righteous and the fate of the condemned. As in prophetic, Deuteronomistic, and wisdom traditions, it was believed that God would reward those who were righteous and punish the wicked. But it was no longer expected that God's justice would be experienced, fully, at any rate, in this life; rather, this would occur at the time of Judgment at the end or consummation of the age. The perspective is essentially that of Daniel 12:1f. We find, typically, a moral and also judicial dualism, reflected in the final destinies to which men will be assigned.

> . . . I know . . . how in the great time (to come) many mansions (are) prepared for men, good for the good, and bad for the bad, without number many. Blessed are those who enter good houses, for in the bad there is no peace nor return.[117]

The righteous are assured that they will inherit the earth: "For the elect there shall be light and joy and peace, and they shall inherit the earth."[118] But it will be a transformed earth, no longer subject to human corruption, Satan, or foreign powers.

The fertility of the ground will be restored, so that field and tree will produce in super-abundance.[119] It will be an era without sin and death or any other corruption. Only good, light and righteousness will remain there (En. 91:17).

> For the righteous the great aeon will begin, and they will live eternally, and then too there will be amongst them neither labor, nor sickness, nor humiliation, nor anxiety, nor need, nor violence, nor night, nor darkness, but great light. And they shall have a great indestructible wall, and a paradise bright and incorruptible, for all corruptible things shall pass away, and there will be eternal life.[120]

No longer will foreign kings or nations lord it over Israel, but these—if they remain at all—will worship God or at least bear gifts of tribute to Israel in that new era.[121] God himself will rule the world, through his Messiah (Ps. Sol. 17) or through the righteous.[122]

The Kingdom of God will then be established throughout the whole creation and for all ages.[123] Necessarily, Satan or Beliar would have no more place there.[124] Some of the sources contemplate a final battle of cosmic proportions in which God and his host of armies overcome and finally defeat Belial and his horde, either before, or in connection with the day of Judgment.[125] In the process, perhaps, the world itself will pass away or be destroyed, or will be so radically transformed that a new world, both heaven and earth, will come in its place:

"And I will transform the heaven and make it an eternal blessing and light; and I will transform the earth and make it a blessing."[126] The idea of a new heaven and a new earth also appears in the concluding chapters of the canonical Isaiah: 65:17; 66:22. Thus the new or transformed earth is referred to not only as the Kingdom of God, but also as the world (or age) to come.[127]

The unrighteous not only will be excluded from the joys of life in the new era: they also must face eternal torment or destruction. This is true alike for sinful men as for Belial and the unrighteous angels. Belial is to be "cast into the fire forever" (T. Levi 25:3), and at the great Judgment, some, at least, of the corrupt angels will be "made an end of."[128]

Several passages state that sinners will be condemned to destruction: "And sinners shall perish forever in the day of the Lord's judgment, when God visiteth the earth with His judgment."[129] Frequently, however, the prospect awaiting the unrighteous is visualized in terms of eternal punishment or retribution.[130] Whether in connection with extinction or eternal torment, the unrighteous are to experience fire. In a few places, it is suggested that this fire will be cast upon the earth either in the course of the tribulation that precedes the Judgment, or as part of the Judgment itself, after the fashion of the rain of brimstone on Sodom.[131] Typically, sinners are pictured in the fires of gehenna or hell, or simply in a place of fire or burning.[132] The idea of judgment by fire is also known in the O.T., notably Isa. 66:15–16, 24.[133] As we have seen, several traditions in various synoptic strata attribute to Jesus the idea that the condemned will experience torment in gehenna or fire.

The time of Judgment. In all instances, the day of Judgment was expected to take place in the future. It would bring to an end the oppression of the righteous and the whole ambiguous course of history that had obtained on earth since the time of Adam. The Judgment will occur at the end or consummation of the present age or world, but before men can enter the new age or world that is to come.

> But the day of Judgment will be at the end of this age and the beginning of the immortal age to come, in which corruption has passed away, sinful indulgence has come to an end, unbelief has been cut off, and righteousness has increased and truth has appeared.[134]

Some of the sources describe signs or clues that would divulge when the time was near. Typically the apocalyptic books were written in the form of visions or "revelations" to relatively ancient figures, and often portrayed, through allegorical or other imaginative scenes and episodes, the course of history from that ancient time down to the period in and for which the book was written. In addition, some of the apocalypses visualize a series of more or less stock cosmic supernatural or eerie phenomena expected to precede the time of final judgment and deliverance:

> And the sun shall suddenly shine forth at night
> and the moon during the day.
> Blood shall drop from wood,
> and the stone shall utter its voice;
> The peoples shall be troubled
> and the stars shall fall.[135]

In some places, however, "signs" are not so much preliminary indications of the progress of events, as *accompanying* phenomena which herald the beginning of the end events, including, notably, the appearance or coming of God, the Son of man, or the Messiah for Judgment. Such signs will leave no doubt that the end is about to occur: "Now I will tell you a very evident sign, that you may understand when the end of all things is coming to the earth. . . ."[136] Or such signs may even be part of the final aggregate of events which include the disclosure of God's Kingdom and the time of Judgment.[137]

At all events, it is characteristic of apocalyptic writing to look for the time of final Judgment and deliverance in the near future. Thus from the standpoint of those living at the time in and for which an apocalypse was written, most of the signs pertaining to the course of history have already occurred; what remain are the final cosmic signs and the events which they herald (e.g., II Esdras 9:1–9).

That the end events are expected in the near future is stated expressly in several places, especially in *II Baruch*; e.g., "For truly my redemption has drawn nigh, and is not far distant as aforetime"; "For the Judge shall come and will not tarry."[138] This is also affirmed in II Esdras: "The age is hastening swiftly to its end"; "Therefore my judgment is now drawing near."[139]

The purpose of the predictions. Preaching or parenesis, or even kerygma, may be written as well as orally presented. This is clear enough in the admonitions and exhortations of the wisdom writings and in such stories as Suzanna, Bel and the Dragon, and Judith, as well as Paul's letters. It is certainly true of the apocalyptic writings which, of course, were intended to be read. Why were they written? Some of them may have been composed in times of persecution or distress, in an effort to understand why these things were happening,[140] and in any case, to urge the religious community to keep the faith. Some of the writings have a more speculative character. But generally the purpose seems to have been parenetic: to call Jewish readers to mindfulness of the Judgment in store for the unrighteous and the blessed life God has prepared for those who have kept the faith and practiced righteousness in their lives. Thus both implicitly and explicitly, the reader is called to repentance and righteousness:

> The consummation, moreover, of the age shall then show the
> great might of its ruler, when all things come to judgment.
> Therefore prepare your hearts for that which before you believed,
> lest you come to be in bondage in both worlds,
> so that you be led away captive here and tormented there.[141]

The Judgment: Apocalyptic Judaism, Jesus and the Modern World-View

The world-view expressed in these Jewish sources is reasonably coherent even if there are some important variations. The time is coming, perhaps very soon, when everyone—both the living, and probably the resurrected dead of earlier generations—would be judged. Either God himself, his Messiah, or the Son of man would be the Judge. Judgment would be based upon men's faithfulness to God and to his covenant, which requires above all else, responsiveness to those in need. The righteous would be granted entrance into the new world, where they would experience love, joy, and peace. Sinners would be condemned to torment if not destruction in gehenna or some other place of fire. Those who read the revelations set forth in the writings were warned, while there still was time, to be mindful of the respective destinies awaiting righteous and sinners, lest they be found among the latter when the time of Judgment comes.

This world-view, with its expectations and exhortations, is not fundamentally different from that which is attributed to Jesus in the synoptic gospels. Certainly there are some differences. Jesus' sayings are, for the most part, less vivid in describing the prospects ahead for the righteous and sinners. He did not elaborate a detailed apocalyptic program of historical and cosmic phenomena preliminary to the final eschatological events—not, at any rate, if the structure of Mark 13 is correctly attributed to the evangelist or the editorial hand of the church. But there can scarcely be any doubt that Jesus, like earlier and contemporary Jewish apocalypticists, looked for that time in the future when men (if not also nations) would be judged on the basis of their faithfulness to God and responsiveness to others. A great many of the synoptic traditions report that Jesus warned his hearers to repent and act in accordance with the will of God while there still was time, so that they might indeed inherit the Kingdom of God and not be condemned to eternal torment or extinction.

In modern times, the notion of such Judgment is certainly out of fashion—except, perhaps, in some theologically conservative quarters where it tends to be reserved for persons or groups on some enemies' list. That Jonathan Edwards should have once preached a sermon entitled "Sinners in the hands of an Angry God" is regarded with amused condescension by those whose humanistic sensibilities are offended by the thought that there might really be any sinners, and that if there were a God, he would or should be angry with them. A few liturgical fragments still echo the earlier expectation: "We believe that thou shalt come to be our Judge."[142] But on the whole, modern Christian and secular interpreters of the historical Jesus have been optimistic about human nature and destiny. They generally do not expect to be judged, certainly not severely, or that anyone else will be either. It is consistent with this modern climate of opinion that in studies of the historical Jesus, his proclamation of the impending day of Judgment has, very largely, been neglected.

III Interim Ethics: Ethics for the Interim

A few decades ago, many Protestants felt that Christian ethics consisted primarily, or even entirely, of applying to various moral and social questions the principles or values that Jesus had taught. Adolf von Harnack's *Das Wesen des Christentums* (1900)[1] and E. F. Scott's *The Ethical Teaching of Jesus* (1936) epitomize this understanding of both Jesus' teaching and the character of Christian ethics. A few books representing this perspective have been written more recently, e.g., L.H. Marshall's *The Challenge of New Testament Ethics* (1946). By and large, however, this viewpoint has been abandoned. The teaching of Jesus is no longer regarded as the head and corner of Christian ethics. Several factors have contributed to this shift in understanding as to the basis and nature of Christian ethics. National and international events have made it plain that the Kingdom of God is not immanent in human history.[2] Moreover, it is clearer than ever that Jesus' teachings do not tell all that we need to know in order to decide and act obediently and responsibly in confronting the complexities of this multi-problem world.[3] Twentieth century theologians, grappling with the freshly revealed and pervasive presence of sin and tragedy in the world, turned with a renewed sense of relevance to both the Old Testament and other portions of the New as points of departure for interpreting Christian faith and life.[4]

Something else happened since the late nineteenth century that further undermined the liberal "ethics of Jesus" idea. This was the perception formulated, notably, by Johannes Weiss, and then by Albert Schweitzer, that Jesus had not been enunciating, promulgating, or inculcating an ethical system or set of precepts for all times after all. They showed instead that Jesus expected and proclaimed a dramatic, world-shaking event: the coming of the Kingdom of God which would put an end to all history within his own lifetime, or, at most, that of his contemporaries. At that time, men would be judged on the basis of their loves, loyalties, and conduct in the meantime—the "interim." It is not surprising that liberal and Platonizing moralists looked upon Schweitzer as if he had committed the abomination of desolation. He had placed a *skandalon* in the path of the benevolent teacher of a permanently valid ethics by declaring that Jesus' ethic was an *Interimsethik*, an ethic for the interim, not one intended for all times, and thus not one intended for us. Schweitzer was fully aware that to recognize Jesus' eschatological orientation would call into question the relevance of his "ethics" for life in the modern world. As we shall see, Schweitzer thought that Jesus' ethics was still fundamental to the moral life. But now it was much more difficult to grasp the meaning and relevance of Jesus' ethics.[5]

Curiously, most of those who discuss interim ethics misread or misrepresent Schweitzer's position. Since Schweitzer's interpretation is basically correct, they tend also to misunderstand the substance and import of Jesus' message to his contemporaries. Typically, the objections raised against the interim ethics theory are aimed at some distortion or caricature of Schweitzer's actual position. Schweitzer's conclusion that Jesus' ethics was an ethics for the interim rests solidly upon the results of his historical-critical research. It is not a question of Schweitzer's mere opinion or personal preference, though several interpreters like to think that this is the case. As we will see, much of the scholarly resistance to Schweitzer's position derives from hermeneutical or ideological concern that it might undermine the felt authority of Jesus for the modern moral life. It is not proposed here that every aspect of Schweitzer's eschatological interpretation should be embraced as final truth. But we do suggest that in understanding and describing Jesus' teaching as *Interimsethik*, an "ethic for the interim," Schweitzer did so accurately. He thereby raised issues with which further attempts to understand the substance of Jesus' teaching and its relevance for the moral life must eventually come to terms.

Interim Ethics: Misinterpretations

A great many of Schweitzer's critics seem to have seen or heard the term "interim ethics" and immediately assumed that they knew what it meant without bothering to read what Schweitzer had said on the subject. At any rate, interpreters commonly proceed to read erroneous notions into the term and then triumphantly point to these errors a. evidence that the interim ethics theory is untenable. T.W. Manson, for example, poses a moral objection:

> If, in the belief that the whole monetary system of the world is going
> to be abolished next week, someone advises me to withdraw all my
> money from the bank and distribute it to charity, he may be giving
> me the best advice in the circumstances; but to dignify his advice with
> the name of "ethics" or even "interim-ethic" is to make a virtue of
> necessity with a vengeance.[6]

This, of course, is not what Schweitzer meant by "interim ethics." It
is instructive to notice that Manson implies that if Schweitzer's interpretation were correct, Jesus' advice would have been unethical; and
that, *ergo*, Schweitzer must have been wrong. This kind of logic per-
vades the reasoning of many critics of interim ethics: in effect, if historically correct, it would be morally or theologically objectionable,
hence it is historically incorrect. Sometimes the arguments (or assertions) are so vague as to be unintelligible; e.g., "Thus, when
[Schweitzer] found the ethical teaching of Jesus a grave difficulty for
his theory, he dismissed it as 'an ethic of the interval'. . . ."[7] In fact,
Schweitzer found Jesus' "ethics" entirely consistent with his theory
of *konsequente Eschatologie*.[8]

Some of the more typical and widespread misconceptions about
Schweitzer's interim ethics theory are as follows: (1) that it entails a
legalistic interpretation of Jesus' teaching; (2) that it treats the content
of Jesus' ethical understanding as if it were derived solely from his expectation of the imminent appearance of the last times; (3) that
Schweitzer meant that the relevance of Jesus' teaching was confined to
that interim period of expectation long ago, and that since Jesus was
mistaken about when the Kingdom would come, his ethical teaching
no longer has any validity; and (4) that since (supposedly) the Kingdom of God was in some sense present, the interim ethics interpretation is wrong, and Jesus' ethics was really an ethics or moral ideal for
the present or "realized" Kingdom. In common, these interpretations
and assertions seem calculated to preserve the relevance of Jesus' ethics
for the Christian life, as understood in liberal Protestantism. For such a
worthy objective, surely Schweitzer's characterization of Jesus' teaching as an ethic for the interim must be rejected!

Legalism

One common objection mistakenly brought against interim ethics is that it makes Jesus the author of a new law or legalism.[9] E.F.
Scott declared, for instance: "In spite, however, of all logical considerations the theory of an 'interim-ethic' may be confidently put
aside. For one thing it rests on the false hypothesis that the intention

of Jesus was to prescribe a number of set rules."[10]

Paraphrasing Scott, E.C. Gardner wrote: "A third reason why this view of an 'interim ethic' is inadmissible is that it rests upon the erroneous assumption that Jesus' intention was to prescribe a set of rigid rules."[11] Neither Scott nor Gardner cite Schweitzer, nor do they say which "set of rules" Schweitzer supposedly ascribed to Jesus. None of the other interpreters who claim that Schweitzer's interim ethics theory makes Jesus' ethics into a matter of "law" or "relative requirements" provides documentation either. This is understandable in view of the fact that Schweitzer nowhere describes Jesus' ethics in these terms. What Schweitzer says is that the central demand of Jesus' interim ethics was for *repentance*, moral renewal, renovation, or transformation.[12]

As early as 1913, Schweitzer noted and attempted to correct his critics' inclination to misrepresent *Interimsethik* as a legalistic ethic.

> In order to prevent further misunderstanding, let it be remembered that the term *"Interimsethik"* coined in the *Skizze des Lebens Jesu* (1901)[13] only signifies that the ethical demands of Jesus taken together, are aimed at the *inner* preparation of those belonging to the coming Kingdom and ultimately their vindication at the Judgment.[14]

It is not interim ethics but the charge that Schweitzer represents Jesus' ethics as a new legalism that rests on a "false hypothesis." It is another question, of course, whether Jesus' ethical teaching was not, in part, at least, a matter of commandment after all. That this is the case has been shown recently by Victor P. Furnish and Paul S. Minear.[15]

Apocalypticism

It is commonly argued that Jesus' teaching cannot possibly have been meant as an interim ethic because many of the sayings contain no explicit reference to the nearness of the end, or because the content of Jesus' teaching, in most cases, is not specifically tied to or based upon that expectation. Bornkamm, for instance, writes: "[The interim ethics] interpretation would appear to make the apocalyptic end of the world the ground of Jesus' demands, whereas the love of our neighbor and of our enemy, purity, faithfulness and truth are demanded simply because they are the will of God."[16]

Similarly, Reinhold Niebuhr urged that the ethic of Jesus definitely is not in the category of interim ethics: "The note of apocalyptic urgency is significantly lacking in many of the passages in which the religio-ethical rigor is most uncompromising. The motive advanced for fulfilling the absolute demands is simply that of obedience to God or emulation of his nature."[17] Schweitzer, however, never claimed that the basic *content* of Jesus' teaching derived from his expectation of the imminent arrival of the Kingdom of God. Rather, the nearness of that time made it all the more urgent for men to repent now and thereby become persons fit to enter the Kingdom when it comes. Jesus' prophetic ethics and the beatitudes do not draw their moral content from the expectation of the Day of the Lord, but they set forth what God requires of those who wish to prepare themselves in prospect of the coming time. "The Day of Judgment puts this moral transformation to the proof: only he who has done the will of the heavenly Father can enter into the Kingdom" (Matt. 7:21).[18]

The basic content of Jesus' ethical proclamation was derived from his understanding of God's will. But his hearers must now repent and continue faithfully to do God's will through acts of love in the time remaining, *the interim* before the coming of the Son of man, Judgment, and the Kingdom of God. Perhaps interpreters commonly see the term *"Interimsethik"* and suppose it to mean an ethic "of" or "from" the interim, whereas it is clear from all that Schweitzer says that he intended it to mean an ethic *for* the interim. Curiously, some of those who object strenuously to the interim ethics theory nevertheless are willing to avail themselves of it selectively in order to try to blunt the edge of some of Jesus' "severe" sayings, for instance, those concerning property or self-renunciation.[19] Moreover, it says nothing against Schweitzer's theory to point out that some of Jesus' sayings are gnomic or sapiential in character[20] and thus not directly tied to his eschatological expectations. It is unlikely that Jesus (or the synoptic editors) would have included an explicit eschatological reference with every saying. The synoptic gospels contain sufficient evidence to make it clear that Jesus did not expect that his hearers would have long to wait until the final eschatological events occurred. In the meantime, the interim, they were to act. Whatever the modern reader may find of current relevance in some or all of Jesus' message, it seems clear enough that all of Jesus' "ethics" was meant for his contemporaries who lived in that interim nearly two thousand years ago.[21]

Validity or Invalidity

A rather strange accusation brought against the "interim ethics" interpretation is that it represents an attempt to "escape" the demands of Jesus for perfection or radical obedience by consigning and confining these demands to an age long past.[22] This charge mistakenly assumes that Schweitzer intended to limit the relevance or validity of Jesus and his ethics to that interim of long ago.

Albert Knudson expresses a similar and more common misreading:

> It has been argued by some modern scholars, such as Albert Schweitzer, that the moral teaching of Jesus was an "interim ethics"—a morality applicable only to the brief period before the advent of the Messianic Age. . . . It turned out, however, that the expected parousia did not come; and hence his ethic, based upon the belief in its imminence, lost its validity.[23]

It is significant that these critics do not quote Schweitzer to the effect that the validity or relevance of Jesus' interim ethic need be confined to that ancient interim. If they had looked, they might have cited numerous statements which indicate Schweitzer's conviction as to the continuing authority and validity of Jesus' teaching for the moral life. For example:

> [Jesus'] individual ethic does not perish with the collapse of eschatology, but thereby loses only the idea of reward and its eudaemonistic conditionality. The powerful demands of world-denial and inner perfection thereby lose nothing of their significance.[24]

But even if Schweitzer had proposed that the significance of Jesus' ethical teaching perished with the eschatological expectation of the early church, and no longer could be considered meaningful or valid in our time, the interim ethics interpretation would not thereby be discredited. For whether *we* find Jesus' teaching significant for the moral life in our time has no bearing upon the historical question as to Jesus' intention and the substance of his message to his contemporaries. Nevertheless, some writers urge the validity they feel Jesus' teaching to have in our time as an argument against the interim ethics theory. Thus W.D. Davies declares, as if thereby refuting the interim ethics theory, "There is much in the teaching of Jesus which . . . is clearly applicable to all times."[25] Likewise, Gustav Aulen could assert: "Jesus' interpretation . . . that the 'love of God' was to be realized in and through 'love of one's neighbor' was certainly no interim ethic."[26]

Earlier, Martin Dibelius had objected, "The interpretation has this in its favor, that for the duration of the brief interim, man can actually exist without making the forbidden provisions. But the theory effectively limits the validity of Jesus' commandments, and is thus beset with difficulties."[27] Dibelius proceeded to suggest that Jesus' ethical teaching was not meant for the interim, but for that time in the future when God's Kingdom would be established. Thus Jesus' teaching was an ethic for the future Kingdom of God. This theory not only presents obvious "difficulties" with respect to the present relevance of such teaching but, more to the point, it has no support from synoptic (or any other) evidence.[28]

Similarly, C.H. Dodd dismisses the eschatological interpretation of the gospels because "this raises a difficulty in regard to the ethical teaching of Jesus." Any difficulties that interim ethics may present need cause no concern, however, Dodd says, for "it has become clear that the sayings cannot be convincingly interpreted in this sense."[29] Dodd was not convinced. One suspects that his whole program of "realized eschatology" was intended to spare the modern reader such difficulties.

John Bright apparently meant to rule out the idea that Jesus intended his teaching for those contemporaries living in the last days of the old or present age. He asks, rhetorically: "But if that be so, what authority at all can they have over us today who live so long after that expected interim has passed?"[30] (As if our desire to find Jesus' authoritative teaching for us could tell us anything in regard to the historical question as to his intent!)

Similarly, it is no argument against interim ethics to point, as Ramsey and Gardner have done,[31] to Schweitzer's own career or the "striking words" with which he concluded *The Quest of the Historical Jesus*. These show that Schweitzer believed that Jesus and his words had continuing significance for the moral life. Such belief is expressed in many of Schweitzer's writings, and is in no way inconsistent with his characterization of Jesus' demands as an interim ethic. It is inconsistent only with a prevalent but mistaken conception of what Schweitzer meant by "interim ethics."

Many writers apparently assume that Jesus' ethical teaching can have no relevance for us unless he himself had *us* in view,[32] or at least claimed a permanent validity for his teaching. It seems important to many writers to affirm that Jesus made such a claim.

> It cannot be granted, then, that Jesus intended to teach nothing more than an "interim ethics." Some of his judgments, as we shall presently see, were necessarily colored by the expectation that earthly conditions would soon be transformed; but for his teaching as a whole he claims a permanent value.[33]

What evidence is there that Jesus ever made such a claim? The argument from silence, advanced by some of these writers, is not impressive: "He never suggests that he is saying something of only temporary relevance."[34]

> Moreover, it is not true that Jesus' ethical teaching was merely what Schweitzer called an "interimsethik." Jesus did not regard his ethical principles as binding only for the brief interim before the Kingdom was to come; they were to have permanent validity for human life! There is not a shred of evidence that he would have wanted to change any of his fundamental ethical principles if he had anticipated that after nineteen hundred years the Kingdom would still not have come.[35]

Since the synoptic evidence indicates that Jesus was looking for the new age within the lifetime of at least some of his contemporaries, it seems that John Knox is more nearly correct when he insists that Jesus "was not thinking of us or of the centuries which separate our time from his."[36] Moreover, Knox correctly observes that to admit this is not necessarily to declare Jesus' teaching irrelevant to our time.

> The question, however, is whether his ethical teaching would have been less absolute in its demand if he had been [thinking of us and our time]. To answer a question about what might have been is always precarious, but I should say that the teaching would not have been essentially different. Perhaps in that event he would have said some things he did not say; I do not believe he would have withheld anything he did say. For Jesus is concerned in his ethical teaching with the absolute will of God and would have declared it in similar terms in any case.[37]

This well-taken point does not, however, constitute an argument against Schweitzer's interim ethics theory. Schweitzer himself said much the same thing over sixty-five years ago.

> Were Jesus to come again in our time, he would certainly no longer think in terms of late-Jewish eschatology, yet the basic character of his ethic would not be different. But with regard to every ethic, philosophical and theological, national and social, which represents the modern "law," he would teach, as then, "Unless your righteousness is better than that of the Scribes and the Pharisees, you cannot come into the Kingdom of heaven . . ." and would demand absolute perfection and absolute surrender.[38]

Futurism

A final argument against interim ethics is that it rests upon, and therefore presumably falls with, the hypothesis that Jesus thought of the Kingdom of God as entirely future. It is true that Schweitzer yielded no ground to claims by mediating interpreters on behalf of realized or even partially actualized eschatology, so far as Jesus' understanding was concerned. Neither do a number of other interpreters.[39] We have suggested earlier that the common tendency to claim that Jesus thought the Kingdom at least partly present in some way is prompted by interest in making Jesus' ideas more presentable to the modern world-view.[40] It is interesting that most interpreters who maintain that for Jesus the Kingdom was both present and future proceed in various ways to dispense with the future aspect more or less completely. Typically they conclude that Jesus' ethic was not significantly related to his futuristic expectations after all, but rather, in the final analysis, "was an ethic of the present Kingdom of God."[41]

It may be that in some sense Jesus *did* think the Kingdom already present, in heaven, perhaps, or in the ground gained through his exorcisms (J. Weiss), or perhaps even "proleptically," in his own person as the one who would come as messianic Son of man (R.H. Fuller). But only a theory of "realized eschatology" that completely eliminates the importance for Jesus of the future coming of the Son of man and day of Judgment can seriously challenge Schweitzer's contention that Jesus meant his teaching and preaching as a summons to repent in the time still remaining—the interim—before the judgment. Few have joined C.H. Dodd in such a radical and questionable exegetical program.[42] C.J. Cadoux, T.W. Manson, A.M. Hunter, Amos N. Wilder, and E.C. Gardner described Jesus' ethics as the morality of the present or "realized" Kingdom of God. They did not thereby disprove that it was also an ethic for the interim that remained before the complete or final coming of the Kingdom. The interim ethics theory is not discredited by claiming that in some way or to some degree the Kingdom of God was present. Even if it was partly present or actualized, its decisive future manifestation, along with the Judgment, remained to occur. In the meantime, life was to be lived in the interim.

Reinhold Niebuhr acknowledged this indirectly. In his view Jesus thought the Kingdom both present and future. History, then, is to be understood as the period or "interim" in which we live, between the coming of Christ and the Kingdom and their second coming.[43] Similarly, Emil Brunner described Christian ethics as necessarily "interim ethic."[44]

The Meaning of Ethics for the Interim

If what Schweitzer understood by "interim ethics" has been generally misrepresented, then what did he mean? It can be stated briefly. Jesus expected and proclaimed that the Kingdom of God was at hand (i.e., *near*). The coming of the Kingdom and time of Judgment would mark the end of the "interim"; it was the decisive event of life-and-death importance for his hearers. Only those who had maintained a transformed moral life in this interim would be admitted to the Kingdom. What was the character of the moral demand that Jesus taught or preached? It was *metanoia:* repentance and moral renewal. Jesus' "whole theory of ethics must come under the conception of *repentance* as a preparation for the coming of the Kingdom." The Beatitudes, for instance, "define the moral disposition which justifies admission into the Kingdom."[45]

How can Jesus' ethical teaching, so interpreted, have meaning for later generations of Christians who live in a world where the Kingdom of God has not come in any identifiable way, and where people no longer look for it to do so, however much they may continue to repeat the prayer, "Thy Kingdom come!"? Many interpreters evidently assume that, in order to salvage Jesus' ethics, they must deny his eschatology. But although Jesus may have been mistaken as to his conception or theory of history, this does not necessarily mean that he was mistaken concerning the basic character of God's intention and demand.[46]

Some of Jesus' sayings, however, do call for actions that are appropriate only under interim or emergency conditions, where little time remained for doing what might otherwise be good and right. How can we otherwise understand Jesus' word to the would-be disciple who wished to bury his father before following after him,[47] or his refusal to permit another to say farewell first to those at home (Luke 9:61)? The Lucan version of both sayings is followed immediately by Jesus' appointment of seventy who were to go out, hastily, through the towns announcing the nearness of the Kingdom of God. Wilder's suggestion that Jesus' instructions for this special mission should be thought of as "discipleship ethics" may be correct; but it is no less a matter of interim ethics. The reason for the disciples' urgent mission was Jesus' conviction that the Kingdom of God and time of Judgment had come near (Luke 10:9–12). In the Matthean account of the instructions to the Twelve, Jesus declares that despite all haste they will not have returned from this all-important mission before the Son of man has come (Matt. 10:23). Even allowing for hyperbole, how else should the eunuch saying (Matt. 19:10–12) be understood than as an exceptional measure that makes sense only in view of the nearness and utter importance of the Kingdom of God? The Lucan version is even more explicit: ". . . those who are accounted worthy to attain to that age [the Kingdom of God] and to the resurrection from the dead neither marry nor are given in marriage . . ." (Luke 20:35).[48] The admonition to make friends by unrighteous mammon in the Parable of the Unjust Steward (Luke 16:1–9) clearly points to the interim and emergency character of the situation,[49] however morally distasteful this may be to modern sensibilities. Similarly, the warning "settle with your accuser on the way to court"[50] plainly indicates the remaining interim as the time for decisive action before it is too late. The sort of conduct commended in the Parables of the Treasure and the Pearl (Matt. 13:44–46) is hardly "ethical" in the context of an enduring world and social order, but was evidently intended to underscore the urgency of appropriate action—giving up all else—for the sake of the Kingdom. Bultmann completely fails to account for such sayings when he claims "[We cannot] view the ethical precepts of Jesus as 'interim-ethic'; for his demands have an absolute character, and are by no means influenced in their formulation by the thought that the end of the world is near at hand."[51]

It is possible that the specific content of some of Jesus' other radical demands is conditioned by expectation that the end of the present age was near, e.g., in the case of Mark 10:21, 29f. and parallels, or Matt. 10:37 = Luke 14:26. Even E.F. Scott was prepared to admit that in the case of "not a few of the sayings on renunciation" there is "an 'interim' element," and that in these instances Jesus was influenced primarily "by the requirements of apocalyptic theory."[52] Even Schweitzer's statements about interim ethics invite the criticism that he did not sufficiently recognize the extraordinary character of some of these sayings. Weiss did not use the term "interim ethics" but aptly characterized the situation with respect to such sayings:

> As in war, when exceptional laws come into force which are not called for in time of peace, so this part of Jesus' ethical proclamation bears a special character. He demands mighty, in part superhuman things; he demands things which under normal circumstances or conditions would be simply impossible.[53]

Nevertheless, Jesus' convictions about God's nature and will determined the main substance of his preaching about the response people should make in the interim before the coming of the Judgment and the Kingdom. This is plainly true in the description of the Great Judgment (Matt. 25:31–46). The same basic moral standard is implicit also in the Parable of the Rich Man and Lazarus (Luke 16:19–31). More is involved than simply a state of emergency or interim crisis. An interim ethics based on different moral premises will necessarily reach different conclusions as to what ought to be done. The particular expectation as to what lies ahead also influences the moral judgment. Those whose moral standard is self-gratification, who lack any hope for the future, are likely to adopt the interim ethic of Epicureanism: "Eat, drink and be merry, for tomorrow we die."[54] The Marxist interim ethic rests on still another value premise and another vision of the future: the inherently righteous proletariat are to be agents and ultimate beneficiaries of the perfect society, where, at last, workers—but no others—will have their reward. The absolute value of this ideal world purportedly justifies an interim Machiavellian ethic of power, deception, revolution, suppression, or any means necessary to constrain its actualization.[55] Obviously Jesus' ethic rests upon other beliefs or affirmations than simply that the end of the present age is near.

Schweitzer himself attempted in several ways to account for the continuing authority which he experienced in Jesus and his words. He referred in particular to Jesus' will, his person or personality and spirit, his ethic or religion of love, and his ethic of self-devotion to others.[56] It is not simply to be assumed that Jesus' eschatological ethic is irrelevant because it was eschatological. Little attention has been given so far to the implications for ethics of the theology of hope.[57] Nevertheless, the hopes of Jesus and the early Church for the fulfillment of God's purposes in time and space may turn out to be more relevant than was thought during the recent decades that were dominated, theologically, by an existentialist and individualistic emphasis on the present, recurrent "Now" of decision.

At all events, as Jesus' teaching is reported in the synoptic gospels it can be properly described as an "ethic for the interim."[58] It can scarcely be understood otherwise. Much of the opposition to this description evidently derives from interpreters' mistaken or distorted notions as to what Schweitzer meant by it. In particular, interpreters have been concerned that if this description were allowed, it would necessarily relegate Jesus' ethics to antiquity. But this opposition has resulted in confusing rather than clarifying the character of Jesus' teaching. It has directed attention away from the radical claim which Jesus made upon his contemporaries, his demand for repentance, moral transformation, the demand that they turn from self-seeking and self-serving to a life based upon seeking first the Kingdom of God and doing his will in responsive love for their neighbors.[59] This demand may well be applicable to the moral life in the context of the modern world. But even if Jesus' ethic-for-the interim could not be regarded as authoritative or meaningful for contemporary life, this would not invalidate the accuracy of the description. Historical research, we suggest, cannot legitimately bend its conclusions to suit the hermenuetical interests or desires of the interpreter.

IV Jesus As Demon-Exorcist: Overpowering Satan

According to the synoptic gospels, one of the main features of Jesus' activity was his campaign against the household of Satan, the demons.[1] And yet Jesus' work as demon-exorcist has received little scholarly attention. This is probably because the idea of demon possession is alien to the viewpoints of both liberal and conservative interpreters of his ministry. *We* do not believe in Satan and demons; surely Jesus could not have done so either!

Albert Schweitzer, Rudolf Bultmann, Morton S. Enslin, Hans Conzelmann, and Wolfhart Pannenberg could recognize Jesus' futuristic eschatological world-view for what it was, problematic as it may be, theologically. But these same interpreters virtually ignore his reported exorcism of demons. Bultmann states that Jesus and his disciples drove out demons in the belief that Satan's power had been broken and the Kingdom of God was about to begin. But then—evidently wishing to attribute to Jesus his own ethical-voluntaristic-humanistic-existentialism—Bultmann goes on to declare that Jesus did not really take Satan and the demons seriously after all: "If it is true that to Jesus the world can be called bad only in so far as men are bad, that is, are of evil will, then it is clear how little the figure of Satan really meant to him."[2] Bultmann's premise, not his logic, is questionable here.

A few interpreters are willing to acknowledge, somewhat hesitantly and cautiously, that Jesus probably did share the beliefs of his contemporaries with respect to Satan and demons, and did understand that he was dealing with them through his exorcisms.[3] Most commentators, however, discuss Jesus' exorcism of demons, if at all, only under the more general rubric of "miracles" or "signs."[4]

Beginning, apparently, with Rudolf Otto, a great many interpreters have come forward with the explanation that the exorcisms meant the "powers of the Kingdom of God are already operative," or showed that the Kingdom of God was "dawning," "breaking in," or, simply, already present. Otto's summary of the import of Matt. 12:28f. = Luke 11:20–22 anticipated the position of many more recent commentators:

> Jesus says: Were I to exorcise by Beelzebub, Satan would be arrayed against himself, which cannot be. Therefore concede that I exorcise by the finger of God. But if this is so, then what I teach holds good, *viz.* that the kingdom of God has already dawned, i.e. God's rule over Satan has already come to pass and Satan himself is already deprived of his power i.e., his armour, since otherwise one could not take away from him his spoil, the demon-possessed. As long as the strong one sits in full armour and is not deprived of his armour, and thus equipped watches his household, no exorcist, not even I, can take from him what he possesses. But just because the kingdom has already dawned, because God has already achieved His victory and stripped Satan of his armour (we might continue: because Satan has already fallen from heaven, but still rages with the remnants of his power here on earth), it is possible by exorcism to take from him his spoil, i.e. those made captive and taken into his possession.[5]

If, in fact, Satan had *already* been defeated and deprived of his power and the Kingdom of God begun on earth, it would be odd to find that he "still rages with the remnants of his power here on earth."[6] What is most remarkable about Otto's statement is that the whole fabrication (including three "i.e.s" and six "alreadys") is placed on the lips of Jesus himself ("Jesus says . . ."). In the same spirit many other interpreters freely attribute all sorts of expressions and understandings to Jesus and the evangelists. The term "already" is read at will into the text, and such expressions as "the inbreaking powers of the Kingdom,"[7] or "signs" of its "dawning" are commonly repeated in the secondary literature, despite the fact they have yet to be found in any text of the gospels.

The whole interpretation of exorcisms as "signs" is unjustified. Despite the inclination of interpreters to read the term "signs" into Matt. 12:28 = Luke 11:20, *casting out demons is not so designated here or anywhere else in the gospels.* Moreover, the synoptic tradition reports several important sayings in which Jesus explicitly disavows signs. According to Luke 17:20, he declares that the coming of the Kingdom would *not* be marked by any accompanying signs. Nevertheless, various interpreters, ignoring the clear meaning of this statement, proceed without evident misgiving to eisegete into the following verse (17:21) the idea that Jesus intended his exorcisms (which are nowhere indicated in the pericope) as "signs of the presence of the Kingdom." Such, however, is decidedly not the meaning of the verse.[8] It is only *false* messiahs and prophets who would offer signs.[9] No sign would be given to Jesus' contemporaries (Mark 8:11f. = Matt. 16:4); or only that of the prophet Jonah (Matt. 12:39 = Luke 11:29), and Jonah had nothing to do with exorcisms. None of the exorcisms reported in the synoptic gospels is described as a "sign." Yet even Bultmann, here following the practice of placing one's own interpretation on Jesus' lips could maintain: "Jesus expected that [the coming of the Kingdom of God] would take place soon, in the immediate future, *and he said* that the dawning of that age could already be perceived in the signs and wonders which he performed, especially in the casting out of demons."[10] Only in the Fourth Gospel, however, does Jesus perform signs in order to arouse belief,[11] but here in order to demonstrate his claim to be Son of God, not the nearness or presence of the Kingdom of God. Moreover, no "signs" in the Fourth Gospel involve exorcisms.[12] Furthermore, Jesus' exorcisms are never designated as "miracles" in any of the gospels. Nevertheless, interpreters continue to apply these categories to Jesus' exorcisms—to the extent that they treat them at all—as if it were obvious that such were their meaning.

The confused state of current interpretation suggests the need for a more careful investigation of the relationship between Jesus' beliefs concerning Satan and the demons on the one hand, and his understanding and expectations concerning the Kingdom of God on the other.

The subject has not been entirely ignored or misrepresented. James M. Robinson and Howard C. Kee have produced excellent studies of Mark's treatment of Satan and demon-exorcism, but neither explicitly considers the question of Jesus' attitude and activity with respect to the demons.[13] James Kallas highlights the dualistic outlook of the Marcan Jesus, but ignores his eschatological beliefs—possibly because he wishes to maintain for dogmatic reasons that Jesus had not been "mistaken."[14] William Manson and Charles E.B. Cranfield both insist that, despite modernist aversion to such dualistic notions, there can be no doubt that Jesus and the early Church regarded his exorcism of demons as one of the central features of his ministry. He was thereby freeing those whom Satan had held in bondage and overcoming the power of Satan. But both Manson and Cranfield regard this activity as eschatological in the sense of manifesting the *presence* of the Kingdom of God, despite the fact that they both state that the manifestation or establishment of the Kingdom was an event which Jesus expected in the future![15] Two other writers have given careful attention to the question of Jesus' understanding of his work as exorcist and the relation of this to his eschatological beliefs and expectations: Johannes

Weiss, *Die Predigt Jesu vom Reiche Gottes* (1892)[16] and Otto Betz' 1958 article, "Jesu Heiliger Krieg."[17] Both hold that Jesus saw his exorcistic activity as preparatory to the coming of the Kingdom of God.

Satan in Apocalyptic Judaism and the Synoptic Gospels

It is generally agreed that first century Jews and Christians took Satan or Belial and the demons seriously. To be sure, by the time the rabbinical tradition was being recorded, beginning in the second and third centuries A.D., Judaism had for the most part abandoned its apocalyptic heritage, and with it the cosmic dualism of the preceding three or four centuries. Even though belief in demons continued, they came to be regarded mainly as minor nuisances. The Qumran writings show what is also apparent from the intertestamental literature: that apocalyptic and dualistic beliefs were current and important among significant segments of Judaism in the final century or two B.C. and at least the first century of the Common Era.[18]

It is difficult for those of us educated in the modern Western world to imagine an era in which Satan and demons were thought of and experienced realistically. It may help us appreciate the plausibility of this world-view if we recall the situation of the Jewish people at the time, and the range of then available conceptual explanations for the ills of mankind generally, and that of the Jewish people in particular. In the prophetic view of history, the triumphs of Assyria and Babylonia over Israel and Judah had been understood as an expression of God's righteous rule in judgment against the sinful nation that had forsaken him and his covenant.[19] Such also was the Deuteronomistic theology of history: it was God who, for cogent reasons, had delivered Israel and Judah over to oppressors.[20] Satan had not yet appeared in the Israelite and Jewish world.[21] There was no need for him. History was understood as the consequence of God's dealings with his people and other nations. However, by the time of Antiochus Epiphanes (c. 170 B.C.), the Jewish people had lived under the heel of foreign rulers for four hundred years. In apocalyptic thought, the continuing dominion of foreign powers was no longer intelligible as an exercise of *God's* rule.[22] Instead, especially when these foreign powers proved hostile to the Jewish people, their dominion was more plausibly understood in connection with the rule of evil cosmic powers. The Book of Daniel and the Qumran *War Scroll* evidence this interpretation of things. The "rulers of this age" came to mean both the kings and emperors who successively lorded over the Jewish homeland, and, more or less synonymously, the satanic "principalities and powers" which—as in Zoroastrian theology—for a while had gained control of the earth.[23]

It is not entirely clear how it was thought to have happened that Satan held sway on earth. Some Persian (Zoroastrian) dualistic motifs seem to have entered the Jewish world-view through Hellenism, if not earlier in the Persian period. Perhaps the Persian tradition of the "up-rush" of the evil spirits had influenced Jewish understanding. Or, again along Persian lines, it may have been supposed that Satan had been thrown out of heaven after having tried to seize control there. Displaced from heaven, he had set up his satanic kingdom on earth. Such, possibly, is the understanding expressed in Rev. 12:7ff., although it may be that what we have here is the seer's vision of Satan's *prospective* ejection from heaven. Or, as in the prologue to the book of Job, it may have been thought that Satan was given authority over the world in order to *test* the Jewish people.[24] In the N.T., Satan is known, among other terms, as "the tempter" or "tester," *ho peirazōn*.

Whatever the theory, the reality of centuries' experience of domination by foreign empires—only temporarily and ambiguously relieved during the Maccabaean era—had convinced many Jews that it was no longer God who ruled over his people and the other nations.[25] However it had come about, synoptic tradition presupposes that Satan holds sway (*exousia*) over the kingdoms of the world (Matt. 4:8f. = Luke 4:5f.) and was attempting to retain and exercise that power over men through his household, the demons.

Once this viewpoint is recognized, it will be seen that little is accomplished by claiming, as many interpreters do, that *hē basileia tou theou* and its Hebrew and Aramaic equivalents mean God's "rule" or "reign" which is "ever-present." From the standpoint of apocalyptic and dualistic Judaism (if not also early Christianity), the human predicament derives precisely from the fact that God does *not* at present rule on earth. Satan rules.[26] Through temptation or affliction, Satan seeks to break down men's trust in God, snatching away their faith.[27] The apocalyptic pattern of understanding parallels the Zoroastrian conception of the current historical era as the last time, when men's loyalties are to determine their ultimate destinies. This pattern also appears in the Qumran idea of the two contending spirits. Jesus reportedly understood that Satan would attempt to gain the allegiance not only of men generally, but particularly of Peter (Luke 22:31f.), and would try to seize or subvert his other disciples and followers as well. Consequently, he instructed them to pray that they might be delivered from temptation or tribulation brought on by the Evil One (Matt. 6:13). Satan had gone so far as to try to gain Jesus' own loyalty or devotion.[28]

Perhaps, for a moment, Jesus feared that Satan had succeeded with Peter (Mark 8:33)!

At all events, if the Kingdom of God is to come, the power of Satan must be overcome. Furthermore, those who will be fit to enter it must first be freed from the clutches of Satan's tyranny. Implicitly, a double process of preparation for the Kingdom of God is taking place through the exorcisms. On the one hand, Satan is being bound. The world is being wrested from his control. The victories that Jesus and his disciples gain over the demons should therefore be seen as clues to the fact that Satan is being defeated, and that consequently the establishment of God's Kingdom on earth is near.[29] Similarly, the healing of the sick meant that the demons (to whom sickness was generally, though not always attributed)[30] were being defeated. And on the other hand, the exorcisms and healings meant that the people of Israel were being cleansed from the afflictions of body and spirit that had held them in bondage to Satan and kept them unfit for the Kingdom of God. In the Kingdom, of course, there would be no place for sin, sorrow, uncleanness, or sickness, much less for unclean spirits or Satan![31] Moreover, those who had suffered disease or illness through no fault of their own—or whose sins had been forgiven—should be enabled to enter the Kingdom of God without having to bring their diseases with them.[32]

The proclamation of the *nearness* of the Kingdom of God and the consequent need for repentance are linked explicitly with the task of exorcising demons. This is true both of Jesus' own activity (Mark 1:15–30), and of the preaching and exorcising mission of his disciples. It is curious that the exorcistic work of the Twelve (and also of Luke's seventy) has been ignored by nearly all interpreters. The missionaries were instructed by Jesus to heal the sick and cast out demons, and to proclaim that the Kingdom of God had come *near:* Matt. 10:7; Luke 10:9–11, 17. Here there can be no question of exorcisms being a "sign" of the *presence* of the Kingdom. Rather, the exorcism of demons, like the preaching of repentance, was a task of the utmost importance *in preparation for* the coming of the Kingdom. This was not necessarily a novel understanding. Though exorcism as such is not mentioned, a similar relationship between repentance and the fate of the Kingdom of Satan is indicated in T. Dan 6:1, 3f.:

> And now, fear the Lord, my children, and beware of Satan and his spirits. . . . Therefore is the Enemy eager to destroy all that call upon the Lord. For he knoweth that upon the day on which Israel shall repent, the Kingdom of the Enemy shall be brought to an end.

A related understanding, perhaps, appears in Acts 3:19, where Peter calls upon his fellow Jewish inhabitants of Jerusalem: "Repent therefore, and turn again, that your sins may be blotted out, that times of refreshing may come from the presence of the Lord." It is another question whether Schweitzer is justified in interpreting Matt. 11:12 to mean that, through preaching repentance and moral renewal, Jesus and his followers are the "men of violence" who compel the Kingdom of God to come.[33]

In Mark, as J.M. Robinson has pointed out, Jesus' struggle against the demons is associated with the power of the Spirit of God.[34] According to Joel 2:28ff., the manifestation of the Spirit was to *precede* the "great and terrible day of the Lord." In Mark 1:15, Jesus proclaims repentance and the nearness—not presence—of the Kingdom, and gathers disciples to be "fishers of men" (1:17), to join him in the work of preaching and exorcism (3:14f.; 6:7–13). Jesus himself is engaged in exorcising demons from the first days of his ministry in Capernaum (1:23ff.) until the end of his ministry in Galilee (9:17–29).

In the so-called Beelzebul controversy (Mark 3:21–30), Jesus refutes the charge of his accusers that he casts out demons by "an unclean spirit," namely, Beelzebul or Satan. Instead, he implies, he exorcises demons by the Holy Spirit (3:28–30) or Spirit of God (Matt. 12:28). Many interpreters of the Beelzebul episode declare that Mark 3:27 means that Jesus understood that he (or God) had already "bound" or defeated Satan—perhaps during the "temptation" in the wilderness. In that case, Jesus' exorcisms would constitute the "plundering" of Satan's house. On the other hand, the term "strong man" could refer to the demon, and his "goods" to the demoniac, now set free from the oppressing demon, or more inclusively, the world which was now being liberated from the reign of Satan and his demons.[35] In this case, exorcism would be equivalent to "binding" the demons, as in Tobit 8:3 and Jubilees 10:7ff. Since Satan worked through his demons, binding the demons meant that Satan himself was being bound. In the Beelzebul controversy, Jesus refers to the demons who were *being* exorcised as "Satan" (Mark 3:23, 26a). There is no basis here or elsewhere for the supposition that Satan previously had been bound.[36] At the end of the "temptation narrative" Satan still remains in command of all the kingdoms of the earth. But by defeating the demons, through the power of the Holy Spirit, Jesus was overcoming Satan's power. The implication of Mark 3:22–27 is that Satan's "house" or "kingdom"—his control of the earth—was coming to an end. This also seems to be the meaning of Luke 10:17f. Upon hearing the disciples report their successes against the demons, Jesus visualizes—logically and as by prophetic inspiration—the ultimate destruction of Satan: "I saw Satan fall like lightning from heaven." Through the exorcisms wrought by Jesus and his disciples, Satan's power is being overpowered, he is being bound, and his eventual doom is certain.[37] The ultimate defeat or "binding" of Satan, however, would occur only at the beginning of the Kingdom of God or the messianic age. Such at any rate is the viewpoint reflected in much of the inter-testamental literature,[38] as well as in Isa. 24:21f. and Rev. 20:2f., 13.

The "Q" saying, Matt. 12:28 = Luke 11:20, placed both by Matthew and Luke in the Beelzebul controversy setting, is often interpreted to mean that exorcism signifies the *presence* of the Kingdom of God.[39] It is noteworthy however, that the Matthean Jesus does not understand that the coming age has begun: Matt. 12:32 distinctly refers to the age to come as a future era. The Lucan Jesus also regularly regards the coming of the Kingdom as a future occurrence.[40] It is *possible* that here, as in the saying at Luke 10:17f., Jesus might have been inspired by the present victories over the demons to speak in joyful or prophetic anticipation of the final victory of God as if it were already a present reality.[41] But one ought not build too much upon the occurrence in this one instance of the verb *phthanein*. It should be observed that the verb is used here with the preposition *epi*, a point ignored by interpreters who claim that the meaning is simply "to arrive."[42] Moreover, in all other places, the Greek verb used to translate Jesus' proclamation of the coming Kingdom is *engizein (epi)*, which normally means to come or draw *near*.[43] On the occasion or occasions when Jesus sends forth his followers to cast out demons and preach repentance and the coming of the Kingdom, they are to announce its near, but future arrival: *ēngiken hē basileia tou theou* (Matt. 10:7; Luke 10:9, 11). Their mission was a matter of life and death for the people of Israel, who now must either make ready for the coming of the Kingdom or forever miss their chance. In the meantime, Satan continued to operate through his demons, causing disease and snatching away the word of faith. This mission of the disciples would be dangerous. But because Jesus had given his followers power or authority *(exousia)* over the unclean spirits, they could hope to prevail.[44] This was no mere polite well-wishing but a necessity for their success, for the demons were still far from being defeated.[45] The Kingdom of God was near, but it had not yet come. Jesus and his disciples had gone on the offensive against the household of Satan. Matthew reports a demon's complaint that this was unfair: "Have you come to torment us *before the time?*" (Matt. 8:29).

Evidently Jesus understood demon exorcism, like the preaching of repentance, to be preliminary and preparatory to the coming of the Kingdom of God. Such is the understanding that typically appears in the Jewish literature as well. Howard C. Kee has shown that the verb *epitiman (ga'ar)*, typically used in Mark's descriptions of Jesus' "rebuking" the demons, appears in the Dead Sea Scrolls and other Jewish sources in connection with the idea of God's activity in bringing the evil powers or agents of Belial (Satan) under control *in preparation for* God's rule in "the eschaton."[46] Of course it is possible that this conception of exorcism was not Jesus' own, but that of the early church or the evangelists. In this case, we should speak of "the tradition's" understanding of the matter. But we have no reason to suppose that Jesus' understanding was significantly different from that which the synoptic tradition attributes to him. Demon exorcism is an important part of Jesus' activity in all three of the synoptic gospels.

Exorcism of Demons: Preparation for the Kingdom of God

We have seen that Jesus and his disciples not only prepared Israel for the coming of the Kingdom by preaching, but also by delivering men and women from their demons and diseases. In the process, they were also preparing for the coming of the Kingdom by overpowering the demons, the kingdom of Satan, thereby working for the day when they (and he) would finally be put out of action. By "force" or "violence" they were clearing the way for the coming of the Kingdom of God.[47] One could even argue, as Rudolf Otto and Floyd V. Filson have done, that Jesus understood the Kingdom of God to be present to the extent that he and his followers, through their exorcisms, were gaining ground, liberating men and recovering territory for the rule of God on earth.[48] *Perhaps* this is the meaning of Matt. 11:12 = Luke 16:16, if not also of Matt. 12:28 =Luke 11:20. Usually, however, the synoptic sources refer to the coming of the Kingdom (along with the Son of man and Judgment) as a future event which God himself would bring about, soon, but in his own time. It seems more likely, therefore, that the meaning here is consistent with that elsewhere in the synoptic tradition: Jesus and his followers were preparing for the coming of the Kingdom both by preaching repentance and by exorcism. Satan and his minions who stood in the way of its coming were being opposed— with violence. Because they were being overcome, it was apparent—to the eyes of faith—that the Kingdom of God would soon come and his rule would soon be established on earth.

Despite neglect of the subject by most modern interpreters, demon-exorcism is a prominent part of Jesus' public activity as reported in the synoptic tradition. There is no evidence to suggest that Jesus did not view the demons in the same way his contemporaries and the synoptic evangelists did: realistically and seriously. Exorcisms are not described as "signs" of the Kingdom, nor are they attributed to the Kingdom or its "power" or "powers," and it is nowhere said that the Kingdom is "dawning" or "breaking in." Nevertheless, demon-exorcism is correctly understood as an eschatological activity, namely, one of preparation for the coming of the Kingdom of God. Jesus casts out demons by the Spirit of God and authorizes his disciples to do likewise as they proclaim that the Kingdom of God has come near. The victims of Satan's power are being released. And from his own success against the demons, along with that of his followers, Jesus draws the joyful assurance that the time for the end of Satan's dominion and for the establishment of God's rule on earth is near. Perhaps a last effort on the part of the Evil One to retain his power, a final tribulation, still had to be endured—unless God chose to bring his Kingdom without tribulation (Matt. 6:10–13). God had not yet caused his Kingdom to come. But when Satan and his demons were finally overcome, God alone—whether with or through his Messiah—would rule over this world. Then the Kingdom of God would have come at last.[49] God's will, and his only, would then be done on earth. All would be delivered from the Evil One, for Satan and his demons would be no more. This important connection between the present exorcism of demons and the future coming of the Kingdom is overlooked by interpreters who neglect the apocalyptic and dualistic world-view of the gospels and instead picture Jesus as a "miracle worker" or *theios anēr* of the sort supposedly common in Hellenism and later Jewish lore.[50]

V Eating and Drinking in the Kingdom of God:

Jesus' Expectation in the Context of Jewish and Early Christian Belief

Apparently Jesus expected that in the coming Kingdom of God he and his followers, together with other righteous persons, would sit at table, eating and drinking. This expectation is not shared by many Christians in the twentieth century. It has not been a significant part of the Christian world-view for several centuries. On the whole, N.T. scholars obligingly have refrained from emphasizing this aspect of Jesus' message and outlook. In general, the synoptic passages where this expectation is evidenced are simply ignored. Occasionally an interpreter acknowledges the existence of certain passages, but then suggests that such ideas should be treated either as vestiges of Jewish belief or as later glosses by transmitters or editors of the tradition.[1] That such ideas might actually have been a part of Jesus' understanding and proclamation to his contemporaries is seldom considered. Interpreters sometimes concede that Jesus may have made such statements, but then go on to explain that he did so intending to symbolize something other than the literal and materialistic ideas seemingly represented.[2] The late Norman Perrin often intimated that references to eschatological table-fellowship symbolize something else.[3] However, Perrin correctly insisted that "the fellowship of the ministry of Jesus, immensely significant though it is, is still only an anticipation of the 'sitting at table with Abraham, Isaac, and Jacob in the Kingdom of God.' "[4]

Schweitzer's seasoned and substantial treatment of this question in *The Mysticism of Paul the Apostle*[5] has largely been neglected. Our concern here is not to argue for Schweitzer's position—which no one has seriously undertaken to refute. We do propose to review the synoptic evidence and show that this expectation is well-attested in the gospel traditions. We shall also suggest that it was congruent both with earlier and more or less contemporary Jewish expectations, as well as with the early churches' hopes for the future. We shall observe that there is little basis for the commonplace assertion that Jewish beliefs, historical Jesus traditions, and early Christian expectations must be regarded as mutually opposed or exclusive.

Eating and Drinking in the Kingdom of God: Synoptic Traditions

Sitting at Table in the Kingdom of God

A number of passages refer explicitly to eating and/or drinking or sitting at table in the Kingdom of God. One such saying, probably assignable to "Q," promises that in days to come many (or "men") will "sit at table in the Kingdom of God" along with the fathers of Israel:

I tell you, many will come from east and west and sit at table with Abraham, Isaac and Jacob in the Kingdom of heaven, while the sons of the kingdom will be thrown into the outer darkness; there men will weep and gnash their teeth. (Matt. 8:11-12)

There you will weep and gnash your teeth, when you see Abraham and Isaac and Jacob and all the prophets in the Kingdom of God and you yourselves thrown out. And men will come from east and west, and north and south, and sit at table in the Kingdom of God. (Luke 13:28-29)[6]

The slight differences between the two recensions can probably be accounted for in terms of the evangelists' respective styles and interests. The versions appear in different contexts. Matthew's is a homily appended, appropriately, at the end of the story of the gentile centurion's faith. Luke's version is part of a collection of sayings about entering the Kingdom of God. One of these directs those who would enter to strive to do so by the narrow door. Another specifically reproaches those who suppose that eating and drinking with Jesus now means that they will have some claim to a share in the table-fellowship of the coming Kingdom.

In both versions, the essential message is the same. The unworthy are solemnly warned of future condemnation to the realm of weeping and gnashing of teeth. Those destined to have a share in the Kingdom are assured that they will sit at table there with the fathers. In both gospels, the pericope functions as a summons to repentance and preparation, so that the hearers/readers might avoid the one destiny, and be numbered among those who are to enjoy the blessings of the other. Neither version says that Jesus himself would be present at table, nor is there mention of the messiah or the so-called "messianic banquet." It may be significant that the saying is not in the form of a parable or allegory. Instead, Jesus simply declares what will take place. Many will come from east and west to sit at table in the Kingdom. Those excluded and condemned will weep and gnash their teeth elsewhere. It is not stated when these things were to happen, though in Luke's version Jesus uses the second person plural, as if these events were going to take place within the lifetime of those who heard Jesus speak.

The Last Supper and Partaking in the Kingdom of God

At the Last Supper, Jesus vows that he will not again drink wine until he does so in the Kingdom of God. Again, the gospels report slightly divergent accounts. Mark's, perhaps, is the earliest: "Truly, I say to you, I shall not drink again of the fruit of the vine until that day when I drink it new in the kingdom of God" (Mark 14:25). Matthew's account adds the words "with you," making clear what may be implicit in Mark, that Jesus expects to be reunited in the Kingdom of God with those who are now at table with him (Matt. 26:29). Luke makes explicit what also is apparent otherwise, that Jesus' vow of abstinence was meant to be effective during the interval "until the kingdom of God comes" (Luke 22:18).

Another saying in the same setting appears in Luke only. Here Jesus vows not to eat the Passover "until it is fulfilled in the kingdom of God" (22:15–16). Whether he ate with them at the Last Supper or abstained, he expected, it seems, to eat the Passover when "it" was fulfilled in the Kingdom of God.[7] That Passover would celebrate not only the deliverance of Israel from Egypt, but entrance into the final inheritance. Quite possibly the Passover observance in Jesus' time already contained this hope for eschatological fulfillment.

Luke's description of the last supper includes still another such saying. To those who have been with him in his trials, Jesus promises: "As my Father appointed a kingdom for me, so do I appoint for you that you may eat and drink at my table in my kingdom, and sit on thrones judging the twelve tribes of Israel."[8] Here Jesus' faithful followers, presumably the Twelve, are assured that they will eat and drink at his table in his kingdom. Implicitly, it would be the Messiah's table, though there is no mention of the so-called "messianic banquet." The fact that these last two sayings are found only in Luke does not mean that they necessarily originated in a later stratum of tradition. As we have noted above (p. 30), special Lucan (and Matthean) traditions may well have been drawn from the earlier common source, "Q". These two sayings do comport with Luke's emphasis on the imminence of the coming Kingdom. However, they do not attempt to explain why the coming of the Kingdom had been delayed, and thus do not appear to have been shaped by Lucan redaction, much less created by the evangelist. Moreover, as we have seen, all four synoptic "sources" report sayings of Jesus which anticipate the coming of the Kingdom in the near future or at the latest, in the lifetime of some of his contemporaries.

The Beatitudes and the Anxiety Saying

Another fairly explicit reference to eating in the Kingdom of God appears in Luke's version of the Beatitudes: "Blessed are you poor, for yours is the Kingdom of God. Blessed are you that hunger now, for you shall be satisfied."[9] In the Kingdom of God, those who had suffered privation during their earthly lives would experience recompense. The same idea appears in the Lucan Parable of the Rich Man and Lazarus (16:19–31).

Likewise, in the "Q" saying about anxiety and the Kingdom, the faithful are assured that their need for food and drink will be satisfied.

Therefore do not be anxious, saying, 'What shall we eat?' or 'What shall we drink?' or 'What shall we wear?' For the Gentiles seek all these things; and your heavenly Father knows that you need them all. But seek first his kingdom and his righteousness, and all these things shall be yours as well. (Matt. 6:31–33)	And do not seek what you are to eat and what you are to drink, nor be of anxious mind. For all the nations of the world seek these things; and your Father knows that you need them. Instead seek his kingdom, and these things shall be yours as well. (Luke 12:29–31)

There is no hint that the food and drink included in the expression "these things" was thought of metaphorically. It is possible, of course, that "these things" referred to the gifts with which God would sustain those who seek his Kingdom during their remaining days in the old world before the Kingdom comes. However, the promise "and these things shall be yours as well," or literally, "given in addition" (*prostethēsetai*), suggests, as do the Beatitudes, that these blessings are to be enjoyed along with the others that will obtain in the coming Kingdom. Perhaps both meanings are implied. The situation or "plot" is somewhat analogous to that of the ancient Israelites in the wilderness. There God promised and provided "bread" or manna to sustain his people on their journey to the Promised Land. Once there, however, in the "land of milk and honey," all their needs and longings would be satisfied.

The Lord's Prayer: Bread for Tomorrow

The second petition of the Lord's Prayer expresses this same hope: "give us today our bread[10] for tomorrow" (Matt. 6:11). The only reason the verse is not translated literally in this way is that it does not make any sense to the reader *unless* the reader recognizes eating as a characteristic feature of the anticipated beatific life of the coming age. Once this is recognized, the meaning becomes clear: "Bring now the time for eating bread in the Messianic age."[11] Thus the petition about bread reiterates and parallels the import of the initial petition, "Thy Kingdom come!" Both ask God to bring about the promised era of redemption, the Kingdom of God or coming age.[12] Another time, someone exclaims in Jesus' presence, "Blessed is he who shall eat bread in the kingdom of God!" (Luke 14:15). Jesus does not take the occasion to repudiate the idea of eating bread in the Kingdom. Instead, according to Luke, Jesus responds with the Parable of the Great Banquet (14:16–24). The parable makes the point that those who do not come when invited to the banquet will have no share in it.[13] It is not clear whether the banquet in the parable was meant to represent the so-called "messianic banquet" in particular. It does suggest something of the sort, as does the Parable of the Marriage Feast in Matt. 22:1–5, 9–10. The Kingdom of God is also represented by a marriage feast in Matt. 25:1–13, though here, as with most parables, the point is not so much to describe the Kingdom, as to urge people to be ready in view of its coming in the near future.

Considered in the context of the sayings we have already examined, along with the several banquet parables, it seems likely that the second petition of the Lord's Prayer has to do with the prospect of eating in the Kingdom of God. It has been reasonably well-established that the probable meaning of *epiousios* in Matt. 6:11 is "coming" or "for tomorrow."[14] The petition does not refer explicitly to the "messianic banquet." Instead, "bread" or "food for tomorrow" seems to refer generally to whatever food it may be that will be enjoyed in the Kingdom of God or Messianic age, as part of the transformed and fulfilled life of that coming great era.

The "Feeding" of the Large Crowds

The prospect of eating bread, and also fish, in the coming age may be implicit in the stories of Jesus' "feeding" the five and four thousand reported in Mark 6:35–44, 8:1–10 and parallels. We have considered elsewhere some of the evidence that seems to justify this conclusion.[15] The expectation that those who lived in the grand days of the Messianic age would feast upon the flesh of the two great "fish" of antiquity,

Leviathan and Behemoth, recurs throughout Jewish sources.[16] In all gospel accounts, Jesus sacramentally distributes pieces of loaves and of two fish to a crowd that has come forward in response to his proclamation and that of his disciples. There is reason to believe that the crowd, together with Jesus and his disciples, were looking for the coming of the Kingdom of God, and that Jesus' distribution of bread and fish fragments is to be understood in connection with this hope. No other interpretation has succeeded in making any sense of Jesus' procedure on these occasions.[17] This interpretation is also supported by the pervasive utilization of bread and fish motifs in early Christian catacomb and other funerary art. It is fairly certain that bread and fish were thought of in connection with the hope for resurrection and participation in the Messianic age.[18] By giving pieces of bread and fish to the people who had come out to him, Jesus was pre-enacting the meal which he believed they would share in the coming Messianic age. Thereby he intended, perhaps, to offer the recipients a place in it.[19] Such a meal, in which Jesus symbolically feeds his followers the food of the Messianic age, is consistent with the second petition of the prayer he taught his followers: "Give us today our bread for tomorrow."[20] Jesus thereby gave those who had heard the message that the Kingdom of God had come near, a foretaste of the "bread for tomorrow" which they would enjoy once the Kingdom had come.

It is possible that Jesus enacted this kind of sacramental distribution on more than one occasion. His entire ministry or public activity was directed to the preparation of his people for the coming Kingdom. He repeatedly proclaimed that the Kingdom had come near, and called on his hearers to repent. Likewise, on many occasions, he undertook to exorcise demons. Mark and Matthew report two different bread and fish meals, perhaps, among other reasons, because two such meals were remembered. Perhaps there were still other such occasions.

The fact that the early Christian communities believed that Jesus had come as Messiah may have prompted the addition of the several baskets of food left over after the "meal" as completed (Mark 6, 8, and parallels). This superabundance of food would have been regarded as proof of Jesus' messiahship. Jewish tradition did not expect that the Messiah would perform miracles. But, as we have noticed, and will further show, Jewish traditions frequently did express the belief that in the Messianic age there would be enough for all to eat, and more.

Eating and Drinking: Jesus' Anticipatory Celebrations

According to one of the "Q" traditions, Jesus characterized his own way of life in the following way: "The son of man came eating and drinking."[21] The context is suggestive: Jesus has just identified John the Baptist (for those who have "ears to hear") as Elijah, the herald of the Messianic age.[22] He then speaks of himself as the son of man—the same term he uses for the messianic figure who is to be revealed at the beginning of the new age—who has come "eating and drinking." Read against the background of those sayings which explicitly mention eating and drinking in the Kingdom of God, it is conceivable that this saying refers not only to Jesus' non-ascetic lifestyle generally, but more specifically to his repeated anticipatory celebration of the coming Messianic time. Again, at the last supper, as we have seen, Jesus evidently invited his followers to share in an anticipatory celebration or pre-enactment of the meal that would be fulfilled in the Kingdom of God. The meal or meals he provided the large crowds in the wilderness seem to have been intended likewise.

On many occasions during his ministry, Jesus ate with "sinners" or other low caste persons whom he seems to have regarded as heirs to the Kingdom. As "bridegroom" who celebrates the coming "marriage" [when he will come as Messiah], Jesus does not fast.[23] Eating and drinking with Jesus would not, as such, assure fellow celebrants of a share in the table-fellowship of the coming Kingdom.[24] But those who were qualified to enter the coming Kingdom, whether on grounds of their experience of privation in the present age, or through repentance and seeking the Kingdom above all else, could look forward in confidence to enjoying the blessings of life together at table in the Kingdom when at last it came.

The Fig Tree Episode: No More Figs Until the Kingdom Comes

There may be a connection between Jesus' prayer or prohibition as to eating figs—the incident generally referred to as his "cursing" the fig tree[25]—and his expectation that food would be abundant in the coming Kingdom of God. Why would Jesus have looked for figs in the first place when, as Mark observes, "it was not the season for figs"? Interpreters who struggle with this seemingly enigmatic episode usually overlook two important considerations. One is the fact that numerous synoptic passages indicate clearly that Jesus was looking for the coming of the Kingdom of God in the near future. It is possible even that as he drew near to Jerusalem he thought that the era of the Kingdom had at last begun or was just about to do so.[26] The other consideration is the fact that a number of O.T. and Jewish sources, as well as N.T. and early Christian traditions, attest the belief that trees would bear fruit continually in the Messianic age.

Ezekiel had predicted a preternatural increase of fertility in the coming era of redemption: "And they will say, 'This land that was desolate has become like the garden of Eden . . .' " (36:35). His vision of the transformed environs of Jerusalem in the Messianic age further elaborates this theme. "There will grow all kinds of trees for food. Their leaves will not wither nor their fruit fail, but they will bear fresh fruit every month . . ." (47:12). Some such expectation appears also in Enoch 10:18–19. Enoch also refers to the tree of life, whose fragrance is beyond all fragrance, and whose beautiful fruit will be for the elect when, in the Messianic age, it is transplanted to the Temple precincts.[27] Probably the most prolific fertility is that visualized in II Baruch (ca. 75 C.E.) with ten thousand- (or billion-) fold productivity of vine and fruit.[28] According to II Bar. 29:2 and 30:1, this period of superabundant produce would take place in the days when the Messiah "shall begin to be revealed," but before his manifestation "in glory." Prolific fertility in the messianic age is also expected in the Talmud. Rabbi Gamaliel (c. 90 A.D.) is said to have declared: "Trees are destined to yield fruit every day. . . . Just as the boughs [exist] every day, so shall there be fruit every day" (Shabbat 30b).

Christian literature attests similar expectation. It was revealed to John of Patmos that in the Messianic age, the tree of life would yield twelve kinds of fruit and do so, like the trees of Ezek. 47:12, every month (Rev. 22:2). Presumably this would include figs, the tree-fruit most typically referred to in biblical traditions. As in Enoch 24–25, these trees of life would be planted in Jerusalem. It was just outside Jerusalem that Jesus stopped to look for fruit, even though it was "not the season for figs" (Mark 11:13). According to Irenaeus, Papias (c. 150 A.D.) reported that Jesus himself had taught that fruit and all kinds of crops would be produced in superabundance in the coming age.[29] It is unlikely that either John of Patmos or Papias provides a reliable account of Jesus' words. But these sayings do show that such ideas were not alien to Jesus' followers in the century following his lifetime. It may be that Jesus did express some such understanding in his parables of growth.[30]

Assuming that Mark 11:14 gives the earliest reading of Jesus' saying about the fig tree, we notice that he did not here "curse" it (as in Matt. 21:19), but rather prayed (or commanded), "May no one any longer eat fruit from you *eis ton aiōna*." This Greek phrase can hardly have served to translate any Semitic expression meaning simply "ever." It probably did translate an expression that referred to either the present or the coming age. Apocalyptic and even rabbinic thought divided history into two ages: the present and the one that was to come. Jesus also seems to have made this distinction.[31] He and his contemporaries were living in the last days of the present age. The coming of the Kingdom of God would mark the beginning of the age to come or Messianic age. Read in the context of this understanding, *eis ton aiōna* probably stands for a Hebrew or Aramaic phrase that meant either "in this age" or "until the age to come." Jesus then would have said, in effect, "May no one any longer eat your fruit in this age" or may no one do so "until the age to come."[32] Such a saying would have been entirely reasonable under the circumstances. He had just entered Jerusalem as Messiah.[33] Immediately afterwards, he went on, again, perhaps, intending to fulfill messianic prophecies, to purify the Temple in preparation for the coming of the Kingdom of God.[34] Finding figs at this time would have confirmed his hope that the Messianic age—when figs and other fruit would always be in season—was about to appear or had already begun to do so. Finding no figs, Jesus may have meant to declare his hope that the coming age would indeed have come by the time it was the season for figs. Either reading would have essentially the same meaning: "May no one again eat of your fruit in this age;" "May the Kingdom of God have come by the time it is again the season for figs." Jesus had taught his followers above all else to seek and pray for the coming of the Kingdom of God, that time that God would give them their bread or food "for tomorrow." Likewise, at the Last Supper, he vowed to abstain from drinking wine until the Kingdom of God had come, thus giving expression to his hope that the Kingdom of God would come by the time for eating the Passover meal.[35]

This proposed interpretation of the fig tree episode is, admittedly, somewhat speculative. But it does take into account the substantial body of evidence which shows that Jesus, like many of his Jewish predecessors and contemporaries, did expect that people really would eat and drink in the Kingdom of God. Then it would always be the season for figs, and for all the other fruit and produce that would abound in that age. Here again, we see that the historical Jesus is not so strange and enigmatic after all *if* we take seriously the nature and implications of his reported eschatological beliefs, and if we allow ourselves to recognize their connection with the beliefs and expectations of apocalyptic Judaism.

Old Testament and Later Jewish Concepts

The hope of eating and drinking amid the transformed conditions of existence in the coming age would have been familiar to any Jew of Jesus' day who was acquainted with the Scriptures and tradition. This does not mean, of course, that Jesus necessarily shared all such beliefs and expectations. But it seems likely that his own understanding was influenced by some of these ideas. It cannot simply be assumed that Jesus' own position necessarily would have been different from or opposed to such Jewish beliefs.

Again and again, the "promised land" is characterized as a land "flowing with milk and honey" as well as supplying other material blessings.[36] The hope of inheriting or coming into the promised land, of course, gave coloration to the later hope for inheriting or entering the Kingdom of God. Various biblical traditions recalled that God had provided good things to eat when man and woman lived in the Garden of Eden,[37] and had supplied his peoples' need for food all during their sojourn in the wilderness (e.g., Exod. 16, Num. 11). In Psalm 78:24–25, the "manna" of the wilderness is also described as "the grain of heaven" and "the bread of angels." The latter terminology also recurs in II Esdras 1:19 and Wisd. Sol. 16:20. Several O.T. traditions associate the offering of sacrifices to God with eating and drinking before him or in his presence.[38] After Canaan had been occupied by Israel, the ideal life is pictured in terms of each man sitting "under his [own] vine and under his fig tree" (1 Kings 4:25). Such imagery also is used to depict the fulfilled life of the Messianic age (Micah 4:4; Zech. 3:10).

In time, perhaps as early as Amos or Isaiah, hope began to emerge that God would restore and transform not only history, but also "nature," the creation. The concluding verses of Amos give expression to this hope.

> "Behold, the days are coming," says the LORD,
> "when . . . the mountains shall drip sweet wine,
>   and all the hills shall flow with it.
> "I will restore the fortunes of my people Israel,
>   . . . they shall plant vineyards and drink their wine,
>   and they shall make gardens and eat their fruit."[39]

Such expectations appear in sayings attributed to Isaiah, e.g., 4:2; 32:15. Second Isaiah likewise looks for the restoration of all creation, particularly the environs of Jerusalem: "For the LORD will comfort Zion; he will comfort all her waste places, and will make her wilderness like Eden, her desert like the garden of the LORD" (Isa. 51:3). The concluding chapters of "Third Isaiah" look for a radical world transformation in which all will be made new.[40] Such expectation comes to the surface in numerous later Jewish and Christian apocalyptic statements, some of which refer explicitly to eating and/or drinking. This kind of belief probably underlies Jesus' anticipation of drinking "new wine" at Mark 14:25. Matthew 19:28 refers to the reordering of the conditions of existence in the coming Kingdom of God as the "rebirth" *(palingene-sia)*, evidently of the world or creation.

The apocalypse of Isaiah contains the famous statement of such hopes: "On this mountain the Lord of hosts will prepare a banquet of rich fare for all the peoples, a banquet of wines well-matured and rich-est fare, well-matured wines strained clear" (Isa. 25:6, N.E.B.). Here we find reference to a future banquet, though no mention of a messiah or *messianic* banquet.[41] In all of the O.T. passages that refer to abundant food and drink, the place where these are to be enjoyed is the earth, albeit a transformed or even "new" earth. Many other O.T. passages evidence similar hopes and expectations.[42]

Almost without exception, the inter-testamental and rabbinic sources look for a material, though transformed world as the place where the fulfilled life of the coming age will be enjoyed. The idea of a new or renewed heaven and earth is reiterated in Jub. 1:29.[43] First Enoch frequently portrays fruitful trees, often associated with the tree of life.[44] Here also we find explicit reference to eating with the Messiah (or Son of man) in the new age:

> And the Lord of Spirits will abide over them,
> And with that Son of man they shall eat,
>   And lie down and rise up for ever and ever. (I En. 62:14).

Again, in T. Levi 18:11, we read of the messianic priest: "And he shall give to the saints to eat from the tree of life." The inter-testamental writings that anticipate super-abundance of the fruits of the earth in the coming age contain few references to the Messiah. In some in-stances, no human or supernatural agency is involved; e.g., at Sib. Or. III: 744–45, "For the Earth, the universal mother, shall give to mortals her best fruit in countless store of corn, wine and oil."[45] The preternat-ural fertility of the earth on the threshold of the Messiah's disclosure is pictured vividly in II Baruch:

> The earth shall yield its fruit ten thousandfold,
> and on each vine there shall be a thousand branches,
> and each branch shall produce a thousand clusters,
> and each cluster produce a thousand grapes,
> and each grape produce a cor of wine.[46]

In the same context, we are told that "those two great monsters," Levi-athan and Behemoth, will be food for those that are left, and also that "the treasury of manna shall again descend from on high, and they will eat of it in those years."[47]

In II Enoch 8 it is revealed that the transformed creation, identified as Paradise, will not be located on earth. Instead, it is to be placed in (or below) the third heaven, "between corruptibility and incorruptibility." There will be found "every tree sweet flowering, every fruit ripe, all manner of food perpetually bubbling with all pleasant smells, and four rivers flowing by with quiet course, and every growth is good, bearing fruit for food.[48] This place, Enoch hears, is prepared as an eternal inheritance for the righteous (9:1) who, presumably, would eat and drink of its bountiful produce.[49] Several passages in II Esdras likewise refer to the fruitful trees of Paradise prepared for the righteous. Among the rewards of the Kingdom which these may look forward to are places "at the feast of the Lord."[50]

We have already mentioned the saying attributed to Rabbi Gamaliel in Shabbat 30b.[51] Such expectations appear in other rabbinic writings.

> Similarly in the Messianic age, He will establish peace for them,
> and they will sit at ease and eat in Paradise . . .
> He will bring them fruit from the Garden of Eden
> and will feed them from the Tree of Life.[52]

Perhaps the most extravagant version of this hope is that found at Kethubot 111b: "In the world to come a man will bring one grape on a wagon or a ship, put it in the corner of his house and use its contents as a large wine cask. . . ."[53]

Only one passage in the Dead Sea Scrolls refers to eating and drinking in the coming age. This is in the *Rule of the Future Community* (IQSa) 2:17–21. Here the Messiah is pictured sitting at table with those others who shall be present in the Messianic age. Even here, it is not a question of "the messianic banquet," but rather of instructions for conduct during recurring meals in the future.[54] This messiah will be subordinate to "the priest at the head of the whole congregation of Israel."[55]

Beliefs, Practices, and Expectations in the Early Church

The Christian community in Jerusalem continued to gather for the "breaking of bread," apparently expecting Jesus' return as Messiah and the coming of the Kingdom of God.[56] Quite possibly some traditions to the effect that the risen Jesus ate and drank with his followers were believed to have fulfilled, at least in part, Jesus' assurances about eating and drinking with them again in the Kingdom of God.[57] Like Paul, the early Christian community may have believed that with Jesus' death and resurrection the New age had begun to dawn.[58] Paul's warning that the Kingdom of God does not mean food and drink may have been aimed at those who supposed that they were already living in the new age.[59] Paul's expectations are also directed toward the future. The church's observance of the eucharist has meaning in connection with its expectation of Jesus' coming (1 Cor. 11:26). This association of eucharist with longing for Jesus' coming as Messiah is evident also in the Didachē,[60] and as late as the Epistle of the Apostles.[61]

The prospect of eating and drinking in the Kingdom of God is anticipated elsewhere in the N.T., notably in the Apocalypse to John. Here "Jesus," risen and exalted as "one like a son of man" (Rev. 1:12–18), instructs John to write to the angel of Ephesus "what the Spirit says to the churches"—evidently to all the churches. " 'To him who conquers, I will grant to eat of the tree of life, which is in the paradise of God' " (Rev. 2:7). Similarly, in Rev. 3:20 we read: "Behold, I stand at the door and knock; if anyone hears my voice and opens the door, I will come in to him and eat with him, and he with me."[62] The idea of a new or renewed heaven and earth is appropriated in Rev. 21:1, 5, with special attention to the new Jerusalem which would come "down out of heaven from God." Through this city would flow "the river of the water of life," on either side of which would be planted the tree (i.e., trees) of life "with its twelve kinds of fruit, yielding its fruit each month."[63]

Irenaeus attributes to "the elders" a statement purporting to come from Jesus himself about "those days":

> The days will come, in which vines will be produced,
> each one having a thousand branches,
> and in each branch ten thousand twigs,
> and on each twig ten thousand shoots,
> and on each shoot ten thousand clusters,
> and in each cluster ten thousand grapes,
> and each grape when pressed will give twenty-five metretes of wine.
> And when one of the saints takes hold of a cluster, another will cry, 'I am a better cluster, take me, bless the Lord through me.' Similarly a grain of wheat will produce ten thousand ears,
> and each ear will have ten thousand grains,
> and each grain ten pounds of clear pure flour;
> And the other fruits and seeds and grass will produce in the same proportion, and all the animals, using the foods which come from the earth, will be peaceful and harmonious with each other, and perfectly subject to man.[64]

It is obvious that this tradition is related to II Bar. 29:5f., and probably represents an expansion of it. Irenaeus himself endorses the expectation of eating and drinking in the Kingdom of God which is to be established on earth. He explains the meaning of Jesus' words at the Last Supper as follows: "He promised that he would drink of the produce of the vine with his disciples, thus showing both the inheritance of the earth, in which the new produce of the vine is drunk, and the physical resurrection of his disciples."[65] Moreover, Irenaeus construed Jesus' sayings at Luke 14:12–14, 18:29f., and Matt. 19:29 in the same sense:

Where are the hundredfold rewards in this age, the dinners offered to the poor, and the suppers for which a reward is received? These things are [to be] in the times of the Kingdom. . . . This is the true Sabbath of the just, in which they will have no earthly work to do, but will have a table prepared before them by God, who will feed them with dainties of all kinds.[66]

Numerous early Roman catacomb paintings depicting people seated or reclining at table with bread, fish, and wine, as well as the recurrent usage of bread and fish images in other early Christian funerary art suggest that the hope for reunion at table in the Messianic age continued into the third and fourth centuries.

The Earlier Hope and Subsequent Modifications

As Christianity became more at home in the world of Greek thought, the hope for re-union at table in the Kingdom of God became less intelligible, for the fulfilled life of salvation was conceptualized primarily as a non-material realm or mode of existence. Understandably, the N.T. passages that gave promise to the hope for eating and drinking in the Kingdom of God were increasingly passed over in silence, or else subjected to allegorical or "spiritual" reinterpretation.

But there is no reason to suppose that Jesus did not mean literally or realistically what he said when he spoke of those who would come from East and West to sit at table with the patriarchs in the Kingdom of God, or of his own hope again to drink of the fruit of the vine at that time. The prospect of eating and drinking accords entirely with Jesus' eschatological message and activity as represented elsewhere in the synoptic sources. Old Testament and Jewish sources corroborate the eschatological character of these beliefs. Such beliefs appear also in the writings of the early Church. It would be possible to argue that the beliefs attributed to Jesus in the synoptic gospels actually originated in the early Church. Buy why should the early community have wished to impute such beliefs to Jesus? Moreover, there is no substantive basis for viewing such sayings as secondary. It is reasonable to surmise that the Church continued for a time to look forward to eating and drinking in the Kingdom of God because Jesus' first followers had learned from him to do so. Afterwards this expectation became less important for the Church. Since the parousia had not occurred within the lifetime of the first and then ensuing generations, Christians were increasingly open to alternative understandings as to their hopes for the future. As Christianity became increasingly a gentile religion, Hellenism provided such concepts and categories. In particular, Hellenism viewed the whole realm of material existence with suspicion and looked for perfection in a wholly spiritual realm. As early as Paul, we can see the beginning of a shift in Christian doctrine from anticipation of reunion at table in the Kingdom of God to hope for heavenly life in a spiritual body.[67] Later, with the emergence of the idea of the immortality of the soul, little place remained for the prospect of eating or drinking in the Kingdom of God.[68]

VI The Historical, Eschatological Jesus and the Modern Quest

Our inquiry has focused mainly upon the characteristic methods and interests of those who have attempted to describe and interpret the historical Jesus to modern readers. In order to appraise the adequacy of interpretations, we must see what interpreters have done with the data. Therefore we have directed our attention to primary sources, particularly the synoptic gospels. Jewish and early Christian writings also provide considerable background information.

Jesus' Eschatological Message and Activity: Basic Findings

Jesus' proclamation of the Kingdom of God as well as other important features of his reported message and activity indicate that his understanding of history was consistently eschatological, indeed, apocalyptic.[1] Moreover, Jesus' message and activity are intelligible only when the underlying eschatological and apocalyptic perspective is recognized. His warning of impending Judgment refers to the coming eschatological assize when the Son of Man, or God himself, would separate the righteous from the unrighteous, and assign them to their respective final destinies. Jesus' message of repentance and radical, responsive love was addressed to those living in the indeterminate but brief interim period of history before the coming of the Kingdom and the time of Judgment. His entire preaching and other activity appear to have been prompted by concern for the ultimate well-being of his contemporaries. He was concerned that as many of them as possible should hear this message and repent so that they might be included with those who would share the blessings of life in the coming Kingdom rather than be found among those forever excluded from its joys. In the meantime, Satan and the demons continued to cause grief. Like his healings, Jesus' exorcisms reflect his care for the well-being of the sons and daughters of Abraham (and, reportedly, some gentiles) in the remaining days of the present age. The exorcisms also were intended to prepare the way for the coming of the Kingdom of God. Jesus, together with his disciples to whom he granted power (*exousia*) over the demons, was engaged in binding the strong man, Satan. The latter's kingdom would indeed have come to an end once the kingdom or rule of God was established on earth. When that time came, those who had heeded the message of repentance and done the will of God would experience the joy of sitting at table with the righteous of all ages and places, eating and drinking in the Kingdom of God. Even if in a few sayings Jesus might have hinted that the Kingdom of God was already somehow present, his characteristic orientation was toward these future eschatological occurrences and their all-encompassing importance for those who lived in his time.

Jesus, Apocalyptic Judaism, and Christian Interpretation

We have also seen that in many respects, Jesus' beliefs and expectations were congruent, though not entirely identical, with those of inter-testamental apocalyptic Judaism. Christian interpreters have ordinarily insisted that Jesus' beliefs were somehow essentially different from, or opposed to, those of Judaism, especially apocalyptic Judaism. This insistence appears to derive more from theological assumptions and desires than from careful analysis of synoptic and Jewish sources. Such interpreters may suppose that since in the Christian canon the New Testament follows directly upon the Old, and the gospels come immediately after the prophets, Jesus and the entire New Testament are to be understood simply as the fulfillment of Old Testament prophetic hopes and expectations.[2] Moreover, Christian interpreters commonly assume that such traditions and hopes point clearly to "the messiah" in whose role Jesus unmistakably appeared. They often assume further that the spiritual messiah, supposedly looked for by the prophets, had little or nothing to do with Judaism.[3] If interpreters do acknowledge a connection between Jesus and Judaism, they generally find the non-apocalyptic thought-world of rabbinic Judaism a more congenial "setting" for Jesus and his message than the "strange" world of Jewish apocalypticism. At all events, Christian interpreters tend to ignore, distort, and belittle Jewish, and even Christian, apocalyptic writings and ideas generally. Such interpreters seem to find it preferable to depict Jesus as over against such strange (or "fantastic") Jewish beliefs and expectations. One technique frequently employed is to equate apocalyptic with wild and fanciful speculations and calculations, and then confidently declare that Jesus' understanding of the coming Kingdom was not only non-apocalyptic but anti-apocalyptic. Jesus, as spiritual messiah, is then said to have proclaimed or embodied a spiritual Kingdom of God.

Interpreters to whom the apocalyptic prospect of coming Judgment is either unfamiliar or repugnant commonly neglect this aspect of Jesus' proclamation. Alternately, Christian interpreters propose to attribute such passages—as many as possible—to putative Jewish (or other unwholesome) influence in the later churches. Then if any of these passages still remain to be considered, such interpreters may suggest, following C.H. Dodd, that what Jesus really meant was that men already pass judgment upon themselves in the present time. In either case, the idea that Jesus proclaimed an actual, future Judgment is avoided. Schweitzer's characterization of Jesus' message as an ethic for the interim has been subjected to a number of curious distortions. Most of these distortions seem to derive from interpreters' unwillingness to believe that Jesus actually meant to address his Jewish contemporaries in regard to their attitudes and behavior during the time remaining before the Judgment. Jesus' and his disciples' exorcisms of demons likewise are generally ignored, or else construed more generally as "miracles" or "signs," without serious attention to the dualistic world-view typical of apocalyptic thought. Finally, to those who choose to ignore Jewish apocalypticism (or even non-apocalyptic Judaism), it usually appears obvious that Jesus would not have been thinking of actual and *materialistic* eating and drinking in the Kingdom of God. Interpreters find it much more meaningful to understand such passages in a symbolic and spiritual sense.

Necessarily, modern critics and historians are not at home in the pre-scientific, and particularly, the eschatological world-view of apocalyptic Judaism and early Christianity. Modern interpreters—particularly those who find Jesus and his message important and authoritative for faith and life—are therefore understandably predisposed to assume that Jesus (and perhaps some of the early Christians) really shared our world-view, and only talked or wrote in apocalyptic terms for rhetorical purposes. Such interpreters are readily persuaded that Jesus and the evangelists used these terms as "symbols," intending to express meanings which are really the same as those *we* find relevant for faith and life in our time. Harnack, Bultmann, Wilder, and Perrin, for example, lean toward this kind of interpretation, despite their scholarly sophistication. Each sets out to express in terms of particular modern categories what it was that Jesus really meant, so that their readers may understand what in Jesus' message to his contemporaries is (or should be) meaningful to us today. But then each goes on to imply or assert

that Jesus himself espoused the substance—or even the terminology—
of their respective modern translations. Some such "demythologiza-
tion" or reinterpretation goes on almost automatically, without reflection, in wider circles of interpretation.

For example, Christians have long been content to repeat the familiar rendering of the petition in the Lord's Prayer, "Deliver us from
evil." The Greek text, however, refers explicitly to "the Evil One." Recently, a number of interpreters who have found A.N. Whitehead's
process theology helpful to their own faith-understanding have ventured to suggest that Jesus' beliefs can be translated without substantial alteration into process categories.[4] Not surprisingly, in the course
of such reinterpretation, Jesus' apocalyptic beliefs and expectations are
either blurred or put to one side. It does seem to be quite difficult for
modern Christian interpreters to accept the fact that Jesus, according to
all the synoptic gospels and their sources, spoke in terms of the beliefs
and expectations of dualistic and apocalyptic Judaism. Evidently interpreters find it even more difficult to believe that Jesus actually thought
(or lived) in accordance with such beliefs and expectations. And nearly
all interpreters are inclined to ignore the fact that Jesus undertook to
address his own contemporaries, not us or our time.

The Quest for a Jesus Without Eschatology

Many interpreters seem to be afraid that if, the eschatological and
apocalyptic aspects of Jesus' outlook and message were taken literally,
the consequences for contemporary faith (whether traditionalist or liberal) would be to say the least disconcerting and possibly disastrous.
Several writers ask, in effect, "What then would Jesus mean to us
if. . . ."[5] To recognize that Jesus was mistaken in his belief that the
eschatological events were soon to occur would present some problems
for traditionalist faith. Such faith, which is grounded substantially in
the Fourth Gospel, commonly ascribes to Jesus all the attributes of deity, including omniscience. Since, in the view of traditionalist interpreters, Jesus could not have been mistaken, his sayings about the
coming Kingdom must have referred to something that did soon occur,
such as his resurrection, pentecost, or the establishment of the Church.
On the other hand, if Jesus really expected people to be judged for their
attitudes and deeds in this Old world, and proclaimed "only" an ethic
for the interim, this would call into question the liberal perspective
which typically looks to Jesus' words as a source of guidance for the
moral life in the modern world. If Jesus really believed that he was
engaged in binding or overpowering Satan and the demons, such be-

lief would be problematic for all modern interpreters who no longer take such beings seriously. Moreover, if he expected that he and his followers would actually eat and drink in the coming age, such expectation would make little sense to the great number of Christians who have long been accustomed to the (non-Jewish) idea that the spiritual ultimately transcends and excludes the merely physical or material dimensions of existence. In short, to every school of modern theology and thought, the historical, eschatological Jesus is *persona non grata*, in Schweitzer's phrase, "a stranger and an enigma."

To avoid this kind of impasse and its attendant theological and ethical problems, interpreters have found it very tempting to try, in one way and another, to skirt, offset, or eliminate the eschatological material in the tradition, and thereby, if possible, avoid or refute the eschatological interpretation of Jesus and his activity. Thus we have seen that interpreters commonly ignore the synoptic passages that report Judgment sayings and exorcisms of demons. Invoking the mystical name of form criticism, interpreters may propose to attribute eschatological passages to a later stage in the development of the tradition. Or, under the banner of redaction criticism, such passages can be assigned to the editors or authors of the gospels. These methods of literary analysis have yielded valuable results. Nevertheless, we suspect that some form and redaction critics have also been prompted by a sense that it is theologically preferable to know too little about Jesus' outlook and message than to know too much about one who entertained the strange eschatological thoughts attributed to him in the synoptic gospels.[6] Again, interpreters often propose that when Jesus referred to the coming Kingdom, or to eating and drinking there, he was speaking *symbolically*—for instance, about religious experience, or about himself as the bread of everlasting life.

Several writers have adopted yet another strategem for avoiding theological difficulties. They assert—numerous synoptic passages notwithstanding—that for Jesus time was no longer important, so that it does not really matter whether the eschatological events are considered to be past, present, or future. Interpreters who find meaningful the Platonic idea of timeless essences are naturally more at home with a Platonic than an eschatological Jesus.

Few interpreters have completely subscribed to C.H. Dodd's view that Jesus understood and proclaimed that the Kingdom of God was already entirely present (except for some further dimension "beyond time and space"). But a large number do hold that Dodd was partly correct, and maintain that Jesus believed and declared the Kingdom to be *both* somehow present *and* a future, eschatological event. This mediating position appears, on its face, to be a fair-minded resolution of the conflicting claims of Weiss and Schweitzer on the one hand, and of Dodd on the other. This resolution is especially appealing to those who find the Aristotelian "mean" (or British "good sportsmanship") more congenial than the purportedly Teutonic disjunctive, "either/or." Thus the futuristic eschatological interpretation is commonly said to be "too extreme," or "one-sided." Consequently, many interpreters seem prepared to adjudge the futuristic eschatological interpretation wrong or "wrong-headed" by definition, without feeling any particular obligation to account for the synoptic evidence that gives rise to that interpretation. In this connection, we have noted the tendency of various interpreters to distort or caricature Schweitzer's position, and then dismiss it as obviously implausible.[7]

The question remains, however, whether the synoptic evidence is such as to sustain the contention that Jesus considered the Kingdom of God both present and future. Though the contrary is occasionally asserted, there are no passages which report that Jesus declared it unambiguously to be present. Moreover, there are no passages in which he declared it to be both present and future. The absence of such passages weighs heavily against the theory that such precisely was what Jesus meant his hearers to understand. There are, however, numerous passages in which Jesus reportedly implied or declared the Kingdom to be a future and indeed imminent event. Moreover, as we have seen, there can be little doubt that he regarded other closely related eschatological occurrences, such as the Judgment and eating and drinking in the Kingdom of God, as still future. Further, Jesus' message or "interim ethics" of repentance and responsive love presupposes the futurity, if not the imminence, of the Judgment and the coming of the Kingdom of God. Jesus' (and the disciples') exorcisms of demons are most plausibly understood as activities carried out in preparation for the still future establishment of God's Kingdom on earth. We have indicated elsewhere that interpreters who hold that Jesus regarded the Kingdom as both present and future have achieved peculiarly little consensus as to *how* he might have understood the relation between Kingdom present and Kingdom future.[8]

We have seen here that these both-and or "two-sided" interpretations tend to become involved in all sorts of curious contradictions, and to necessitate creation of various idiosyncratic neo-logisms and other hermeneutical inventions, devices, and distinctions. Thus interpreters may speak of a first and second coming of the Kingdom—without explaining the relation between the one and the other—even though the synoptic sources refer only to its *coming.* Or interpreters assert both that Jesus proclaimed or manifested the "irrupting," "dawning," or "inbreaking" of the Kingdom in the present, and that he declared that it would "irrupt," "dawn," or "break in" in the future. One commentator feels constrained to disavow "all logical considerations" in order to maintain that Jesus' moral message was not a matter of interim ethics, but then goes on to urge that *some* of Jesus' sayings may properly be discounted because they *were* based upon his expectation of imminent eschatological events.[9] Jesus' exorcisms are said to be "signs" of the presence of the Kingdom, even though exorcisms are nowhere so characterized in the primary sources. Again, the exorcisms are said to show that the "powers of the Kingdom" were already operative, even though this expression does not appear in the gospels, which do, however, expressly represent the coming of the Kingdom of God "with power" as a future eschatological event. Those who read the gospels to mean that the Kingdom was present usually do not explain why Satan and the demons were still present in this new era. Various interpreters who claim that Satan had already been "bound" early in the course of Jesus' ministry nevertheless acknowledge that Satan still continued to be potent and operative afterwards. An interpreter who grants that Matt. 6:11 refers to the bread of the Messianic age feels justified in asserting that the same words simultaneously refer to "earthly bread to meet the hunger and need of the present day."[10] And a great many (especially Christian) interpreters realize that Jesus was speaking to his Jewish contemporaries, but also urge that he really intended his message for "us."

This confused, if not contradictory, pattern of interpretation appears to derive from a single source. Interpreters find it very difficult to refrain from attributing to Jesus himself the interpretations they experience as meaningful. Rather than allow him merely to speak his own lines and do his deeds in the setting of early first century Palestinian Judaism, interpreters proceed to credit Jesus with having anticipated those conceptions of his message and activity which they find relevant to contemporary faith and life. Having paid respects, perhaps somewhat hurriedly, to the historical, though theologically or morally problematic,[11] elements in the tradition, interpreters typically go on to emphasize the more relevant or convenient features which they have come to believe represent, in the final analysis, the essence of Jesus' intention and message. This relevant essence usually is expressed in terms familiar to one or another of the modern philosophical or theological schools. It also normally rests on a shallow exegetical foundation.[12] Thus Jesus is represented, finally, by Harnack as the proponent of liberal piety and ethics ("the Fatherhood of God and the infinite value of the human soul"); by Bultmann as the one who summoned his hearers to the recurrent existential crisis of decision and radical obedience; and by the "new questers" as the original exemplar and sponsor of the "understanding of the meaning of existence" evoked by the Church's kerygma.

These several mediating solutions attempt to combine critical historical research with theological interests. It is widely recognized that texts of all sorts are read by persons who necessarily are related to a community of shared understanding, values, and concerns. To acknowledge this, however, does not—as is sometimes asserted—justify dismissing the question as to what Jesus intended when he addressed his own contemporaries. There are two separate questions: what did the historical Jesus mean, and what does he mean for us? Those who are concerned with the second question may also be concerned with the first. But when, as commonly happens, inquiry as to the first is guided and shaped by interest in the second, the results are apt to be distorted by the interpreter's desire to find the right sort of Jesus. Fidelity to truth, including the truth about the historical Jesus, requires that the first question be considered as much as possible without regard to desirable or undesirable results. Distinguishing these two questions does not, of course, resolve the evidentiary problem as to which traditions, if any, can be regarded as relatively reliable accounts of Jesus' actions and words. However, unless these two quesions are distinguished, there is little to prevent interpreters, consciously or otherwise, from ignoring or interpreting away evidence that is theologically distasteful, or from investing ambiguous evidence with the meanings that most appeal to their own point of view. Even when the questions are distinguished, the interpreter may still be tempted to determine in advance what kind of historical Jesus is to be found and then proceed to read the evidence accordingly. But interpretation is less likely to succumb to this temptation if the historical and theological tasks are differentiated and the interpreter's conception of the historical Jesus is continually tested by reference to the primary evidence.

The Jesus of History and the Gospels: The Eschatological Jesus

The early churches and evangelists also had their interests. They were not writing "objective history" but were reporting remembered teachings and episodes in accordance with their own beliefs and concerns. To some degree their interests can be identified, and a good many particular traditions can be assigned to their hands as editors or even authors. It is theoretically possible that all of the traditions originated in the early Church, and that nothing remains which can be regarded as evidence for the deeds and words of the historical Jesus. Even if this should prove the case, the Jesus of the Church's earliest recollections was the eschatological Jesus. It is unlikely that such a Jesus would have been entirely invented by the earliest Church. Perhaps a radical *either/or* is unnecessary here. The historical, eschatological Jesus may have been remembered somewhat accurately in the early Church's traditions.[13] At all events, interpreters are not now in a position to choose between an eschatological and a non-eschatological Jesus, but only between an historical, eschatological Jesus and a non-historical, but nevertheless eschatological one. Schweitzer stated the matter dramatically when he wrote that the Jesus of the rationalist and liberal "lives" of Jesus "never had any existence."[14] More precisely, it could be said that the primary sources, the synoptic gospels, do not give us any information about such a Jesus, or about any other non-eschatological Jesus. It does not follow that the historical, eschatological Jesus can have no meaning "for us." But that is another question.

VII The Eschatological Jesus and Modern Faith:
Theological and Moral Reflections

The Eschatological Jesus: Traditionalist and Liberal Reactions

We have seen that interpreters located within the Christian tradition tend to bypass or downplay the eschatological aspects of Jesus' message, expectation and activities. Many apparently assume that Christian faith or ethics would be undermined or even irreparably damaged should it turn out that Jesus really believed and proclaimed that the Kingdom of God and Judgment would come upon the generation of his contemporaries. It simply does not occur to traditionalist interpreters who subscribe to the high christology of the Fourth Gospel that Jesus might have been mistaken about anything, particularly anything so important as the coming of the Kingdom of God. How could Jesus, who was one with God—indeed, was God—be in error?[1] Traditionalist theology, influenced, perhaps by the metaphysical dualism underlying much of Greek thought, has also tended to posit the ultimacy of spiritual, as opposed to physical realities. Hence traditionalist interpreters do not often contemplate the possibility that Jesus understood the Kingdom of God as a realm in space and time where those still alive at its coming would sit at table, eating and drinking with the resurrected righteous dead of earlier generations. When noticed at all, passages evidencing such expectations are construed either as metaphors intended to symbolize intangible realities of some sort, or else as accretions from the thought-world of Jewish-Christianity. Since Jesus—in the view of traditionalist theology—was a Christian, not a Jew, it seems natural to suppose that he would have discarded such Jewish ideas as a physical or worldly Kingdom in favor of spiritual or otherworldly meanings. Thus eating and drinking traditions are usually understood sacramentally, in accordance with the eucharistic beliefs and practices of later Christianity. Traditionalist theology has experienced no difficulty in understanding Jesus' reported exorcisms as evidence of his identity as the Christ or supernatural Son of God, and generally has supposed that Jesus so regarded them also.

Liberal or modernist schools of theology, which typically are optimistic as to human nature and destiny, also found the eschatological Jesus uncongenial and therefore implausible. Jesus' warning of impending Judgment seemed too pessimistic and inconsistent with the liberal doctrines of human goodness and progress. Modernist interpreters were particularly offended by Schweitzer's proposal that Jesus meant his ethical teachings for those living in the brief interim before the coming of the Kingdom of God and the Judgment. If Jesus expected these decisive events within the lifetime of the generation then alive, he would not have intended his teaching for the guidance and direction of Christians living in later centuries. Yet liberal faith regarded Jesus as the great teacher of timeless truths and founder of the Kingdom which gradually but surely would be established on earth as the result of moral and social reform inspired by his gospel of love. Such a Jesus was infinitely more welcome to liberal theology than the apocalyptic, if not fanatical figure portrayed by the eschatological school. Surely that school must be mistaken! The idea that Jesus might have understood that he was casting out demons in order to free their victims from Satan's power and prepare the way for the coming Kingdom of God would have been just as strange to liberal as to traditionalist Christianity. It occurred to few interpreters of either school. Liberal-oriented interpreters do sometimes suggest that Jesus' exorcisms were carried out as a concession to the superstitions of his contemporaries, but are really to be understood as expressions of his gospel of love, along with his healings of the sick. Similarly, liberal interpreters occasionally intimate that Jesus' meals are to be regarded as illustrations of caring and sharing love. Only rarely does an interpreter propose that Jesus might actually have expected the righteous and impoverished of this age to eat and drink together in the next. A Kingdom beyond caste has never been popular with Christians in the comfortable pew, whether traditional or liberal.

Notwithstanding the serious concerns of traditionalist and liberal faith, we have found it likely that Jesus thought, prophesied and acted in accordance with the eschatological pattern of belief and expectation described in the earlier chapters. We would have preferred to reach other conclusions. As Schweitzer observed many years ago, "The ideal would be that Jesus should have preached religious truth in a form independent of any connection with any particular period and such that it could be taken over simply and easily by each succeeding generation of men."[2] But he did not do so.

It would be possible, of course, for Christian faith to continue to bypass the question of Jesus' eschatological intention and message, and to ground itself on something else. Traditional Christianity has long been accustomed to rely upon the faith of the church, beginning with the formulations by Paul[3] and, especially, by the author of the Fourth Gospel. To be sure, traditionalist theologians have not been concerned to distinguish Pauline expressions from the sayings of Jesus, and generally have been content to assume that the Fourth Gospel can be taken as an accurate account of Jesus' message and activity.[4] Consequently, traditionalist theology has not been particularly aware that its own faith-understanding may differ significantly from that of the historical Jesus. Rudolf Bultmann, on the other hand, found it theologically important to insist there was a substantial difference between Jesus' understanding and the so-called kerygma of the church. Bultmann was concerned lest the former might somehow "legitimate" the latter and so encroach upon the radical character of faith. For Bultmann it was quite enough "that" the "Christ-event" had occurred. Several of Bultmann's pupils, the so-called "new questers," on the other hand, wished to bridge the gap between the historical, eschatological Jesus and the existentialist kerygma of the church which they found meaningful for faith, and so ventured to reinterpret the "historical" Jesus accordingly. In their view, Jesus' message, like the church's kerygma, was intended to evoke the possibility of a new understanding of existence.

The historical Jesus and his teachings were of greater importance for liberal faith and ethics than for traditionalist Christianity. Liberal interpreters, therefore, have been considerably more troubled by recognition that Jesus preached and lived in the strange, eschatological thought-world evidenced in the synoptic gospels. Weiss considered it possible to continue to adhere to the liberal understanding without claiming Jesus as its founder.[5] Schweitzer attempted to identify certain elements in Jesus' ethic that were unrelated to his eschatological outlook and to find in these the basis for modern religion.[6] For the most part, liberal interpreters were less bold, and tended to accommodate their portrayals of Jesus' message and activity to their religious and moral concerns. In the process, typically, the eschatological features of Jesus' message and outlook were so neglected or attenuated as to lose any real importance, even for Jesus. Thus liberal-oriented interpreters could picture Jesus as teacher of timeless truths or proclaimer (if not founder) of the Kingdom of God in the hearts of men or social reform after all.

In general, both traditionalist and liberal interpreters have sought to establish the relevance of Jesus for contemporary faith or ethics by ignoring or deemphasizing the eschatological features of the synoptic material. Since the synoptic gospels are virtually the only sources we have for learning anything about the historical Jesus, both traditionalist and liberal theologies have tended to create (or accept from their predecessors) representations of Jesus that are more indebted to theological interest than to historical research. Neither theological school has been especially conscious of the distinction, hence theological interest tacitly has been allowed to blur or mingle with historical judgment. As a result, neither school has recognized the extent to which its theological position has been rooted elsewhere. Both schools, for the most part unconsciously, have proceeded as if it were necessary to dispense with the eschatological Jesus in order to preserve the Christianity each knows. Yet both schools wished to enjoy the sense of security inherent in the assumption that their respective theological positions corresponded more or less precisely to what Jesus had in mind. Understandably, neither school has been quick to recognize that the only Jesus portrayed in the synoptic gospels is the strange, eschatological Jesus. Lacking a supposedly authoritative universal church, Protestants have been tempted ever since the Reformation to look for final authority in an inerrant Bible or/an infallible Jesus.[7] Both traditionalist and liberal-oriented interpreters have persistently endeavored to devise concepts and categories that would relieve Jesus of the error of having declared that the Kingdom of God was about to appear.

The Historical Jesus and Christian Faith

Faith-Understanding Need Not Depend on Jesus' Beliefs

To acknowledge that Jesus was mistaken in this expectation does not necessarily threaten the foundations of Christianity. Traditional faith, following the Johannine doctrine of the incarnation, has long affirmed that the Word became flesh, or, in the formula of Chalcedon, that Jesus was fully man, as well as fully God. Some interpreters have suggested that Jesus' limitation to human knowledge is a reasonable corollary to belief in the incarnation. The Fourth Gospel also affirmed Jesus' omniscience, as well as other attributes of deity, and thereby created a theologically (if not also psychologically) problematic image.[8] If Jesus did enjoy divine or supernatural knowledge and foreknowledge, his conduct, hopes, and prayers would have been more matters of staging than genuine expressions of his cares and concerns.⁹ The synoptic gospels do not portray a divinely omniscient Jesus, but do indicate fairly clearly and consistently that he looked for the coming of the Kingdom of God and the Judgment in the near future.

Neither is it theologically necessary for Jesus to have anticipated every aspect of later Christian faith-understanding. It is possible, for instance, that he did not believe himself to be the messiah or Christ. Even if historically reliable tradition left no doubt that he had so believed, this would not prove that he was the messiah. He might have been mistaken. On the other hand, the church's belief that he was the messiah would not be proven wrong even if Jesus did not so regard himself. The earliest Christian theologian, Paul, shows little interest in what Jesus may have thought or said, but was fully convinced that Jesus was the Christ, who, by his death and resurrection, had brought about an entirely new basis for faith and life. Believers were already "in Christ," "new creatures," even though history had not yet come to its end. Subsequent Christian theologies also attempted to formulate the experienced reality of this new situation. The concluding verses of Matthew's gospel promised the abiding presence of the risen Jesus until the end of the present age. This promise has been cherished especially by later Christian pietism which commonly affirmed the nearness of Jesus in the life of faith. The Jesus of the Fourth Gospel gave assurance of the coming and continuing support of the "Counselor" or Holy Spirit. Later Christian mystics referred to the indwelling Christ, and Quakers spoke of the "inner light." Late nineteenth century Protestant liberals characterized the essence of Christianity as the communion of God with the human soul. None of these conceptualizations appears to be directly dependent upon evidence as to what Jesus himself may have believed or proclaimed. But they need not, on that account, be regarded as invalid. Instead, they express the experienced meaning of faith in the context of particular Christian communities. These and other formulations may still be quite adequate expressions of the faith-understanding of many Christians today.

The Historical Jesus Did Not Endorse All Later Doctrines and Theories

At the same time, if the evidence as to Jesus' eschatological convictions is accorded full recognition, a good many customary assumptions and claims must be excluded. Jesus was not thinking out our theologies before us, legitimating in advance any current version of either traditionalist or liberal faith. He appears to have expected the Kingdom of God to come within the lifetime of his contemporaries. If so, it is unlikely that he intended to establish a church or churches to continue for centuries afterwards either to dispense the sacraments or proclaim the divine word. Neither Catholic nor Protestant polities can be validated by reference to Jesus' intent, however justified they may be on other grounds. Millenialist churches correctly recognize that Jesus was looking for the end of history, but err when they assert that he predicted or revealed that this end would take place in *their* time. Jesus was not publishing timetables to inform some later generation when the end was near. Instead, he was summoning his own generation to repentance because he believed the end of the age already was near. Popular theories to the effect that modern events constitute "signs of the times" are at best naïve attempts to clothe dubious human speculations with biblical authority. They also involve the arrogant assumption that history hitherto has had little or no meaning, since the "Bible prophecies" refer only to our own time.[10] Jesus did not proclaim that the Kingdom of God would come at some point in the then distant future. Nor is it likely that he believed or declared that it was then present or immanent in some way. There is no reason to think that Jesus regarded himself as the incarnate word (Barth), or as divine power or logos conforming the world to himself (Bonhoeffer, Teilhard). He intended neither to summon his hearers to a new existential self-understanding ("new questers") nor to elicit religious experience (Perrin). He did not proclaim that the Kingdom of God was to be found in the hearts of men (Harnack), in the reconstitution of society by moral effort (social gospel), or the "secular city" (Cox). Nor does the evidence sustain theories to the effect that he was or had been a member of Qumran, or that he understood himself as a revolutionary, magician, or even superstar.

If the other features of Jesus' eschatological outlook which we have considered are taken seriously, it may be necessary to recognize that several other familiar doctrines or concepts cannot accurately be ascribed to him either. Jesus evidently believed that all of his contemporaries, except, perhaps, the Twelve, would have to pass before the throne of Judgment. He proclaimed neither the traditionalist message of forgiveness to all who believe,[11] nor the liberal gospel of the inherent value of the human soul. Moreover, those who find Jesus' "ethical teaching" a source of guidance for life in our time are not justified in claiming that he intended this teaching "for us." The historical Jesus evidently did not visualize the continuation of the world beyond the lifetime of his own generation; he was not issuing a program for life in the world for succeeding centuries; and he did not set forth a "system" of ethics, "sublime" or otherwise.[12] His "ethics" was for the interim remaining before the time of Judgment and the coming of the Kingdom of God, and consisted of various sayings and parables summoning his hearers to repentance and responsive love. Interpreters who venture to declare what Jesus meant to say "to us" thereby short-circuit the process of interpretation. Much of what Jesus said may indeed be meaningful to us, but so far as we can tell, he was not thinking of us or of our time.

The commonly held theories that Jesus performed exorcisms and other "miracles" in order to demonstrate that he was the Christ or to manifest the presence of the Kingdom of God are without foundation in the historical tradition. Only in the Fourth Gospel does Jesus perform miracles to prove anything, and there it is to prove that he is the divine Son of God. Nothing in earlier Jewish tradition suggests that the messiah was expected to perform miracles, or that doing them would demonstrate the doer's messiahship. The synoptic Jesus refused to perform signs, but understood exorcism in connection with his belief that the time when God's Kingdom would be established on earth was near. By defeating the demons, he was preparing for that time, and also freeing the afflicted from the tyranny of the demons' power. It is unlikely that Jesus regarded the exorcisms as a sign of the presence of the Kingdom, though he may well have seen them as indications that it soon would come. Satan had not yet been overcome on earth, but his kingdom was coming to its end. There would be no place for Satan or demons in the Kingdom of God.

Finally, it does not appear that either Protestant or Catholic sacramental theories can be justified by reference to Jesus' understanding. Though baptized by John, Jesus himself baptized no one.[13] The synoptic Jesus did not instruct his followers to repeat the last supper in after years as a memorial service.[14] Neither did he declare the eucharistic elements to be tangible means of grace for those who partook of them.[15] Instead, he evidently regarded the last supper as an anticipation of the eating and drinking that would obtain in the Kingdom of God, in which he and his followers, together with the righteous of all generations, past and present, would soon take part.

It does not follow, of course, that the faith of Christians in later times must be confined to those beliefs and affirmations that can plausibly be attributed to Jesus. Christians are free, as we have suggested, to take Paul, John or other canonical or post-canonical understandings as points of departure for their own faith. We have been suggesting, however, that modern theologians, interpreters, and other writers might well make more of an effort to distinguish between their own preferred interpretations and Jesus' message and understanding as represented in the synoptic gospels.

Interpreters who are Christians might reasonably be expected to wish to honor Jesus by trying to learn what they can about him; yet often they seem more concerned to preserve or promote their own theological point of view. Theologians, like other human beings, desire certainty and security. They no longer build empires and palaces, but may still find it tempting to make icons in the form of doctrinal formulations. Icons purportedly represent transcendent reality, but in fact are always made to human specifications. As Paul Tillich and H. Richard Niebuhr pointed out some years ago, believers are easily persuaded to identify their particular community's symbols or representations of transcendence with that which is experienced and affirmed as transcendent. Thus adherents of supposedly monotheistic religions such as Christianity and Islam continually lapse into the worship of idols and icons. John C. Meagher has suggested recently that the principal task of exegesis and historical research is the often thankless one of helping theology break off its love affair with such icons, by "letting the past . . . say what it would prefer to say, rather than what we might prefer to hear."[16] From historical research and exegesis we learn that Jesus did not direct attention to himself, much less to doctrines about himself. Instead, he called his hearers to repentance in view of the eschatological events soon to occur. Proponents of both traditionalist and modern faith have generally been under the impression that this Jesus could mean little to those living in the modern world.

The Relevance of the Historical, Eschatological Jesus for Faith and Ethics in the Modern World

We suggest that Jesus' eschatological beliefs and hopes need not be viewed with embarrassment merely because we find them untenable in our time when literally construed. As we have seen, the method frequently pursued has been to attribute to Jesus the special viewpoint found meaningful to the interpreter and to his or her theological school. Almost invariably, Jesus' eschatological orientation is ignored or substantially altered in the process. This procedure may evidence tacit recognition that there are aspects of Jesus' message and outlook significant for contemporary faith despite his eschatological beliefs. But it also fails to differentiate historical tradition from interpretation, and typically results in imputing to Jesus beliefs and concepts that actually originated in later times.[17] Moreover, such procedure is likely to occasion the neglect of those elements in Jesus' faith-understanding that do not conform to the interpreter's point of view. We suggest that Jesus' eschatological message and hopes may well give expression to certain affirmations of importance to Christian faith in our own time.

In proclaiming that the Kingdom of God had come near, Jesus was not speculating as to times and seasons. He was expressing his conviction that God both intended and was able to make things right on earth. Jesus said little about love as such and less about justice. But he expected that the poor and oppressed, together with the righteous—those who directed their concern toward the well-being of others—would inherit and enjoy the blessings of life in the coming Kingdom. This proclamation also entailed a realistic appraisal of the historical situation. The secular world, the world that loves neither God nor neighbor (or only those neighbors of the same tribe),[18] lives according to the principle of self-love, which comes to expression, typically, in injustice and oppression. This appraisal more nearly corroborates the human condition in the 1980s than do modern euphoric claims that the Kingdom of God is immanent in the hearts of men or human society, or that the secular society has "come of age." The power and inclination of nations, corporations, and even individuals[19] to pollute and destroy life on earth while questing for glory, profit, or pleasure is revealed anew each day. Jesus seems to have shared the prophetic-apocalyptic conviction that God would soon make his righteousness manifest, and establish the final and everlasting era of justice, love, and peace throughout the whole creation.[20] The decisive question for faith is not when and how, but whether God ultimately is and will be sovereign over history and the universe. Jesus' hope and confidence that, despite appearances, God soon would reorder historical existence in accordance with his will may again inspire those who hunger and thirst for righteousness and peace in our own era.

Augustine and later Christian mystics seem to have abandoned the expectation that God would establish his reign on earth, and looked instead for final peace and joy in the community of saints in the heavenly city, or individually, in experiencing the beatific vision. The Calvinist-Puritan tradition, however, radically reaffirmed the sovereignty of God over all history, and held that it was not enough to leave secular man to his own vices and devices. Consequently, the Puritans believed and undertook to demonstrate that some approximation of God's will could be achieved on earth.[21] Even in attempting to establish the holy commonwealth, however, the Puritans did not claim to be building the Kingdom of God on earth.[22] The experience of communion with God and the affirmation of God's sovereignty may be basic aspects of the Christian faith. But it is inaccurate and misleading to designate such experiences and affirmations as the Kingdom of God. To describe the heavenly communion of saints as the Kingdom of God is to miss the fundamental conviction of Jesus (and of the earlier prophetic faith) that God's rule would obtain not only in heaven, but on earth. To emphasize mysticism or other forms of individual religious experience, is to neglect the communal or social dimension that pervaded Jesus' hopes for the Kingdom. The Kingdom Jesus proclaimed was neither otherworldly nor individualistic.

On the other hand, to assert, as modern interpreters have been inclined to do, that Jesus thought the Kingdom of God already present on earth, raises serious questions for contemporary faith and ethics. To say that the Kingdom of God is now present on earth prompts the question of theodicy: if this world is ruled by God, such a god is either unjust and uncaring, or else impotent to establish his will. Clearly, wills other than God's are done on this present earth. Likewise, to affirm that God's Kingdom is already established on earth would seem to give unwarranted sanctification to the palpably self-serving and brutal ethics of mankind and nations, and the cruelty and suffering still common in the realm of other living things. Swords have not yet been beaten into ploughshares, nor has the lion yet lain down with the lamb. To affirm, amid the ambiguities of historical existence, that the Kingdom of God is present is also to call into question the integrity of the biblical hopes and promises for the future. Is there to be no better ordering of life in the world than what we see around us today? Some interpreters indulge in the speculation that the Kingdom was present in Jesus' time, but since has gone away. Others propose to distinguish between the Kingdom that was partly present and the completed Kingdom yet to come. But such artificial rationalizations in turn raise further troublesome problems,[23] and have no basis in the synoptic traditions. A theology that takes God's righteousness and power seriously may find it important to insist that the Kingdom of God has not been established on earth, and that under God's rule, when it is established, the conditions of life on earth will be very different from those at present. So, at all events, Jesus himself appears to have believed. Conversely, the once so-called death of God theology may be seen as a plausible expression of the disillusionment that was inevitable to occur among those persuaded by the premature claim that God's Kingdom or reign was already established on earth.

Jesus' expectation that the Judgment would take place at the beginning of the new age indicates his awareness of a great gulf between human self-love, on the one hand, and love for God and his righteousness on the other. This expectation and awareness are in sharp contrast to modern sentimental optimism as to human nature and destiny. Liberal theology never quite decided whether Jesus was supposed to have held that the Kingdom of God was present in the hearts of *all* men. Generally, this theology seemed to share Harnack's view that love for God and neighbor would more or less follow automatically once men understood Jesus' gospel of the Fatherhood of God and the infinite value of the human soul. Secular liberals, of course, were willing to dispense with God altogether, either on the happy, if illusory, assumption that love and righteousness would flourish all the more apart from religion, or, alternatively, pursuant to shrewd awareness that self-interest could become the true guide to life only in the absence of restraint by religious and moral standards. Whether naïvely or cynically, modern secular culture prefers to think that things go better when "anything goes."[24] Jesus' anticipation of coming Judgment, on the other hand, expresses the conviction that God is neither indifferent to the attitudes and actions of his people in their interactions with others, nor incapable of bringing his love and justice to bear accordingly.

In trying to comprehend the meaning of Jesus' death, it is understandable that early Christians, familiar with Jewish sacrificial traditions and practices, came to understand it as an offering for the sins of the world. Jesus may have characterized his prospective death as "a ransom for many."[25] But it is unlikely that he would have endorsed such routine weekly clerical pronouncements to modern congregations as, "In Jesus Christ, you are forgiven." The relation between "faith" and "works" has been a topic for troublesome controversy at many periods in the history of Christianity. Jesus himself reportedly held that it was not enough to profess that he was Lord (Matt. 7:21). Only those who had shown forth their love for God in lives of responsive service to others would withstand the Judgment and be called to enter into eternal life in the Kingdom of God. Jesus consistently assumed that his hearers had the ability to hear and do the will of God. Modern behaviorist and sociological determinists, on the other hand, see no place for God, human responsibility or morality, since in their view, human behavior is merely a set of responses to conditioning or environmental stimuli. Such theories, of course, serve to justify any type of behavior, including that of the determinists, and are just what those already dedicated to relentless pursuit of their own purposes and pleasures have been waiting to hear. Any kind of ethics or moral expectation, however, presupposes some degree of freedom and responsibility on the part of those who act or refrain from acting. Jesus did not go about bestowing unqualified blessings upon all who turned out to see him. Instead, he constantly summoned his hearers to decision. The Kingdom of God and Judgment were coming soon, perhaps at any time. His hearers were to "repent" or "turn" then and there from their pride and

self-love, to God and their neighbors, those in need of care or attention. Jesus did not intend his "ethics" for us; but his sayings and
parables may nevertheless have meaning to us. The basic triadic relationship, God-neighbor-self, is essentially the same now as in his
time. Jesus' understanding that God desires and requires compassion
or affirmative caring for others, is not contingent upon the expectation
that history is about to end.[26] The fact that Jesus' ethics was "interim
ethics" does not mean that his moral message is without meaning in
our time. All ethics is interim ethics. Each person lives within the quite
finite span of his or her own lifetime. The persons and other living
beings who can be helped or harmed by our care or lack of it today may
be gone tomorrow. We do not have an indefinite span of time in which
to take effective action. Nations, even democracies, do not live forever.
The lifespan of humanity, of other living species, indeed, of planet
earth, our whole solar system, or the entire cosmos as we know it, also
is finite. What we do or neglect to do in a particular moment often
cannot be undone or done over. The sense of urgency in Jesus' sayings
and parables may prompt a greater sense of the uniqueness and importance of our own moral responsiveness to those about us while we
have opportunity to act.

At the same time, Jesus' certainty that history and that which lies
beyond history ultimately rest in the hands of God can liberate those
who share this confidence from the anxiety and sorrow that otherwise
readily engulf people who are aware of the tragedies of unfulfilled
lives, injustice, misery, and death that are inevitably part of existence
in history. The lives about us and the policy decisions and personal
actions affecting them are of great importance. But even when we have
done what we can, it is finally God who can and will bring about his
own resolution to the seemingly hopeless predicaments of history, in
his own way and time. By this faith we live and hope. In the
meantime, the interim, the foremost ethical question remains the same
now as in the time of Jesus: do we care about others, or only about
ourselves? Just as Jesus pointed his hearers from pretention and preoccupation with self to concern for others, his words and his deeds can
also point us to those about us in the world in which we live.

Jesus' exorcisms of demons mean little to us today, and so this aspect of his ministry usually is ignored or passed over quickly. Yet in
exorcising demons, he was evidently prompted by the same consideration that guided all of his other activities: care for the well-being of
others. He not only taught, but also lived a life of responsive love. His
primary reason for exorcising demons—and for commissioning the
Twelve to do so as well—was to prepare the way for the coming of

God's Kingdom. This itself was a great labor of love. Satan and the demons were understood to be among the leading sources of misery in his day. Overcoming their power, ridding the earth of their oppression, was an important part of Jesus' work and that of his followers. In some such sense, Christians today may also find themselves called to liberate life from all sources of pain, terror, and oppression, and to make the earth a place more fit for the establishment·of God's just and loving sovereignty. Faith now, as in Jesus' time, calls for recognition of the presence of evil in the world, and continued efforts to reduce its power to harm and destroy. Were it not for some confidence in the final triumph of God's power and purposes, we might well despair in the face of the manifold and persistent forces of evil in our time such as "unconquered" disease, nuclear peril, world hunger, and the pride and cruelty of ethnic groups and nations.

Jesus' expectation that the righteous would eat and drink together in the Kingdom of God indicates that he affirmed the goodness of physical life in the material world, albeit, a transformed material world. Here he concurred with earlier prophetic and apocalyptic hopes. If recent liberal theologians have been inclined to regard the secular world too uncritically, traditionalist Christians have chronically been tempted to view the material world with suspicion and to visualize the "real" world as entirely spiritual in character. Thus traditionalist Christians, like Hindus and Buddhists, have often shown an indifference to life in this world. There was no metaphysical dualism in Jesus' own outlook. In his view, the world was good. The creation was the gift of God for all living things, for which he cared and would care in the age to come. If Jesus' own beliefs are in any way normative for Christian faith, they may have some significance for the attitude of modern Christians toward "the world." If the fulfillment of life is believed to be in the world, a transformed world, Christian faith and life in the meantime might well include the appreciation, enjoyment and affirmation of the creation, through sharing its blessings with others now, and preserving and enhancing these blessings for the generations that come after us. Those who hold this faith should have no hesitation in joining with others in our time who are deeply concerned to protect "the environment." There in no basis in Jesus' understanding for disparaging the world in favor of a spiritual realm to be entered by some *via negativa*. Jesus himself was no ascetic (Matt. 11:19). The primitive Christian belief that he was raised from the dead shows that the early church likewise looked for new life in the transformation, not the abandonment, of physical existence. Jesus' "ethics" summoned his hearers to concern themselves not only with the spiritual, but also with the physical well-being of those they encountered in this life.[27]

Non- or anti-Christian interpreters, necessarily do not expect or desire to find anything significant in Jesus or his sayings. Some of them may write with conscious animus, hoping to prove Jesus a madman or fraud. Those of secular persuasion who lack such animus seem to have considerable difficulty understanding that Jesus acted on the basis of religious beliefs and hopes that were important to him. Jesus' eschatological beliefs, which are both religious in substance and alien to modern thought, seem especially incomprehensible. Since such interpreters do not, themselves, find these beliefs meaningful or compelling, they may honestly fail to understand how anyone else, including Jesus, could have found them so.[28] Consequently, such interpreters contrive to explain Jesus in some way that does make sense to them, e.g., as a would-be revolutionary, drug cultist, or magician.

What can Christians make of the enigmatic, eschatological Jesus? According to Matthew, Jesus' own disciples were continually asking themselves who he was, and yet were strongly influenced by his authority. Later Christians have been guided both by the authority of his words, and by a sense of his continuing lordship and presence. Paul referred both to certain traditions which he had "from the Lord" (1 Cor. 7:10–11, 11:23) and to his own encounter with the risen Lord. The Fourth Gospel promised that, when Jesus left the Counselor would come, and later Christianity came to affirm the presence of the Holy Spirit which, in the West, was said to "proceed" from both the Father and the Son (so formulated in the "Nicene" Creed). In Luke-Acts, and implicitly in the Fourth Gospel, the risen Jesus is said to have ascended to heaven. Matthew, on the other hand, contains no ascension tradition, and reports that the risen Jesus promised to be with his followers "to the close of the age" (Matt. 28:20). Pietistic Christianity has maintained that Jesus was directly accessible to each person as friend and savior. The mystery of Jesus remains for us all. He insisted on distinguishing between God and himself, and refused even to be called "good," for only God was good (Mark 10:18). Yet without having so intended, his insights into God's will that come to expression in his various sayings and parables about human behavior in a very different society nearly two thousand years ago, continue to address us with a directness that moves us to try to put them into effect in our own lives.

We can know only in part who Jesus was. Yet we can know enough of his intention and of the direction of his confidence, loyalty and love to realize that we too do well to make the same kind of choice he presented to his hearers: to choose between serving God and all other masters, and to turn to our neighbors with responsive love in the various and often complex contexts of our own time. Jesus' faith was directed toward the God who transcends all limitations of time and history, yet values everything and everyone: the lilies of the field, the birds of the air, adults and children, women and men, Jews, Samaritans and gentiles, rich and poor. This God is both righteous and merciful, and therefore desires and requires righteousness and compassion from his people in their interactions with one another. Jesus expected that God's justice and love would soon be revealed in the Judgment and the establishment of his rule on earth in the peaceable Kingdom. This expectation was not fulfilled. But if the God in whom we trust is the same as the One proclaimed by Jesus, we too may experience the eager longing and confidence that he will, in his own way and time, make things right. In the meantime, we live in the presence of our neighbors and other companions in being for whom, we believe, he cares, and for whom, in the miracle of grace that frees us from concern only for ourselves, we find that we can come to care as well. We do not thereby establish the Kingdom of God on earth. But we may be so bold as to trust that he can use even our small acts of obedience, justice, and love for his own purposes, which surely encompass, but far surpass our best human hopes and understanding.

Abbreviations

Bauer, Lexicon	W.F. Arndt and F.W. Gingrich, trs. and eds., *A Greek-English Lexicon of the New Testament* (Univ. of Chicago Press, 1957)
E.T.	Title of English translation
HJKG	R.H. Hiers, *The Historical Jesus and the Kingdom of God* (Univ. of Florida Press, 1973)
HThR	*Harvard Theological Review*
IB	*Interpreters' Bible*
IDB	*Interpreters' Dictionary of the Bible*
JAAR	*Journal of the American Academy of Religion*
JBL	*Journal of Biblical Literature*
JBR	*Journal of the Bible and Religion*
JR	*Journal of Religion*
JThSt	*Journal of Theological Studies*
KGST	R.H. Hiers, *The Kingdom of God in the Synoptic Tradition* (Univ. of Florida Press, 1970)
LCC	Library of Christian Classics
N.E.B.	New English Bible
N.T.	The New Testament
NTA	E. Hennecke and W. Schneemelcher, eds., *New Testament Apocrypha* (Westminster, 1963, 1965)
NTS	*New Testament Studies*
NovT	*Novum Testamentum*
O.T.	The Old Testament
RB	*Revue Biblique*
RSV	Revised Standard Version
SBT	Studies in Studies in Biblical Theology
SJT	*Scottish Journal of Theology*

Str.-B H.L. Strack and P. Billerbeck, *Kommentar zum neuen Testament aus Talmud und Midrasch* (Munich: Beck, 1922–28)

TD G. Kittel, G. W. Bromiley, eds., *Theological Dictionary of the New Testament* (Eerdmans, 1964—)

USQR *Union Seminary Quarterly Review*

ZNW *Zeitschrift für die neutestamentliche Wissenschaft*

Notes

Preface

1. E.g., *Godspell, The Gospel According to St. Matthew, Jesus Christ Superstar, Jesus of Nazareth, Jesus, In Search of Historic Jesus.*

2. See Roland H. Bainton, *Behold the Christ* (Harper & Row, 1976).

3. Christianity, itself, of course, originated in the Near East, and has had a significant place in non-Western cultures as well.

4. Notably, in the work of Erasmus and Reimarus, respectively. Publication of the latter's "fragment" *On the Intentions of Jesus and His Disciples* by G.E. Lessing in 1778 may be seen as marking the beginning of the "quest for the historical Jesus," a quest that is now over 200 years old.

5. A closely related reaction, especially in the late 1960s, was the rise of interest in cults, particularly those that supposedly mediate Eastern truths through some authoritarian teacher other than parents or Western "Establishment" figures or institutions. See Harvey G. Cox, *Turning East: The Promise and Peril of the New Orientalism* (New York: Simon & Schuster, 1977).

6. Albert Schweitzer, *Von Reimarus zu Wrede: Eine Geschichte der Leben-Jesu-Forschung* (Tübingen: Mohr, 1906), later translated as *The Quest of the Historical Jesus.*

7. By "eschatological" we refer to the several decisive events expected to occur at the end of the present age according to the first three gospels. These events include the coming of the Kingdom of God, the appearance of the Son of man, the coming time of Judgment and other matters that will be considered.

8. *The Kingdom of God and the Synoptic Tradition* (1970), referred to in this study as *KGST*. See esp. chaps. 2–7, 9, 11.

9. For analysis of these passages, see *KGST*, pp. 72–76, 82–92. See also *The Historical Jesus and the Kingdom of God* (1973), referred to in this study as *HJKG*, esp. pp. 12–36.

10. See the introductory essay by D.L. Holland and myself in Johannes Weiss, *Jesus' Proclamation of the Kingdom of God* (Fortress, 1971), esp. pp. 24–49. The term "apocalyptic" is used here to refer to the sev-

eral expected eschatological events described above in note 7. In addition, "apocalyptic" connotes the expectation of entirely supernatural deliverance, perhaps in the near future. The apocalyptic perspective views the present time (in and for which the apocalyptic message was written or spoken) as calling for utmost faithfulness and righteousness, since only those who are faithful and righteous will enjoy the benefits of the coming supernatural deliverance.

11. See Klaus Koch's comment: "What is written about apocalyptic today usually culminates in the flinging down of swift wholesale judgments which close inspection shows go back to the secondary literature of the era before the First World War. . . . It is hard to detect any study of the primary texts, at least in continental theology" (*The Rediscovery of Apocalyptic*, SBT 2d ser., no. 22 [London: SCM, 1972], p. 123).

12. Weiss is regarded more favorably by many interpreters; yet his position is not very different from Schweitzer's. Both maintained that Jesus thought, preached, and acted in expectation that the Kingdom of God and related eschatological events would occur within the lifetime of the generation of his contemporaries.

13. Dodd proposed that Jesus understood that the Kingdom was, for all intents and purposes, already present. Consequently, it was not necessary to think that Jesus had been mistaken, since, according to Dodd, he had declared the Kingdom present, and it *was* present.

14. See R.H. Hiers, *Jesus and Ethics* (Westminster, 1968), esp. Chaps. III–V. It is curious that Bultmann's interest in the significance of Jesus for ethics has largely been ignored.

15. See Chapter VII, below.

16. The first three gospels, Matthew, Mark, and Luke, are commonly designated as the synoptic gospels. When looked at together, they present a similar account of Jesus' message and activity. It is widely agreed that Matthew and Luke each used Mark's gospel as the main source for their narratives, that Matthew and Luke each added (or composed) additional traditions of their own, and drew some 200 verses consisting of sayings from an otherwise unknown source commonly called "Q".

17. The Gospel According to John is more of a faith statement by a particular Christian or congregation, around 100 A.D. Even the synoptic gospels are understood to reflect the interests of the communities where they were composed, as well as the particular concerns or viewpoints of their editors or authors.

Chapter I

1. We agree with Van A. Harvey's observation that " 'the historical Jesus' is actually an ambiguous term because it may refer both to the actual Jesus and to the Jesus that is now recoverable by historical

means" (*The Historian and the Believer* [Macmillan, 1966], p. 266). Necessarily, we must work primarily with the latter meaning.

2. H.H. Wendt, *The Teaching of Jesus* (1890; Scribner's, n.d.); Martin Kähler, *The So-Called Historical Jesus and the Historic Biblical Christ* (1892, 1896, Fortress, 1964). Kähler's position continued to surface in later conservative circles. See Joseph C. Weber, "Karl Barth and the Historical Jesus," *JBR* 32 (1964): 350–54.

3. Ernst Issel, *Die Lehre vom Reiche Gottes im neuen Testament* (Leiden: Brill, 1891).

4. Otto Schmoller, *Die Lehre vom Reiche Gottes in den Schriften des neuen Testaments* (Leiden: Brill, 1891).

5. Johannes Weiss, *Jesus' Proclamation of the Kingdom of God* (1892; Fortress, 1971).

6. Rudolf Bultmann, *Jesus Christ and Mythology* (Scribner's, 1958), p. 11.

7. Weiss, *Jesus' Proclamation*, pp. 92–96.

8. *Ibid.*, p. 80.

9. Its impact in Britain and America was not felt immediately. Several writers continued to assume the validity of the liberal viewpoint. See, e.g., B. Harvie Branscomb, *The Teachings of Jesus* (Abingdon, 1931); and Harvey Cox, *The Secular City* (Macmillan, 1966), pp. 96–98.

10. Adolf von Harnack, *What Is Christianity?* (Harper, 1957), p. 52ff.

11. E.g., Norman Perrin, *Rediscovering the Teaching of Jesus* (Harper & Row, 1967), p. 160f.; *Jesus and the Language of the Kingdom* (Fortress, 1976), pp. 43–56. See Leander E. Keck, *A Future for the Historical Jesus* (Abingdon, 1971), pp. 60–65, 196f., n. 18. Keck describes Wilhelm Herrmann's attempt to synthesize liberal theology with the eschatological orientation of Jesus, and recent similar efforts by Ernst Fuchs and Gerhard Ebeling.

12. Norman Perrin has provided two excellent descriptions of these efforts: *The Kingdom of God in the Teaching of Jesus* (Westminster, 1963); and *Jesus and Language*. No such gap was noticed in those "conservative" Christian circles where historical research was anathema and the rule prevailed that "Scripture must be explained by Scripture." Thus, e.g., Gerhard Maier, *The End of the Historical Method* (Concordia, 1977). Likewise, with few exceptions, historical research was *verboten* and inoperative in Roman Catholic scholarship, particularly from the time of Pius X until John XXIII and the Second Vatican Council. Alfred Loisy was the most notable exception.

13. *The Mystery of the Kingdom of God* (Macmillan, 1914, 1950).

14. A. and C. Black, 1910; Macmillan, 1950. The expanded revision, *Geschichte der Leben-Jesu-Forschung* (Mohr, 1913, 1951), remains untranslated. Schweitzer's most recent version of his understanding of

the historical Jesus is *The Kingdom of God and Primitive Christianity* (Seabury, 1968), esp. pp. 68–130.

15. Schweitzer's term was *konsequente Eschatologie*. E.g., Hans Küng, *The Church* (Sheed and Ward, 1967), p. 55; John Wick Bowman, *Which Jesus?* (Westminster, 1970), p. 35; Walter Schmithals, *The Apocalyptic Movement* (Abingdon, 1975), p. 62f.; Gustaf Aulen, *Jesus in Contemporary Research* (Fortress, 1976), p. 104.

16. E.g., Ernst Käsemann, *New Testament Questions of Today* (Fortress, 1969), p. 42; James M. Robinson, "Introduction" to the Macmillan edition of Schweitzer's *Quest* (1969), p. xiii; Howard Clark Kee, *Jesus in History* (Harcourt, Brace & World, 2nd. ed., 1977), p. 27.

17. E.g., Edward Schweizer, *Jesus* (John Knox, 1971), p. 25. Schweizer says that Schweitzer's Jesus saw the world as "blackened with the smoke of a coming apocalyptic conflagration." To support this contention, Schweizer cites Bornkamm, but not Schweitzer! The interpretive strategy instanced here might be termed exaggeration *ad absurdum*. Other distortions of Schweitzer's "interim ethics" category are considered in Chap. III.

18. William Wrede, *Das Messiasgeheimnis in den Evangelien* (1901), E.T., *The Messianic Secret* (J. Clarke, 1971).

19. E.g., Mark 10:35–37; 9:1; 13:30; 14:62; Matt. 10:23; 11:10–14.

20. J.M. Robinson claimed that Schweitzer and the "old" questers proceeded with a "positivistic" historiography and otherwise attempted to derogate Schweitzer's work, intending, perhaps, to insinuate the relative legitimacy of the "new" quest. See James M. Robinson, *A New Quest of the Historical Jesus*, SBT no. 25 (SCM, 1959), pp. 32–34, 38–40, and Robinson's "Introduction" to *The Quest* (1969), p. xxiv.

21. A remarkably accurate early account of Schweitzer's position is to be found in a review by Geerhardus Vos, in *The Princeton Theological Review* 9 (1911): 132–141. Vos rejects some features as "phantastic," but urged that Schweitzer's findings could be used to rescue Jesus from the liberals and to support evangelical theology (p. 140).

22. For instance, Millar Burrows, Hans Conzelmann, Martin Dibelius, Morton S. Enslin, Robert M. Grant, Erich Grässer, and Krister Stendahl.

23. R. Bultmann, *Jesus Christ and Mythology* (Scribner's, 1958), p. 13. See, e.g., Robert M. Grant, "The Coming of the Kingdom," *JBL* 67 (1948): 297–303; Millar Burrows, "Thy Kingdom Come," *JBL* 74 (1955): 1–8.

24. So Dodd maintains in his last and popularly written book on the subject, *The Founder of Christianity* (Macmillan, 1970), p. 55ff. But he also suggests that it had for Jesus a future and transcendent dimension: "The Kingdom of God, while it is present experience, remains also a hope, but a hope directed to a consummation beyond history" (p. 115). For a brief but trenchant criticism of Dodd's position, see

A.W. Argyle, "Does 'Realized Eschatology' Make Sense?" *Hibbert Journal* 60 (1953): 385–87. Many others also have argued for the equation, person and work of Jesus = Kingdom of God; e.g., Bertil E. Gärtner, "The Person of Jesus and the Kingdom of God," *Theology Today* 27 (1970): 32–43. See also Jack D. Kingsbury, *Matthew, Structure, Christology, Kingdom* (Fortress, 1975), p. 156f.

25. See, e.g., Karl Barth, *The Humanity of God* (John Knox, 1960), p. 47: "Jesus Christ . . . is in his Person . . . the Kingdom of Heaven which is at hand." See also Weber, "Barth and Jesus," p. 352. In his introduction to the script of the television film *Jesus of Nazareth*, William Barclay says that the film and book version tell "the story of Jesus . . . simply and straightforwardly." In fact, the script alternates at will between synoptic and Johannine sources, interpolates numerous fictitious personae, episodes, and characterizations, and avoids any mention of Jesus' futuristic eschatological hopes and expectations (William Barclay, *Jesus of Nazareth* [Ballantine Books, 1977]). See also Lee Roddy and Charles E. Sellier, Jr., *In Search of Historic Jesus* (Bantam, 1979).

26. Bultmann's sketch of the life and message of Jesus [*Jesus and the Word* (Scribner's, 1934, 1958)] was not so much an historical study as a statement of the importance of Jesus' summons to radical obedience for our own time.

27. See R. Bultmann, "The Primitive Christian Kerygma and the Historical Jesus," in Carl E. Braaten and Roy A. Harrisville, eds., *The Historical Jesus and the Kerygmatic Christ* (Abingdon, 1964), pp. 15–42.

28. This curious and misplaced anxiety has been a central feature in several discussions of the "new quest." See Van A. Harvey and Schubert M. Ogden's critique, "How New Is the 'New Quest of the Historical Jesus'?" in Braaten and Harrisville, *Historical Jesus;* V. Harvey, *Historian and Believer*, p. 198f.; and L. Keck, *A Future*, p. 126.

29. M. Kähler, *So-Called Historical Jesus*, p. 46ff.

30. Earlier, in the nineteenth century, David Strauss and Bruno Bauer had expressed radical skepticism as to the historical value of all four gospels. In part, they seem to have been prompted by their disillusionment with Christianity.

31. On these topics, see, e.g., R. Bultmann and Karl Kundsin, *Form Criticism* (Harper, 1962); Edgar V. McKnight, *What Is Form Criticism?* (Fortress, 1969); Norman Perrin, *What Is Redaction Criticism?* (Fortress, 1969).

32. V. Harvey, *Historian and Believer*, p. 275.

33. Thus, e.g., Hans Conzelmann, *Jesus* (Fortress, 1973), p. 16. Yet on the following page, Conzelmann acknowledges that "Jesus moved almost exclusively within the framework of Palestinian Judaism"! Klaus Koch comments critically concerning this "method of reduction" which "led to a general exclusion from the very outset, of everything in the gospels which sounded apocalyptic as being alien to Jesus." *The*

Rediscovery of Apocalyptic, SBT (2nd Ser.), no. 22 (London: SCM, 1972, p. 68f.) See also Leander E. Keck, "Introduction," to D. F. Strauss, *The Christ of Faith and the Jesus of History* (Fortress, 1977), p. *cvf.*

34. For discussion of such criteria, see *HJKG,* pp. 109–111. See also Aulen, *Jesus,* p. 31f., regarding the tendency of some recent critics to find more historically accurate material in the gospels.

35. *HJKG,* pp. 1–117.

36. E.g., Aulen, *Jesus,* p. 148. The implicit suggestion seems to be that the fewer apocalyptic sayings assigned to him, the less apocalyptic Jesus was, and the less problematic he becomes for modern faith.

37. J.M. Robinson, *New Quest,* pp. 92–100, 104ff.

38. E.g., J.M. Robinson, *New Quest,* pp. 118f., 122f.; Ernst Käsemann, *Essays on New Testament Themes,* SBT no. 41 (SCM, 1964), p. 45; Günther Bornkamm, *Jesus of Nazareth* (Hodder & Stoughton, 1960), p. 66f.

39. E. Käsemann, *New Testament Questions,* p. 51. See Koch's discussion of Käsemann's position in *Rediscovery,* pp. 75–78. Eta Linnemann, *Jesus of the Parables* (Harper & Row, 1967) is an extreme example of the "new questers" desire to import realized eschatology into the Jesus traditions in order to bring him into line with the church's *kerygma.* She proposes that Jesus' parables gave (and give) the hearer "the possibility of a new self-understanding." Nothing significant remained to happen in the future.

40. Käsemann, *New Testament Questions,* p. 122: ". . . The sole content of the call is that we should accept and hold fast the promise of the God who is at hand."

41. V. Harvey, *Historian and Believer,* pp. 164–203. See also V. Harvey and S.M. Ogden, "How New is the 'New Quest'?" pp. 197–242.

42. See also, e.g., G. Bornkamm, *Jesus,* p. 233f. Like Bultmann, the "post-Bultmannian" new questers are inclined to de-emphasize apocalyptic and futuristic expectations in the world-view and *"kerygma"* of the early church.

43. Koch, *Rediscovery,* p. 68f.

44. *Ibid.,* p. 125.

45. E.g., Ferdinand Hahn, *et al., What Can We Know About Jesus?* (Fortress, 1969); H. Zahrnt, *Historical Jesus;* Joachim Jeremias, *The Problem of the Historical Jesus* (Fortress, 1964); Jacob Jervell, *The Continuing Search for the Historical Jesus* (Augsburg, 1965); James F. Peter, *Finding the Historical Jesus* (Harper & Row, 1966); Reinhard Slenczka, *Geschichtlichkeit und Personsein Jesus Christi* (Vandenhoeck & Ruprecht, 1967); and Otto Betz, *What Do We Know About Jesus?* (Westminster, 1968). See also Etienne Trocmé, *Jesus as Seen by His Contemporaries* (Westminster, 1973).

46. *In Search of the Historical Jesus* (Scribner's, 1969). See also F. Thomas Trotter, ed., *Jesus and the Historian* (Westminster, 1968).

47. *Jesus in His Time* (Fortress, 1971).

48. *Jesus in History*. See also Wayne G. Rollins, *The Gospel Portraits of Christ* (Westminster, 1963). Another redaction history study of exceptional inclusiveness and quality is John Reumann, *Jesus in the Church's Gospels* (Fortress, 1968).

49. By Gösta Lundström (John Knox) and Norman Perrin (Westminster). Lundström's book had been published earlier in Swedish. Schweitzer's *Mystery* and Wrede's *Messianic Secret* likewise were published on the same day, in 1901.

50. Rev. ed., *The Presence of the Future* (1974).

51. Reumann, *Jesus*, pp. 142–198. See also Joachim Jeremias, *New Testament Theology: The Proclamation of Jesus* (Scribner's 1971).

52. Aulen, *Jesus*, pp. 99–120. Even Conzelmann, who insists that for Jesus the Kingdom was entirely future, argues that the question when the Kingdom comes is, finally, "invalid" (*Jesus*, p. 76). Similarly, N. Perrin questions "whether it is legitimate to think of Jesus' use of the Kingdom of God in terms of 'present' and 'future' at all" (*Jesus and Language*, pp. 40, 197). Likewise, Aulen argues that "for Jesus there was no basic difference between the present and the future" (*Jesus*, pp. 104, 149). These interpreters wish to say that Jesus' futuristic expectations need not be a problem to modern faith. Somehow they manage to ignore the contradiction between their recognition of the decisive importance for Jesus of the future, and their assertion that time was of no real consequence to him. Logic is less important, it seems than presenting readers with a Jesus already adapted to modern faith-understanding.

53. See, e.g., Aulen, *Jesus*, pp. 87, 91, 102, 151. On this tendency, see Koch, *Rediscovery*, p. 69ff. Lack of interest in recognizing, let alone explaining such inconsistencies, seems to derive from dogmatic considerations. As historian, the interpreter is willing to recognize the futuristic character of Jesus' reported orientation; as theologian, he is more concerned with its presentist character. Unconsciously, perhaps, the conflict is resolved by subordinating logical consistency to theological affirmation.

54. See, e.g., Küng, *The Church*, p. 69: "Since the reign of God has been preached, has begun and is already effective—through and in Jesus—in the present, the hope for a consummated and revealed reign of God is not an empty and unfounded hope directed to the future alone." Küng is evidently referring to "the hope" of modern Christians.

55. E.g., Jervell, *Continuing Search*, p. 57. The same equation is made, among others, by Harnack, Bultmann, Barth, Fuchs, Käsemann, Dodd, Linnemann, Perrin, Kingsbury, and August Strobel. Thus, it is proposed, Jesus proclaimed that *God* was near—an understanding presumably more meaningful to modern believers. Evidently readers need

no longer consider Jesus' message of the coming Kingdom. Significantly, such interpreters do not feel called upon to justify their equating "Kingdom of God" with "God."

56. This kind of assertion fails to reckon with the fact that in the synoptic tradition and the N.T. generally, it is understood that Satan, the demons, and the Romans roam and rule the earth in the present age, and that the establishment (or re-establishment) of God's rule on earth regularly is sought and prayed for as a future occurrence. Interpreters who wish to claim that Jesus held the Kingdom of God to be present rely, trustingly, on Strack-Billerbeck's *Kommentar* and Kittel's *Theologisches Wörterbuch*. These authorities pay little regard to apocalyptic inter-testamental sources, but rather, promote the view that Jesus and early Christianity are to be understood in the context of the Old Testament and, particularly, Rabbinic Judaism. The rabbis had virtually abandoned the apocalyptic viewpoint by the time the Talmud was written down. Consequently, the Talmud provides Christian interpreters a more congenial "background" for N.T. research than that afforded by the more nearly contemporary Jewish apocalyptic writings.

57. Thus Fuchs, Ebeling, Käsemann, and Zahrnt. Keck's trenchant comment on Ebeling could have wider application: "The farther one reads, the more one suspects that Jesus is portrayed as the first post-Bultmannian Lutheran" (*A Future*, p. 66).

58. E.g., Otto Betz, Hans Conzelmann, Norman Perrin, Harald Riesenfeld. Despite the popularity of the assumption, neither the Messiah nor the Kingdom of God is characterized by exorcisms or works of healing in any Jewish sources. Cf. Morton Smith, "Prolegomena to a discussion of aretologies, divine men, the Gospels and Jesus," *JBL* 90 (1971), p. 96: "Because of his miracles [Jesus] was thought to be the Messiah."

59. With somewhat enthusiastic exaggeration, Aulen declares: "Nothing in contemporary research is more evident than that Jesus appeared and acted as 'the enigmatic representative of the Kingdom of God,' " (*Jesus*, p. 156). Cf. Dodd, *The Founder*, p. 115: "Nothing [in the teaching of Jesus] is more clearly original or characteristic than his declaration that the Kingdom of God is here."

60. N. Perrin, *Rediscovering*, p. 74. See also N. Perrin, *The New Testament, An Introduction* (Harcourt Brace Jovanovich, 1974), p. 300f.; *Jesus and Language*, pp. 43ff., 194ff., 198f. Edward Schillebeeckx suggests that for Jesus the Kingdom was manifested in his followers' conversion and conduct (*Jesus, An Experiment in Christology* [Seabury: 1979] p. 154).

61. E. Schweizer, *Jesus*, pp. 24, 29.

62. See George Wesley Buchanan, *The Consequences of the Covenant* (Leiden: Brill, 1970), p. 47f.: "These scholars have strained to propose theories that acknowledged, on the one hand, that Jesus expected

the Kingdom to come momentarily, and on the other hand, did not require them to admit that Jesus was mistaken at this point."

63. See, for example, Dodd, *Founder*, p. 113ff., and Perrin, "Eschatology and Hermeneutics," *JBL* 93 (1974): 3–14. Perrin's *Jesus and Language* is devoted to an explication of this line of interpretation. He proposed to distinguish two types of symbols: "steno-symbols" (which bear a one-to-one relation to a single referent), and "tensive symbols," which have multiple and indeterminate referents. According to Perrin, Jesus deliberately used "Kingdom of God" in the latter sense, "to evoke the myth of God acting as King" (pp. 42f., 196). Perrin's *theological* interest in promoting this distinction is apparent when he explains, "If Kingdom of God is a tensive symbol in the proclamation of Jesus *then the mythology of Jesus has not been discredited by the subsequent course of history*" (p. 78, emphasis added). See also A. Wilder's *Early Christian Rhetoric* (Harvard, 1971), esp. pp. 80–87.

64. E.g., J.D. Kingsbury, *Matthew*, p. 152. We suggest that Matt. 12:28 = Luke 11:20 can be read to support such interpretations only by very selective exegesis. See *KGST:* 30–35.

65. Küng, *The Church*, pp. 59, 75.

66. See Chap. IV.

67. Such interpreters typically refer to Luke 17:20–21 for authority. We have contended elsewhere that this passage is not concerned with speculations or calculations as to when the parousia *will* occur. The question, rather, is how people will know when it has come (*KGST*, pp. 22–29).

68. E.g., Küng, *The Church*, pp. 50, 61.

69. *Jesus and the Origins of Christianity* (Harper & Row, 1932, 1960), vol. II, pp. 569–72. For a more adequate understanding of the character and development of apocalyptic, see Koch, *Rediscovery*, and Paul D. Hanson, *The Dawn of Apocalyptic* (Fortress, 1975). See also Lars Hartman, "The Function of Some So-Called Apocalyptic Timetables." *NTS* 22 (1975): 1–14; and Lou H. Silberman, "Apocalyptic Revisited: Reflections on the Thought of Albert Schweitzer," *JAAR* 44 (1976): 489–501.

70. For further such instances and analysis, see Koch, *Rediscovery*, pp. 98–101.

71. Jackson Lee Ice, *Schweitzer: Prophet of Radical Theology* (Westminster, 1971), p. 126ff.

72. The "radical theologians" tried to do both. See, e.g., T.J.J. Altizer, *The Gospel of Christian Atheism* (Westminster, 1966), pp. 25, 71, 105ff.

73. See W. Pannenberg, "Appearance as the Arrival of the Future," *JAAR* 35 (1967): 111–113; Johannes Metz, "Creative Hope," in Martin E. Marty and Dean G. Peerman, eds., *New Theology no. 5* (Macmillan, 1968), p. 138.

74. Pannenberg recognizes that Jesus really did believe and an-

nounce that the Kingdom of God would come in his own generation: *Jesus—God and Man* (Westminster, 1968), p. 226. This imminent expectation, he writes, "is no longer an option for us in its original sense" (p. 242). For an excellent critical review of the treatment of eschatology in 20th century theology, see C.E. Braaten, *History and Hermeneutics* (Westminster, 1966), pp. 160–179. See also Koch, *Rediscovery*, pp. 101–111, especially with respect to Pannenberg's program.

75. See especially Braaten, *Eschatology and Ethics.*

76. Critics for decades have generally agreed that—whatever else they might be—the gospels are not biographies. This view has been challenged recently by Charles H. Talbert, *What Is a Gospel?* (Fortress, 1977). Talbert refutes F. Overbeck's claim that the early church's eschatological perspective precluded use of Graeco-Roman literary forms. Talbert does not, of course, propose that the evangelists were interested in reporting brute facts.

77. Matthew's gospel represents a church which, though adjusting to the fact that history was continuing, still expected the parousia events within the lifetime of some of its members. See *KGST:* 72–76, 78–82. It is also clear that the Marcan community was oriented toward the future eschatological era: e.g., Paul J. Achtemeier, *Mark* (Fortress, 1975), pp. 54f., 107f.; Howard Clark Kee, *Community of the New Age* (Westminster, 1977), pp. 107, 109f. It is now established that Luke likewise expected the parousia to occur in the near future. See R.H. Hiers, "The Problem of the Delay of the Parousia in Luke–Acts," *NTS* 20 (1974): 145–155; and A.J. Mattill, Jr., *Luke and the Last Things* (Western North Carolina Press, 1979).

78. Reinhold Niebuhr, *The Irony of American History* (Scribner's, 1952), p. 151f.

79. See Peter L. Berger and Thomas Luckmann, *The Social Construction of Reality* (Anchor, 1967). A Christian *theologian* may properly understand the purpose of N.T. studies to consist of *proclamation* rather than historical research or reconstruction: Paul J. Achtemeier, "On the Historical Critical Method in New Testament Studies," *Perspective* 11 (1970): 301ff. Achtemeier observes that the principal N.T. methodologies—form, historical and redaction criticism—were developed "to this end" (*ibid.,*p. 303).

80. Aulen puts the matter well: "At stake can be nothing other than to record, without other ends in mind, what can be said about Jesus that is trustworthy" (*Jesus*, p. 159). See also Paul Tillich, *The Dynamics of Faith* (Harper & Row, 1958), pp. 85–89.

81. Joseph Fletcher, *Situation Ethics* (Westminster, 1966), p. 139; Altizer, *Christian Atheism*, pp. 136, 156; Cox, *Secular City* (1965), p. 110ff.

82. William E. Phipps, *Was Jesus Married?* (Harper & Row, 1970). Phipps argues that since all eligible Jewish men were supposed to

marry, it would have been reported if Jesus had *not* been married. Jesus is the dominating but purposeless manipulator in Hugh J. Schonfield, *The Passover Plot* (Bernard Geis, 1966), and the near-Zealot in S.G.F. Brandon, *Jesus and the Zealots* (Scribner's, 1968). See, also W. Wink, "Jesus and Revolution," *USQR* (1969): 37–59; Buchanan, *Consequences of the Covenant*, pp. 42–90. But see Erich Grässer, "Zum Verständnis der Gottesherrschaft," *ZNW* 65 (1974): 3–26. Barrows Dunham describes Jesus simply as a political revolutionary (*Heroes and Heretics* [Dell, 1963], p. 51ff.). Nazi theologians had their Jesuses too. See Martin Hengel, *Was Jesus a Revolutionist?* (Fortress, 1971), pp. 34–36. As to tendencies in black theology, see John H. Hayes, *Son of God to Super Star* (Abingdon, 1976), pp. 170–183.

83. E.g., T. Lorenzmeier, S. Schulz, E. Bloch, D. Solle and H.-W. Bartsch. See Grässer's critique, particularly of Lorenzmeier's position, in "Zum Verständnis." Grässer's comment on Bartsch's claim that Jesus regarded the Kingdom of God as both "exclusively God's doing" and a "utopia" brought about by human agency, could be applied to the operations of many other interpreters: "Well may the cultured among the despisers of theologians complain regarding this exegetical slalom, 'Nothing they desire can be made untrue in their eyes.' . . . Yet where the texts themselves are clear, the desire for opportune interpretation ought not warrant befogging them in a smoke-screen" (pp. 20–21, note 47).

84. See p. 9 and *KGST*: 6–21.

85. Concerning this dilemma, see also John G. Gager, *Kingdom and Community*, p. 6f., and his article: "The Gospels and Jesus: Some Doubts about Method," *JR* 54 (1974): 244–272.

86. See *supra*, pp. 7–10, especially with respect to existentialist and "symbolic" constructions of Jesus' message.

87. See Perrin, *Jesus and Language*, pp. 107–127.

88. Peter L. Berger has suggested that the tendency in modern theology to emphasize individual subjectivity or consciousness derives largely from contemporary secular and neo-liberal influences (*The Sacred Canopy* [Anchor, 1969], pp. 164–168).

89. See Perrin's review of such interpreters in *Jesus and Language*, pp. 132–181.

90. Keck, *A Future*, pp. 186, 206, 216–219, 249. Keck also explains that "Kingdom" really meant God's "righteousness" or "rule" (pp. 66, 221, 234).

91. E.g., Achtemeier, *Mark*, pp. 60, 68f., 110; Kee, *Community*, pp. 108, 148, 176.

92. Achtemeier, *Mark*, p. 109f. See also the "Twelve Theses on Eschatology," adopted by the 1978 General Assembly of the Presbyterian Church in the United States, esp. Thesis no. 3.

93. Kee, *Community*, pp. 145, 174f. The term "consummation of

the age" appears a few times in Matthew, where it evidently functions as a synonym for "coming of the Kingdom and God." None of the gospels contains the expression "consummation" (or "fulfillment") of the "Kingdom of God."

94. Kee nevertheless declares that Mark *explicitly* differentiated two stages of entering the Kingdom: now, and in the coming age (*ibid.*, p. 109).

95. Still another strategy could be mentioned. This might be described as the affirmation of complex, if not incomprehensible, propositions. (One hesitates to say obfuscation.) A few examples: (1) "Precisely in the light of a future goal, not something that has begun but something that will be completed, the future reign of God, man in the *present* is challenged to a radical decision, the present is for him the 'last days,' the eschaton" (Hans Küng, *The Church* [Sheed & Ward, 1967], p. 69). (2) "Thus the understanding of language as that which presents the possibilities from which reality if actualized identifies in Jesus' language itself the locus of God's reign—not in the present as a reality, nor as an apocalyptic reality near or far, but as the structuring of reality that reveals it as immediate to God, 'God's creation'" (James M. Robinson, "Jesus' Parables as God Happening," in F. Thomas Trotter, ed., *Jesus and the Historian* [Westminster, 1968], p. 145).

96. Marc Bloch, *The Historian's Craft* (Vintage, 1953), p. 126.

97. To the degree that the dynamics involve beliefs and values, the term "cognitive" is a misnomer. John Gager has recently utilized cognitive dissonance theory in attempting to understand the impetus for missions in early Christianity (*Kingdom and Community*, p. 39ff.). In effect, what we are suggesting here is that much of modern NT "research" has been shaped by interpreters' concern to reconcile or adjust their perceptions of the historical tradition to the claims of their faith-understandings.

98. *What is Christianity?*, pp. 54, 179f.

99. Koch, *Rediscovery*, p. 11.

Chapter II

1. Adolf von Harnack, *What Is Christianity?* (Harper, 1957), pp. 146, 214.

2. The subject does not come up in Harnack's description of Jesus' message. Shailer Mathews did not find it in Jesus' teaching, either: *Jesus on Social Institutions* (Fortress, 1971).

3. Johannes Weiss, *Jesus' Proclamation of the Kingdom of God* (Fortress, 1971), pp. 96–101.

4. Albert Schweitzer, The Mystery of the Kingdom of God (Macmillan, 1950), pp. 54–56, 124–27; *The Kingdom of God and Primitive Christianity* (Seabury, 1968), p. 107.

5. C.H. Dodd, *The Parables of the Kingdom* (Scribner's, 1961), pp.

60–84, 161–63. See also John A.T. Robinson, *Jesus and His Coming* (Nashville: Abingdon, 1957), pp. 36–82.

6. Joachim Jeremias, *The Parables of Jesus* (Scribner's, 1963), pp. 162–88. See also Jeremias, *New Testament Theology* (Scribner's, 1971), p. 122ff.

7. T.W. Manson, *The Teaching of Jesus* (Cambridge University Press, 1951), pp. 269–77.

8. W.G. Kümmel, *Promise and Fulfillment*, SBT no. 23 (London: SCM, 1957), pp. 43–48.

9. Another exception is Morna D. Hooker, *The Son of Man in Mark* (Montreal: McGill University Press, 1967), pp. 148–73. See also the more theologically oriented discussion by Russell Aldwinckle, *Death in the Secular City* (London: Allen & Unwin, 1972), pp. 101–119.

10. E.g., Vincent Taylor, *The Gospel According to Mark* (London: Macmillan, 1955), William Manson, *Jesus The Messiah* (Westminster, 1956), D.E. Nineham, *The Gospel of St. Mark* (Penguin, 1973), and Norman Perrin, *The New Testament* (Harcourt Brace Jovanovich, 1974). Thus also most European writers, e.g., Maurice Goguel, *Jesus and the Origins of Christianity* (Harper, 1960), Harald Riesenfeld, *The Gospel Tradition* (Fortress, 1970), Etienne Trocmé, *Jesus as Seen by His Contemporaries* (Westminster, 1973).

11. E.g., Perrin, *Rediscovering*, p. 191, explained that such sayings offer "general reassurance to men that, if they have responded to the challenge of Jesus' present, they may have confidence in God's future." More recently, Perrin stated that all sayings pertaining to eschatological Judgment are inauthentic, and derive from the earliest Palestinian Church: *New Testament*, pp. 47, 300. See also Hans Küng, *The Church* (Sheed & Ward, 1968), p. 51.

12. Rudolf Bultmann, *Jesus and the Word* (Scribner's, 1958), pp. 78–81, 121; *Theology of the New Testament*, Vol. I (Scribner's, 1954), p. 14f.

13. Rudolf Bultmann, *Primitive Christianity* (Meridian, 1956), p. 90; *Jesus Christ and Mythology* (Scribner's, 1958), pp. 16–18.

14. Bultmann, *Mythology*, pp. 23, 26.

15. E.g., Günther Bornkamm, Hans Conzelmann, Ernst Fuchs, Ernst Käsemann. Thus also James M. Robinson.

16. Jürgen Moltmann, *Theology of Hope* (Harper & Row, 1967); Wolfhart Pannenberg, *Jesus God and Man* (Westminster, 1968); *Theology and the Kingdom of God* (Westminster, 1969).

17. Carl E. Braaten, *Christ and Counter-Christ* (Fortress, 1972); *Eschatology and Ethics* (Augsburg, 1974).

18. Thus, e.g., William J. Dalton, S.J., *Aspects of New Testament Eschatology* (Univ. of Western Australia Press, 1968), p. 7: ". . . God is primarily a God who loves, a God who saves. Hence any eschatological statement set in the context of future judgment must take into account the *inadequacy* of this context and must allow for this inadequacy if

conclusions unworthy of God are to be avoided." (Italics added.) For further analysis, see Alan M. Fairhurst, "The Problem Posed by the Severe Sayings Attributed to Jesus in the Synoptic Gospels," *SJT* 23 (1970): 77–91.

19. E.g., John 3:17; 2 Cor. 5:19; Rom. 11:32–36.

20. Bultmann, *Jesus and the Word*, p. 78ff.

21. E.g., Bultmann, *Primitive*, pp. 87–89; Hans Conzelmann, *The Theology of St. Luke* (Harper & Row, 1961), p. 121f.; Günther Bornkamm, *Jesus of Nazareth* (London: Hodder & Stoughton, 1960); p. 91ff.; Kümmel, *Promise*, p. 33ff. See Chap. I, p. 9. Interpreters sometimes claim that whereas John the Baptist proclaimed a future day of Judgment, such thoughts were far from Jesus' mind.

22. See Klaus Koch, *The Rediscovery of Apocalyptic*, SBT, 2nd ser., no. 22 (London: SCM, 1972).

23. Cf. Mark 9:43–47; 10:17–30. The same distinction is implicit in Matt. 11:11 = Luke 7:28. See *KGST*: 57–65.

24. See also similar sayings, deriving, perhaps from Mark 8:35 or "Q", that appear at Matt. 10:39; 16:25; Luke 9:24; 17:33.

25. See Weiss, *Jesus' Proclamation*, p. 111f.

26. The RSV editors' judgment that the "best ancient authorities" omit Mark 9:44 and 46 may have been influenced by the gruesome, as well as repetitious, character of these verses. They are included in several early manuscript traditions.

27. See also Judith 16:17.

28. Aldwinckle suggests that the idea of eternal punishment is "impossible to reconcile with what Jesus tells us elsewhere about the character of God," but does not discuss Mark 9:43–48 (*Death*, p. 115ff.).

29. Cf. the second person plural in Mark 13:28f.

30. Mark 13:30; cf. 9:1.

31. See the excellent discussions of the eschatology of "Q" by Richard A. Edwards, *A Theology of Q* (Fortress, 1976), pp. 37–57, 147ff., and Howard Clark Kee, *Jesus in History* (Harcourt Brace Jovanovich, 1977), pp. 91–111.

32. See John A.T. Robinson, "Elijah, John and Jesus" in his *Twelve New Testament Studies*, SBT no. 34 (London: SCM, 1962), pp. 28–52; also *HJKG*: 47–51.

33. Occasionally it is argued that Matt. 11:11f. (Luke 7:28; 16:16) mean that Jesus denounced the Baptist or his "method." But see *KGST* Chaps. 4 and 7.

34. Luke 16:1–9. See R.H. Hiers, "Friends by Unrighteous Mammon," *JAAR* 38 (1970): 30–36.

35. Cf. Tobit 12:12ff.; Wisd. Sol. 3:1ff.

36. Cf. II Esdras 7:12f., 60f.

37. Cf. Matt. 24:37–39 = Luke 17:26f.

38. Cf. Matt. 25:31–46; Tobit 12:13–15.

39. E.g., Mark 8:27 and parallels.

40. Cf. Amos 1:9f.; 3:1f.

41. So also Matt. 10:5–15 = Luke 10:3–12.

42. That "something greater" was the final preaching of repentance, the only sign that would be given, associated by Jesus with John the Baptist who was prophet and more than prophet; namely, Elijah. It is possible that Jesus also hereby meant to refer to himself as well, either in his own role as Elijah, or as the soon-to-be-revealed Son of man. See *KGST*: 51–65; *HJKG*: 48–59, 86–89.

43. See also Matt. 23:35f. = Luke 20:50f.: Mark 13:30 = Matt. 24:34 = Luke 21:32; and Mark 14:62 = Matt. 26:64.

44. See Chap. V.

45. That there would be twelve thrones, one for each of those judging the tribes of Israel, may have given rise to the tradition that Jesus had chosen twelve disciples. Thus Johannes Weiss, *Earliest Christianity*, Vol. I (Harper, 1959), pp. 46–48. But it may be that the "dogmatic" number twelve goes back to Jesus himself.

46. As it stands, there seem to be a number of interpolations. Matthew alone refers to wise men and scribes, crucifying, scourging and persecuting them, and Luke alone mentions "apostles."

47. The view, common among some Christian interpreters, that "this generation" refers to Jews of any and all times is a classic example of special pleading. Whether it reveals implicit anti-semitism, this theory functions to explain away the theological difficulties attendant upon the fact that the generation of Jesus' contemporaries passed away without the fulfillment of the expected parousia events.

48. Cf. Matt. 23:34f., which delimits the time of persecution for which "this generation" must pay to the period ending with Zechariah the son of Barachiah (2 Chron. 24:20ff.). Here, as in other places, Luke adapts tradition to take into account the fact that some time has elapsed since Jesus proclaimed his message, but at the same time hold open the prospect of eschatological fulfillment in the lifetime of his *readers*. See R.H. Hiers, "The Problem of the Delay of the Parousia in Luke–Acts," *NTS* 20 (1974): 145–55.

49. Thus also Luke 21:34f. and 17:20f. See *KGST*: 22–29.

50. See 1 Thess. 5:2; Rev. 3:3; 2 Pet. 3:10a. This familiar image in the primitive church derived, very likely, from Jesus' saying. See Paul S. Minear, *Commands of Christ* (Abingdon, 1972), pp. 152–77.

51. The references to "hypocrites" and "weeping and gnashing of teeth" seem to be Matthean touches.

52. Luke 19:14, 27; cf. 21:20–28. See Hiers, "Problem of the Delay."

53. Matt. 25:29 = Luke 19:26. See also Mark 4:25 = Matt. 13:12 = Luke 8:18.

54. The Gk. *praeis* means "humble, lowly, unassuming." See also

the "Q" saying at Matt. 23:12 = Luke 14:11 = Luke 18:14.

55. Cf. Wisd. Sol. 3:1–9.

56. See *KGST*: 66–71; *HJKG*: 64–70.

57. See discussion of Matt. 11:21–23 = Luke 10:13–15 above.

58. Cf. Matt. 9:37f. = Luke 10:2f.

59. See *KGST*: 79.

60. Cf. II Esdras 7:36.

61. See also Matt. 24:31 and 13:41. The angels are not so-designated in Mark or "Q". Also, some "M" traditions anticipate that there is or will be an intermediate Kingdom of the Son of man, e.g., Matt. 13:41–43. Cf. 1 Cor. 15:24–28; Rev. 20:4–6.

62. Cf. II Esdras 7:33ff.

63. Matt. 22:1–10; cf. Luke 14:16–24.

64. Cf. Matt. 7:23; Luke 13:27.

65. See, e.g., *KGST*: 72–77; *HJKG*: 11–46.

66. Some (especially Catholic) interpreters think that by this expression, Matthew meant the church. E.g., Rudolf Schnackenburg, *God's Rule and Kingdom* (Herder & Herder, 1963), p. 167. Cf. Küng, *The Church*, pp. 94, 96.

67. Cf. Job 29:12–17; 31:16–20; Tobit 1:17; Sirach 7:32–35.

68. Cf. Luke 19:11. See Hiers, "Problem of the Delay."

69. Luke 3:9 = Matt. 3:10; Luke 3:16f. = Matt. 3:11f.; cf. Luke 12:50.

70. Burton H. Throckmorton, Jr., ed. (Nelson, 1967), p. 116.

71. Cf. Isaiah's parable or "song" of the vineyard: Isa. 5:1–6.

72. Cf. Matt. 3:10 = Luke 3:9; Matt. 7:19; 2 Pet. 3:9f.

73. Luke 14:7–11; cf. Prov. 25:6f.

74. See Hiers, "Friends by Unrighteous Mammon," *JAAR* 38 (1970): 30–36.

75. That the poor would inherit the Kingdom is here assumed, as elsewhere in Luke, e.g., Luke 6:20. Cf. Mark 10:23; James 2:5.

76. Luke 17:20f. is often interpreted, without regard to context, as evidence for "realized eschatology." For exegesis, see *KGST*: 22–29.

77. See also Luke 21:34–36.

78. Thus also Matt. 7:7–11 = Luke 11:9–13. Cf. 1 John 4:16f.

79. Why Luke should have included two collections of such sayings is not clear. One (17:20–18:8) is set in or near Galilee; the other (21:8–36) in Jerusalem, apparently at the Temple.

80. Such also is the probable meaning of Luke 17:20f. and Matt. 24:26f. = Luke 17:23f.

81. E.g., Dan. 12:1; Joel 2:30–32; addn. to Esther 11:5–9.

82. Matt. 6:10, 13 = Luke 11:2, 4b; cf. Mark 14:35–39 and parallels. It is not necessary, however, to attribute to Jesus the detailed schema of the synoptic apocalypse, with its various phases or periods of suffering and tribulation. See *HJGK*: 24–26.

83. Mark 8:38–9:1; 13:29f. and parallels; Matt. 12:38–42 = Luke 11:29–32; Matt. 23:35f. = Luke 11:50f.; Matt. 10:23; Luke 18:7f.; 21:34, 36.

84. Mark 13:24–27, cf. 10:37–40; Matt. 24:37–39 = Luke 17:26f.; Matt. 24:44 = Luke 12:40; Matt. 25:31–46; Luke 18:8; 21:36. God is to be Judge in Matt. 18:35, and also perhaps in 22:13; but cf. 25:13 and 40 where the "king" seems to be the Son of man, enthroned for Judgment.

85. Matt. 13:41; 16:28, cf. 20:21; Luke 22:30; 23:42, cf. 19:15.

86. Matt. 13:41; 16:27; 24:31.

87. See *HJKG*: 74–76. Paul's admonition to Corinthian churchmen may have been based on such a saying of Jesus, only given universal scope: "Do you not know that the saints will judge the world?" (1 Cor. 6:2). This understanding may have been informed by Dan. 7, where it is revealed that when "one like a son of man" is given "dominion and glory and Kingdom," the righteous, "the people of the saints of the Most High" will also be given kingdom and dominion over all the nations (Dan. 7:18, 27). See also Wisd. Sol. 3:8; and Rev. 2:26f.; 20:4.

88. See however Matt. 3:10 = Luke 3:9, and esp. Matt. 3:11f. = Luke 3:16f., where the Baptist prophesies that the coming one will baptize with fire and burn the chaff "with unquenchable fire."

89. Matt. 5:22; 13:36–43, 49f.; 25:41. See also Matt. 7:19; 13:30. In Luke, see 9:54; 12:49; 16:24; 17:29f.; 23:31.

90. Matt. 8:12; 13:42, 50; 22:13; 24:51; 25:30.

91. Matt. 5:22, 29, 30; 10:28; 23:15, 33.

92. Mark 9:43, 45, 47 = Matt. 18:8f.

93. Matt. 5:3–11; Luke 6:20f., 24–26.

94. Mark 8:38 = Luke 9:26.

95. Mark 13:2 and parallels.

96. Matt. 9:15 = Luke 10:12. See also Matt. 11:21–23 = Luke 10:13–15; and Mark 6:11.

97. Matt. 23:35f. = Luke 11:50f.

98. Matt. 10:31–33; 12:32 = Luke 12:8–10.

99. Mark 2:3–12. Verses 10 and 11 probably are to be regarded as a Marcan explanation to the reader. It underscores the authority with which Jesus speaks and acts, and possibly was meant by Mark to suggest that such authority is characteristic of the Son of man-Judge. Cf. Mark 1:22, 27.

100. Most notably, perhaps, Mark 10:37–40. Possibly it is implicit also in Matt. 25:31–46. Luke reports that the early church looked for Jesus as the eschatological judge: Acts 10:42; 17:31. See Schweitzer, *Kingdom of God and Primitive Christianity*, pp. 102–108.

101. E.g., Hos. 2:16–20; Isa. 2:2–4; 11:1–10; 19:19–25; Jer. 31:31–34; Hag. 2:6–9, 21–23; Zech. 2:10–12; 3:6–10; 14:1–21.

102. See Paul D. Hanson, *The Dawn of Apocalyptic* (Fortress, 1975).

103. En. 45:3; 55:4; 61:8; 62:2, 5; 69:27, 29. In 62:2, the Son of man

is seated by the Lord of Spirits; in 69:29, he seats himself.
104. E.g., En. 46, 49, 50, 62, 69:27–29.
105. Cf. Judith 16:17.
106. En. 1:7–9; 25:4; T. Benj. 10:8f. See also II Bar. 28:7–29:1; 83:2.
107. II Bar. 21:22–25; 24:1f.; 30:2f.
108. See also En. 63:1–3.
109. E.g., Isa. 2, 19, 49; Jonah 1–4.
110. II Bar. 72:1–5; Sib. Or. III:652–54, 741–60, 772–82.
111. T. Benj. 9:2–4; 10:5, 9f.; 11:2f. See also En. 48:4.
112. En. 10:4–6, 11–16; 18:12–19:1.
113. En. 58:2f.
114. En. 98:9f.; also see 38:1–4; 103:3–8; II Bar. 54:21; Wisd. Sol. 3:1–19; II En. 61:1–3.
115. II En. 44:4f.; cf. Matt. 25:34–40; Matt. 7:2 = Luke 6:38. See also II En. 9:1; 10:1–6; 50:1–5; 51:1–3; 52:1–15. Concern for the poor and needy is central in these passages, and also in several places in I Enoch, esp. chaps. 94–99, which are also reminiscent of various sayings of Jesus, particularly as given in Luke.
116. E.g., En. 41:1f.; 94:6–10; 96:1–8; 97:1–10; 98:7f.; 99:1–16; II Bar. 48:38f.; II Esdras 7:70–74, 77; Wisd. Sol. 4:20–5:16.
117. II En. 61:2f. Cf. Luke 16:9b; John 14:2f.
118. En. 5:7; also Sib. Or. IV:45f., 181–192. Cf. Matt. 5:5.
119. II Bar. 29:5f. See also 29:4, 7f.; En. 10:18f.; II En. 8:1–8; Sib. Or. III: 741–54.
120. II En. 65:8–10. See also En. 10:16f., 20, 22; 58:3f.; Ps. Sol. 17:29. Cf. Zech. 14:6f.
121. En. 10:21; 38:4–6; 48:4f., 8–10; T. Dan 5:13; T. Levi 18:9; T. Benj. 9:2; 10:5, 9f.; 11:2f. Some of these passages may be Christian interpolations.
122. Wisd. Sol. 3:7f.; cf. Dan. 7:21, 27.
123. As. Moses 10:1; Sib. Or. III: 767–71.
124. Jubilees 23:29; 50:5; T. Levi 25:3; As. Moses 10:1.
125. T. Levi 3:3. See also T. Dan 5:10; En. 91:15; Sib. Or. III: 63–92.
126. En. 45:4f. See also En. 72:1; 92:14, 16; Sib. Or. IV:171–91.
127. II Bar. 44:12, 15; II Esdras 8:1.
128. En. 19:1. See also 54:1–6; 56:1–4. Other angels, perhaps, were to be punished for a set number of years in a kind of purgatory (En. 18:11–16; 21:2–6), while others would be punished, again in fire, forever (En. 21:7–10).
129. Ps. Sol. 15:12, 14; see also 14:6; 15:15; En. 45:6; 53:2; 62:2; 69:27; 77:1f.; 98:9f.; Sib. Or. III:761.
130. En. 22:11; T. Reub. 5:5; II En. 10:1–6; 40:12f.; IV Macc. 9:9; 10:11; 13:15 (cf. Matt. 10:28). Cf. also Rev. 20:9–15.
131. Sib. Or. III:669–92; IV:173–78. Cf. Matt. 11:24 = Luke 10:12; Matt. 10:15; Luke 12:49.

132. Book of Noah (Enoch) 108:2–6; Sib. Or. III:761; IV:40–44; As. Moses 10:10; II Bar. 44:15; 48:39, 43; 59:2; 83:13; II Esdras 7:36, 38; IV Macc. 9:9; Zad. Doc. 2:4. Note that in II En. 10:1–6, both cold and darkness as well as fire are involved; similarly, in Matthew, "outer darkness" is said to be an alternate or additional place of punishment.

133. Cf. Joel 2:30; Mal. 3:2f.; Judith 16:17.

134. II Esdras 7:43f. See also As. Moses 1:17f.; II Bar. 83:1f.; 83:7.

135. II Esdras 5:4f. See also 5:6–12; Sib. Or. III:801–04; As. Moses 10:5; cf. Joel 2:30f.

136. Sib. Or. III:796ff. See also IV:171–75; V:344–59; II Esdras 9:1f.

137. E.g., As. Moses 10:1–10; n.b., vv. 4–6.

138. II Bar. 23:7; 48:39. See also 82:1f. and 85:10.

139. II Esdras 4:26; 8:61. See also the extended discussions and metaphors in 4:27–52.

140. E.g., II Esdras 4:22–25.

141. II Bar. 83:7f.; see also En. 50:1–5; T. Levi 19:1; T. Judah 20:1–5; Sib. Or. IV:162–78; II En. 38:3–46:3; II Bar. 84:2–11; 85:4–9, 11–15; II Esdras 9:7–13. On the parenetic character of Jewish apocalyptic, see Koch, *Rediscovery*, p. 25f.

142. *Book of Common Prayer*, "Te Deum." See also the "Venite": "For he cometh to judge the earth, and with righteousness to judge the world, and the peoples with his truth" (Ps. 96:13). This line has been deleted from the version of the "Venite" in Morning Prayer, Rite Two, *Proposed Book of Common Prayer* (Seabury, 1977), p. 82. The "Apostles" and "Nicene" creeds, still used by many Christians, affirm that Jesus is the one who "shall come" to "judge the quick and the dead."

Chapter III

1. E.T., *What Is Christianity?* (Harper, 1957).

2. Perhaps the last important representative of the earlier viewpoint was Harvey Cox, in *The Secular City* (Macmillan, 1965), e.g., pp. 110ff., 121–23; and rev. ed. (1966), p. 95ff.

3. Though not developing an integrated theory of ethics, several mid-twentieth century theologians pointed to Jesus' teachings as *commands* which are to be obeyed in our time: Dietrich Bonhoeffer, *The Cost of Discipleship* (1937); Hans Windisch, *The Meaning of the Sermon on the Mount* (Westminster, 1950); Paul S. Minear, *Commands of Christ* (Abingdon, 1972). Joseph Fletcher has emphasized Jesus' command or teaching of love, though he also describes love rather imprecisely as an "intrinsic" value.

4. The O.T., with its emphasis on justice, community, and the judgment of God in and at the end of history was particularly important in Reinhold Niebuhr's writings on moral theology. For Karl Barth and Rudolf Bultmann, the emphasis was more on the grace of God as

understood in the N.T. by Paul and John. For ethics, however, Bultmann also referred to Jesus' proclamation of radical obedience to God in the form of radical love of neighbor. Neither Barth nor Bultmann had much to say about the relevance of Christian ethics for political or social issues.

5. See p. 55ff., and Albert Schweitzer, *The Philosophy of Civilization* (Macmillan, 1960), p. 146f.

6. T.W. Manson, in H.D.A. Major, T.W. Manson, and C.J. Wright, *The Message and Mission of Jesus* (Dutton, 1938), p. 329. The same kind of objection could be raised against many of the admonitions that do appear in the gospels: e.g., Matt. 5:20; 7:24–27; 13:44–46; 18:7–9; 25:1–46; Mark 10:17–30; Luke 12:57–59; 16:1–9. But the test of historical research is not whether its conclusions offend one's moral sensibilities. Other Protestant writers intimate that there must be something morally (and thus also somehow historically) wrong with an interpretation that allows Jesus to have held before his contemporaries the prospect of "rewards," e.g., R. Bultmann, *Jesus and the Word* (Scribner's, 1958), pp. 78f., 121; E. Clinton Gardner, *Biblical Faith and Social Ethics* (Harper, 1960), p. 60. See G. de Ru, "The Conception of Reward in the Teaching of Jesus," *NovT* 8 (1966): 202–222, and R.H. Hiers, *Jesus and Ethics* (Westminster, 1968), pp. 96–99.

7. A.M. Hunter, *The Work and Words of Jesus* (Westminster, 1950), p. 12.

8. See Albert Schweitzer, *The Mystery of the Kingdom of God* (Macmillan, 1950), pp. 53–60; *The Kingdom of God and Primitive Christianity* (Seabury, 1968), pp. 81–87, 96–101.

9. Thus, e.g., Albert Knudson, Amos N. Wilder, T.W. Manson, C.H. Dodd, A.M. Hunter, Rudolf Bultmann, and Günther Bornkamm.

10. E.F. Scott, *The Ethical Teaching of Jesus* (Macmillan, 1936), p. 43. Willingness to dispense with logical considerations is a recurrent characteristic of critics who wish to refute the eschatological interpretation of the historical Jesus.

11. Gardner, *Biblical Faith*, p. 63. See also Joachim Jeremias, *The Sermon on the Mount* (Fortress, 1963), pp. 9–12. Interim ethics is wrong, Jeremias argues, because it treats the Sermon on the Mount as law. And this is wrong because "every legalistic understanding of the Sermon puts Jesus within the realm of late Judaism." Jeremias, like many other Christian interpreters, assumes *a priori* that Jesus had to be different from the Judaism of his day. In his *Quest of the Historical Jesus* (1906), Schweitzer showed how this assumption appears in Baldensperger and still earlier spiritualizers of Jesus' statements and ideas.

12. Schweitzer, *Mystery*, p. 53ff.; *The Quest*, p. 368f. See Millar Burrows, "Old Testament Ethics and the Ethics of Jesus," in J.L. Crenshaw and J.T. Willis, eds., *Essays in Old Testament Ethics* (KTAV, 1974), p. 233ff. Burrows points out that Jesus was not calling for a new moral-

ity, but for repentance and fidelity to O.T. ethics, especially as represented in the prophetic tradition.

13. E.T., *The Mystery of the Kingdom of God.*

14. Albert Schweitzer, *Geschichte der Leben-Jesu-Forschung* (Tübingen, Mohr, 1913, 1951), p. 594f.

15. Victor P. Furnish, *The Love Command in the New Testament* (Abingdon, 1972); Minear, *Commands of Christ.*

16. Günther Bornkamm, *Jesus of Nazareth* (Hodder & Stoughton, 1960), p. 223. Cf. Herman Ridderbos, *The Coming of the Kingdom* (Presbyterian & Reformed Publishing Co., 1962), p. 471.

17. Reinhold Niebuhr, *An Interpretation of Christian Ethics* (1956), p. 58. See also *The Nature and Destiny of Man* (Scribner's, 1941), vol. II, p. 50f., where Niebuhr demythologizes Jesus' ethics from all eschatological entanglements, attributing to him instead as "the real fact" a series of splendid Niebuhrian concepts.

18. Schweitzer, *Mystery*, p. 54. See also *Out of My Life and Thought* (Holt, 1933), pp. 53–55; and *Kingdom and Primitive*, p. 86: "To do God's will, which cannot be confined to commandments and prohibitions, but makes its demands on men's hearts as unlimited will-to-love: this is the profound, spiritual, inward-looking ethic required for entry into the Kingdom." See also *Philosophy of Civilization*, p. 146.

19. C.J. Cadoux, *The Historic Mission of Jesus* (Harper, n.d.), p. 126f.; E.F. Scott, *Ethical Teaching*, p. 52f. Cf. Alan M. Fairhurst, "The Problems Posed by the Severe Sayings Attributed to Jesus in the Synoptic Gospels," *SJT* 23 (1970): 77–91.

20. E.g., G. Sevenster, Hans Windisch. Amos N. Wilder suggests that Jesus' sayings combine and transcend the wisdom and apocalyptic categories (*Early Christian Rhetoric* [Harvard, 1971], pp. 78–81).

21. Thus Maurice Goguel put the matter several years ago: "The moral teaching of Jesus is only addressed to men who are living in that period, both tragic and fruitful, which is the last in the history of the world." *Jesus and the Origins of Christianity* (Harper, 1960), II: 581.

22. John Knox, *The Ethic of Jesus in the Teaching of the Church* (Harper, 1961), p. 39; John Bright, *The Kingdom of God* (Abingdon, 1953), p. 222f.

23. Albert Knudson, *The Principles of Christian Ethics* (1943), p. 43. See also Bornkamm, *Jesus*, p. 223; Paul Ramsey, *Basic Christian Ethics* (Scribner's, 1954), p. 31; Gardner, *Biblical Faith*, p. 62; Norman Perrin, *The Kingdom of God in the Teaching of Jesus* (Westminster, 1963), p. 36; cf. George E. Ladd, *Jesus and the Kingdom* (Harper & Row, 1964), p. 121; Ridderbos, *The Coming*, p. 471.

24. Schweitzer, *Geschichte*, p. 596. See also p. 640f.; *Mystery*, p. 56f.; *The Quest*, p. 402f.; *Life and Thought*, p. 53ff.

25. *The Sermon on the Mount* (Cambridge Univ. Press, 1966), p. 143f.

26. *Jesus in Contemporary Research* (Fortress, 1976), p. 92.

27. Martin Dibelius, *The Sermon on the Mount* (Westminster, 1940, p. 49). See also J.F. Peter, *Finding the Historical Jesus* (Harper & Row, 1965), p. 42f.

28. See Goguel, *Jesus* II: 581, "The ethic of Jesus is not a system of legislation for the Kingdom of God. . . . Those who will be admitted into it will instinctively know the will of God, and will accomplish it without effort." See also Ramsey, *Christian Ethics*, p. 31: "Jesus' teachings obviously were intended to apply in a world in which there is striking, hostility, persecution, and oppression; not in the kingdom only, where there will presumably be no more blows on the cheek, no more impression into military service, nor need for borrowing."

29. C.H. Dodd, *The Parables of the Kingdom* (Scribner's, 1961), p. 79.

30. Bright, *Kingdom of God*, p. 223. Thus also Hans Conzelmann, *Jesus* (Fortress, 1973), p. 59f.: "If that were the case, Jesus' ethics would stand, but would also fall, with the imminent expectation of the end." Conzelmann evidently thought that Jesus' ethics do or should "stand." See also Heinz Zahrnt, *The Historical Jesus* (Harper & Row, 1963), p. 53.

31. Ramsey, *Christian Ethics*, p. 30; Gardner, *Biblical Faith*, p. 63.

32. Ridderbos grants that it is doubtful whether Jesus had in view a perspective extending over centuries. Nevertheless, he urges, Jesus "has commanded *us* very emphatically to watch for the approach of the great day" (*The Coming*, pp. 476, 488, emphasis added). Similarly, Conzelmann, *Jesus*, p. 60ff.

33. Scott, *Ethical Teaching*, p. 45. See also Bright, *Kingdom of God*, p. 223; R. Bultmann, *Theology of the New Testament*, vol. I (Scribner's, 1954), p. 20; George F. Thomas, *Christian Ethics and Moral Philosophy* (Scribner's, 1955), p. 30; Georgia Harkness, *Christian Ethics* (Abingdon, 1957), p. 63.

34. Harkness, *Christian Ethics*, p. 63.

35. Thomas, *Christian Ethics*, p. 30. Proponents of this view might have seized on Mark 13:31 = Matt. 24:35 = Luke 21:33. However, this saying evidently means that Jesus' "words" will still have authority when the Kingdom comes, after the present "earth and heaven" have "passed away." Cf. Paul's observation that love will endure "when the perfect comes" (1 Cor. 13:8–10).

36. Knox, *Ethic of Jesus*, p. 46.

37. *Ibid.*

38. Schweitzer, *Geschichte*, p. 596. Bultmann's conceptualization of the ethical substance of Jesus' message in terms of "radical obedience" is often misunderstood in some of the same ways as Schweitzer's "interim ethics" theory. For instance, critics commonly assume that by radical obedience Bultmann meant a more intensified legalism. Also, the fact that Bultmann regarded Jesus' ethic of "radical obedience" as

basic to the moral life of modern Christians is commonly overlooked.

39. For example, R. Bultmann, Walter E. Bundy, Fritz Buri, Miller Burrows, Martin Dibelius, M.S. Enslin, M. Goguel, R.M. Grant, E. Grässer, and M. Werner.

40. See chapter one. J.K. Mosley wishes to affirm that the Kingdom was present for Jesus "at least in some way," for if it was entirely future, "how can there be any point to the strivings of man's ethical life?" ["Eschatology and Ethics," *JThSt* 40 (1939): 343f.].

41. Amos N. Wilder, *Eschatology and Ethics in the Teachings of Jesus* (Harper, 1950), p. 160. See also Hunter, *Work and Words*, p. 77; Cf. Perrin, *Kingdom of God*, p. 206. H.P. Owen urges that Jesus' message of repentance was grounded in his proclamation and embodiment of the presence of the Kingdom: "Eschatology and Ethics in the New Testament," *SJT* 15 (1962): 369–82.

42. Dodd recognizes that, in Matt. 7:22f., "the scene is expressly laid on 'that day'—the Day of Judgment to come," and yet goes on to conclude that Jesus' meaning was "that by their conduct in the presence of this tremendous crisis they would judge themselves as faithful or unfaithful, wise or foolish (*Parables*, p. 138f.). Bishop Robinson also virtually eliminates the prospect of Judgment: John A.T. Robinson, *Jesus and His Coming* (Abingdon, 1957).

43. R. Niebuhr, *Nature and Destiny*, Vol. II: 47–52, 288ff. However, there is no biblical basis for the idea of a second coming of the Kingdom of God. Cf. Ridderbos, *The Coming*, pp. 141f., 288, 417. It is a question of its *coming*, not *second* coming.

44. Emil Brunner, *The Divine Imperative* (Lutterworth, 1937), pp. 123, 601f.

45. Schweitzer, *Mystery*, p. 53f. For Schweitzer's most recent and complete account of Jesus' ethics, see *Kingdom and Primitive*, pp. 93–101.

46. Thus H. Richard Niebuhr, *Christ and Culture* (Harper, 1951), p. 21f. For analysis of ways in which Schweitzer described the relevance of Jesus for modern ethics, see Henry Clark, *The Ethical Mysticism of Albert Schweitzer* (Beacon, 1962), pp. 77–85; Jackson Lee Ice, *Schweitzer: Prophet of Radical Theology* (Westminster, 1971), pp. 126–51; and Hiers, *Jesus and Ethics*, pp. 45–78. Cf. Jack T. Sanders, "The Question of the Relevance of Jesus for Ethics Today," *JAAR* 38 (1970): 131–46; *Ethics in the New Testament* (Fortress, 1975), pp. 1–29. Sanders argues that Jesus' ethical teaching is inextricably bound to his imminent eschatology.

47. Matt. 8:21f. = Luke 9:59f.

48. Cf. Paul's similar "interim ethic," 1 Cor. 7:25–31. Some of these sayings may represent a widening or intensification of the earlier tradition's interim ethics. Yet these sayings about sexual or marital abstension are not completely out of line with the synoptic sayings commanding radical renunciation of family ties for the sake of the

Kingdom. Ice gives a thoughtful review of such sayings (*Schweitzer: Prophet*, p. 161f.).

49. See R.H. Hiers, "Friends by Unrighteous Mammon," *JAAR* 38 (1970): 30–36.

50. Matt. 5:25–27 = Luke 12:58f.

51. R. Bultmann, "The Study of the Synoptic Gospels," in F.C. Grant, ed., *Form Criticism* (Harper, 1962), p. 73. Bultmann clearly wished to disengage Jesus' eschatological message from the future for the sake of the understanding of existence and ethics of those living "in the present" (*ibid.*, p. 73f.). On Bultmann's interpretation of Jesus' "ethics," see Hiers, *Jesus and Ethics*, pp. 82–114.

52. Scott, *Ethical Teaching*, p. 52.

53. Johannes Weiss, *Die Predigt Jesu vom Reiche Gottes*, rev. ed., (Göttingen: Vandehoeck & Ruprecht, 1900), p. 139.

54. Thus Ramsey, *Christian Ethics*, p. 45.

55. Will Herberg, *Judaism and Modern Man* (Meridian, 1959), p. 178.

56. See Hiers, *Jesus and Ethics*, pp. 45–76.

57. But see Carl E. Braaten, *Eschatology and Ethics* (Augsburg, 1974), esp. chap. 1.

58. Cf. Georgia Harkness, *Understanding the Kingdom of God* (Abingdon, 1974), p. 38: "Thus [Schweitzer's theory of] the 'interim ethic' has met with minor support, and I know of no one who takes it seriously today." See also Aulen, *Jesus*, p. 104: "It does not now occur to anyone to describe Jesus' 'ethic' as 'interim ethic.'" Harkness and Aulen seem to be saying that if "no one" considers the theory correct, it must be wrong. This kind of "Gallup poll" approach to historical research avoids both the troublesome task of weighing primary evidence and responsibility for defending questionable conclusions.

59. See *HJKG*: 16–24.

Chapter IV

1. See also Acts 10:38; cf. 1 John 3:8.

2. R. Bultmann, *Jesus and the Word* (Scribner's, 1958), p. 56; see also p. 27f., and R. Bultmann, *Jesus Christ and Mythology* (Scribner's, 1958), pp. 13–15. Günther Bornkamm also "demythologizes" (or psychologizes) the demons away: the demoniacs, he says, are freed from "the fetters of their obsession"; for those freed from the demons, "a world has come to its end." *Jesus of Nazareth* (London: Hodder & Stoughton, 1960), pp. 60, 62.

3. H.D.A. Major, "Incidents in the Life of Jesus," in H.D.A. Major *et al.*, *The Mission and Message of Jesus* (Dutton, 1938), pp. 30–32, 63f.; V. Taylor, *The Gospel According to Mark* (London: Macmillan, 1955), p. 239. Taylor explains Jesus' belief in demons as "part of the conditions necessary to a real incarnation."

4. E.g., A.M. Hunter, *Introducing New Testament Theology* (London: SCM, 1957), pp. 28–31; Bornkamm, *Jesus*, p. 130ff.; Heinz Zahrnt, *The Historical Jesus* (Harper & Row, 1963), p. 113; G. Ebeling, *Word and Faith* (Fortress, 1963), p. 226ff.; R.H. Fuller, *Interpreting the Miracles* (Westminster, 1963); H. Van der Loos, *The Miracles of Jesus* (Leiden: Brill, 1965); J. Reumann, *Jesus in the Church's Gospels* (Fortress, 1968), p. 199ff.; Harald Riesenfeld, *The Gospel Tradition* (Fortress, 1970), pp. 72, 84f.; E. Schweizer, *Jesus* (John Knox, 1971), p. 43ff.; Hans Conzelmann, *Jesus* (Fortress, 1973), pp. 32, 48f., 55; but cf. J. Kallas, *The Significance of the Synoptic Miracles* (London: SPCK, 1961). In *Jesus the Magician* (Harper & Row, 1978), Morton Smith urges that all four gospels represent Jesus as a "miracle worker" or "magician," but Smith never quite focuses on the matter of demon exorcism, and pays no attention to the dualistic and eschatological milieu in which the synoptic exorcisms appear. Like the 18th and 19th century rationalist interpreters before him, Smith thinks that everything important has been said once it is declared that the "miracles" are to be understood naturalistically. See, e.g., p. 149.

5. Rudolf Otto, *The Kingdom of God and the Son of Man* (London: Lutterworth, 1951), p. 101f.; see also pp. 102, 104, 107. Similarly: W. Manson, *Jesus the Messiah* (Westminster, 1946), p. 64; C. K. Barrett, *The Holy Spirit and the Gospel Tradition* (London: SPCK, 1947), pp. 68, 92; Bornkamm, *Jesus*, pp. 130f., 149; Zahrnt, *Historical Jesus*, p. 113; and L. E. Keck, *A Future for the Historical Jesus* (Abingdon, 1971). pp. 126, 183.

6. See Erich Grässer, "Zum Verständnis der Gottesherrschaft," *ZNW* 65 (1974): 20, "Wo die Gottesherrschaft *da* ist, geschieht kein Machtkampf mit Satan mehr, sondern liegt er abgeschlossen zurück."

7. The editors of the *New English Bible* even felt free to insert the word "already" in their translation of Matt. 12:28 and Luke 11:20. Assertions by commentators to the effect that the "powers of the Kingdom of God" were present or operative are especially strange in view of Mark 9:1 which certainly means that the Kingdom had not yet come "with power" *(en dunamei)*. See also Mark 13:26.

8. See *KGST*: 22–29.

9. Luke 17:23; Matt. 24:23–26; Mark 13:21f.

10. Bultmann, *Jesus and Mythology*, p. 12f. Italics added.

11. John 2:23; 4:54; 10:38; 12:18; 20:30; cf. Acts 2:22.

12. The Johannine Jesus did not exorcise demons, a point to be understood, perhaps, in connection with the general tendency of the Fourth Evangelist to "demythologize" the tradition in the direction of a "realized eschatology." But cf. 1 John 3:8; 5:19.

13. J.M. Robinson, *The Problem of History in Mark*, SBT no. 21 (London: SCM, 1957); H.C. Kee, "The Terminology of Mark's Exorcism Stories," *NTS* 14 (1968): 232–46. The most important earlier study is Otto Bauernfeind, *Die Worte der Dämonen im Markusevangelium* (Stutt-

gart: W. Kohlhammer, 1927). Bauernfeind urged that most of these sayings were in the pre-Marcan tradition, and arose out of the struggle
between the realm of Satan and Jesus. Bauernfeind did not, however,
connect Jesus' exorcism of demons with his sense of eschatological urgency, or his work of preparation for the Kingdom of God. See also
Campbell Bonner, "The Technique of Exorcism," *HThR* 36 (1943):
39–49, and Jeffrey Burton Russell, *The Devil: Perceptions of Evil from
Antiquity to Primitive Christianity* (Cornell Univ. Press, 1977), pp.
174–248.

14. James Kallas, *Jesus and the Power of Satan* (Westminster, 1968),
pp. 89, 92. See, however, his earlier studies, *Synoptic Miracles*, and *The
Satanward View* (Westminster, 1966). In the latter he writes that what
Jesus "really meant by his phrase, the Kingdom of God," was "a new
world cleansed of evil powers . . . where Satan would be destroyed and
the whole world re-created" (p. 17).

15. William Manson, *Jesus and the Christian* (Eerdmans, 1967) here-
after cited as Manson, *Jesus*, esp. pp. 77–88; C.E.B. Cranfield, *The Gospel According to Saint Mark* (Cambridge Univ. Press, 1959), esp. pp.
58–80. Cranfield proposes to overcome this apparent contradiction by
referring to the presence of the Kingdom in Jesus as a "veiled manifestation" (p. 66).

16. E.T., *Jesus' Proclamation of the Kingdom of God* (Fortress, 1971),
esp. pp. 74–81.

17. *NovT* 2 (1958): 116–37.

18. See Str.-B. IV/I: 501–35, "Zur altjüdischen Dämonologie"; also
J. Weiss, *Die Predigt Jesu vom Reiche Gottes* (Göttingen: Vandenhoeck &
Ruprecht, 1900, 1964), pp. 26f., 230–35; W. Grundmann, *Der Begriff der
Kraft in der neutestamentlichen Gedankenwelt* (Stuttgart: W. Kohlham-
mer, 1932), pp. 47–55; and Paul Volz, *Die Eschatologie der jüdischen Ge-
meinde*, 2nd ed. (Tübingen: J.C.B. Mohr, 1934), pp. 8ff., 68, 83–89.

19. E.g., Isa. 10:5ff.; Jer. 5–6; and esp., Isa. 40:1–2.

20. E.g., Judges 2:11–15; 3:7–14.

21. Satan's only appearances in the canonical O.T. are in the prologue of Job, Zech. 3:1f., and 1 Chron. 21:1; and even here, Satan is not
yet an independent cosmic power. Cf. Wisd. Sol. 2:24. For related references and discussion, see M. Burrows, *An Outline of Biblical Theology*
(Westminster, 1946), p. 124ff.

22. On the influence of post-exilic circumstances on the rise of
Jewish apocalyptic eschatology, see Paul D. Hanson, *The Dawn of
Apocalyptic* (Fortress, 1975), pp. 25f., 405f.

23. E.g., Dan. 2:31–45; 7:2–28; Jubilees 10:6–8; Enoch 21:1–10;
IQM 1:1–7; Rev. 12-13. See Volz, *Eschatologie*, pp. 68, 84; Manson,
Jesus, p. 78f.; Betz, "Heiliger Krieg," p. 117ff., and Matthew Black,
"The Eschatology of the Similitudes of Enoch," *JThSt* 3 (1952):2.

24. Job 1–2; cf. Dan. 2:37ff.; Luke 4:5f. One rabbinical theory was

that the demons first gained power over men in the days of Enoch in consequence of men's worship of idols (Str.-B. IV/I: 521). See also Jubilees 7:27; 10:1–3, 6–11. Cf. Judges 2:21f. Before Satan was postulated, it had been God who tested Israel.

25. See Volz, *Eschatologie*, pp. 7f., 83–89. Such is the viewpoint represented typically in the apocalyptic inter-testamental literature, including the Qumran War Scroll (IQM). It is also characteristic of many of the N.T. writers: e.g., Rev.; 1 Pet. 5:8; Gal. 1:4; 2 Cor. 4:4; Eph. 6:12; 1 John 5:19. Even in the Fourth Gospel, Satan is described as "the ruler of this world" who menaces Jesus' followers if not Jesus himself: 12:31; 13:2; 14:30; 17:15; cf. 10:12, 28f.

26. See M. Burrows, "Thy Kingdom Come," *JBL* 74 (1955), esp. p. 7f. Cranfield characterizes the situation by stating that, for Jesus and then current Jewish thought, God's Kingship was viewed as hidden and ambiguous; in the future, it would be revealed decisively and unambiguously (*St. Mark*, pp. 64f., 168).

27. Matt. 13:19. See also Mark 4:14ff., and the role of Satan in Job 1–2; and 1 Pet. 5:8; Eph. 6:16; James 4:7; and 1 Tim. 5:15. Note the sense of the verb *harpazein* in Matt. 13:19 and cf. 11:12, 12:29, Mark 4:15ff., and John 10:12. See also Str.-B. IV/I: 523, 527; Manson, *Jesus*, pp. 78f., 82f.; Cranfield, *St. Mark*, pp. 59, 138; and *KGST*: 36–42.

28. Matt. 4:8f. = Luke 4:6f. Cf. Luke 22:28 where Jesus refers to the "trials" (*peirasmoi*) which he and some of his disciples have already experienced. See also Jesus' prayer, with his disciples, that they might be spared the final temptation (*peirasmos*) which was associated, at least in Matt. 6:13, with the activities of the "Evil One": Luke 11:4; Mark 14:38f. and par.

29. This, we suggest, is the basic meaning of Matt. 12:28 = Luke 11:20. For exegesis, see *KGST*: 30–35. See also Luke 10:17ff.; Matt. 10:1, 7ff.

30. Str.-B. IV/I: 524ff.; Otto Betz, *What Do We Know About Jesus?* (Westminster, 1968), pp. 58–71.

31. As. Mos. 10:1; Isa. 33:24; 35:5–10; 65:18ff. Note also the ancient tradition concerning the exclusion of the blind and lame from the Jerusalem Temple: 2 Sam. 5:6–8. The promised restoration of sight to the blind (etc.) in Isa. 35 was to be in *preparation* for the exiles' return to Zion.

32. Cf. Mark 9:43–47; Matt. 5:29f.

33. See A. Schweitzer, *The Mystery of the Kingdom of God* (Macmillan, 1950), pp. 63, 65f., 147f.; and *The Kingdom of God and Primitive Christianity* (Seabury, 1968), p. 123f. But cf. *Mystery*, p. 86: "Through his conquest of the demons, Jesus is the man of violence who compels the approach of the Kingdom." For exegesis of Matt. 11:12, see *KGST*: 36–42.

34. Robinson, *Problem of History*, p. 26ff.

35. See *KGST*: 43–49. See also Howard C. Kee: "Jesus' exorcisms have the effect of binding the 'Strong Man' [Satan] and thus presage the end of his control" (*Community of the New Age* [Westminster, 1977], p. 108).

36. Cranfield, for instance, maintains that Jesus himself, as the stronger one, had already bound Satan, but also that "Satan is clearly still strong," without resolving the tension between the two propositions (*St. Mark*, p. 137f.). Similarly, Conzelmann remarks that the meaning of Mark 3:23ff. is that Satan "is bound," but shortly afterwards, notes that "there is no doubt that . . . Satan rules" (*Jesus*, pp. 56, 58).

37. For exegesis of Luke 10:17f., see *KGST*: 50–56. See also *HJKG*: 59–64.

38. E.g., Enoch 10:11f.; 54:1–56:4; T. Levi 18:12; T. Zebulon 9:8.

39. E.g., Van der Loos, *Miracles*, p. 251ff. Cf. N. Perrin, *Jesus and the Language of the Kingdom* (Fortress, 1976), p. 42: "This saying shows that Jesus claimed that his exorcisms were a manifestation of the power of God as king." See Grässer's critique of recent theologically and politically interested interpretations of the saying, "Zum Verständnis," pp. 3–26.

40. Contrary to Conzelmann's thesis in *The Theology of St. Luke* (Harper & Row, 1961). See Fred O. Francis, "Eschatology and History in Luke–Acts," *JAAR* 37 (1969): 49–63; *KGST*: 22–29; and R.H. Hiers, "The Problem of the Delay of the Parousia in Luke–Acts," *NTS* 20 (1974): 145–155.

41. Thus Weiss, *Predigt* (1900), p. 90.

42. E.g., Jack D. Kingsbury, *Matthew: Structure, Christology, Kingdom* (Fortress, 1975), p. 141f. See Kenneth W. Clark, "Realized Eschatology," *JBL* 59 (1940): 377. Clark refers to the appearance of the expression in Judges 20:42 (LXX) and states: "This is precisely the form and syntax of Matt. 12:28 = Luke 11:20, and the context makes plain beyond all doubt the sense of pursuit and imminent contact. . . ."Cf. Obadiah v. 15 (LXX).

43. See Clark, "Realized Eschatology," pp. 367–83.

44. Mark 6:7 = Matt. 9:1 = Luke 9:1; cf. Luke 10:19; Matt. 16:18f.

45. See Matt. 12:43–45 = Luke 11:24–26.

46. See Kee, "Terminology," pp. 232–46. Thus Mark 1:25 = Luke 4:35; Mark 3:12 = Matt. 12:16 = Luke 4:41; Mark 9:25 = Matt. 17:18 = Luke 9:42. Cf. Luke 4:39 where Jesus "rebukes" the fever, Mark 4:39 and par. where he "rebukes" the stormy sea, and Mark 8:33 where he "rebukes" Peter (Satan). See also Volz' discussion of Jewish references to the preliminary exorcistic work to be carried out by the hidden messiah or Son of man: *Eschatologie*, pp. 189ff., 208f., 216.

47. Matt. 11:12 = Luke 16:16. (See *KGST*: 36–42.) Cf. Schweitzer, *Mystery*, p. 86 and W. Manson, *Jesus*, p. 84. See also S. Legasse, "L'

'Homme fort' de Luc 11:21–22," *NovT* 5 (1962): 5–7.

48. So also Johannes Weiss and Otto Betz, cited above, notes 15 and 16. See Manson, *Jesus*, p. 192f.: "Jesus by driving back the forces of the enemy is clearing a space for the Reign of God." In this case, however, exorcism would still be more a matter of preparation for the coming or establishment of the Kingdom than a mark of its presence. Manson aptly observes that in the synoptic gospels it is understood that the presence of the demons results in "the frustration of God's will to establish His reign"(p. 79).

49. Thus also Gustaf Aulen, *Jesus in Contemporary Historical Research* (Fortress, 1976), p. 102: ". . . Satan . . . is the enemy, and the breaking in of the Kingdom of God depends on his removal." Cf. Rev. 11:15.

50. So, e.g., Smith, *Jesus the Magician*, and even Paul J. Achtemeier, *Mark* (Fortress, 1975), pp. 71–81; Geza Vermes, *Jesus the Jew* (London: Collins, 1973).

Chapter V

1. E.g., W.F. Albright and C.S. Mann, *Matthew*, Anchor Bible (Doubleday, 1971), pp. 93, 323f.

2. See Sherman E. Johnson in *IB* 7:341 on Matt. 8:11: "The *metaphor* is the great banquet in the days of the Messiah." (Ital. added.) Or Hans Küng, *The Church* (Sheed & Ward, 1968), p. 50: "Images like that of the feast are not literal descriptions of the Kingdom of God, but are intended to emphasize its reality: they point not to pleasures of the table, but to communion with God and with one's fellow men." Arthur C. Cochrane concludes that such sayings mean that "the saints will . . . *see* what now they can only *believe*, namely that in Jesus the Kingdom has come . . . and that he himself is the food of eternal life" (*Eating and Drinking with Jesus* [Westminster, 1974], pp. 101–106).

3. *Viz.*, "The perfect relationship that will exist between God and that blessed eschatological community." See Norman Perrin, *The Kingdom of God in the Teaching of Jesus* (Westminster, 1963), pp. 80, 85; and his *Rediscovering the Teaching of Jesus* (Harper & Row, 1967), p. 188f. Thus also P. Vielhauer in *NTA* II: 608: "The image of the banquet [is] the symbol of community with God."

4. Perrin, *Rediscovering*, p. 163. See also pp. 106–08, 161–64.

5. Macmillan, 1960, p. 237–53. See also pp. 253–92.

6. See Mishna Rabbah on Exodus 25:8: "[God] as it were sits above the patriarchs, and the patriarchs and all the righteous sit in His midst . . . and He distributes portions to them."

7. It is not clear whether "it" (*hotou*) refers to the Passover or, more generally, to the conditions of existence, all of which would be "fulfilled," transformed, renewed or made perfect in the Kingdom of God. Both meanings may be implicit. Thus also G. Dalman: "Our

Lord, of course, did not think of the sacrificial service of the future . . . but of the Meal of the Kingdom of God itself . . .": *Jesus–Jeshua* (KTAV, 1971), p. 130. So also Erich Grässer, *Das Problem der Parusieverzögerung in den synoptischen Evangelien und in der Apostelgeschichte* (Berlin: Töpelmann, 1960), p. 53f.: "The next repetition is to take place in the Kingdom!" And see Joachim Jeremias, *New Testament Theology* (Scribner's, 1971), p. 137: "If Jesus refuses to taste wine 'until the kingly reign of God comes' (Luke 22:18), then this coming must be really near."

8. Luke 22:29–30; cf. Matt. 19:28. The relation between eating and drinking, and ruling is not explained. Those who were to be part of the King's (Messiah's) court presumably would engage in both activities. See also Rev. 3:21–22.

9. Luke 6:20–21. Cf. Matt. 5:3–6. See also Luke 16:25–26.

10. "Bread" (Gk., *artos*, like the Heb., *lechem*) may mean, more inclusively, "food."

11. Even Cochrane partly recognizes this, though he spiritualizes away the meaning of "future bread": "The prayer for bread for the morrow is therefore a prayer that Jesus will one day come in such a way that we will be able to *see* what now we can only *believe*, namely, that he is the Bread of eternal life" (*Eating and Drinking*, pp. 113–114). Like most theological traditionalist interpreters, Cochrane here (and elsewhere) refers without hesitation to the Fourth Gospel in order to substantiate his interpretation. He seems to be saying that Jesus' real concern was what "we" should be able to believe or hope for.

12. See also Luke 18:1–8, where the disciples are again urged to pray for the coming of the parousia. N. Perrin pointed out the similarity between the Lord's Prayer and the Jewish Kaddish prayer of the same period: "May he establish his Kingdom in your lifetime and in your days and in the lifetime of all the house of Israel, even speedily and at a near time" (*Jesus and the Language of the Kingdom* [Fortress, 1976], p. 28). And yet Perrin finally described the meaning of the Lord's Prayer in vague existential and humanistic rather than specifically eschatological or even Jewish terms: Its petitions are "explorations of fundamental possibilities for the experience of God as King in human life" (*ibid.*, p. 195).

13. Cf. O. Glombitza, "Das grosse Abendmahl," *NovT* 5 (1962): 10–16. Glombitza sees the pericope as an instance of Lucan teaching, to the effect that those who would eat bread in the Kingdom must share what they have now.

14. See Schweitzer, *Mysticism*, pp. 239–41, and other literature cited in Bauer, *Lexicon*, p. 297. See also Geoffrey Wainwright, *Eucharist and Eschatology* (London: Epworth, 1971), pp. 30–34.

15. *HJKG*: 64–70. Also, R.H. Hiers and C.A. Kennedy, "The Bread

and Fish Eucharist in the Gospels and Early Christian Art," *Perspectives in Religious Studies* 3 (1976): 21–47.

16. Notably: Isa. 27:1; II Esdras 6:49–52; II Bar. 29:4; Baba Bathra 74b–75a. In II Bar. 29:3–4 it is understood that the appearance of Leviathan and Behemoth, evidently as "food for all that are left," will mark the period in which the Messiah "shall *begin* to be revealed," but prior, perhaps, to his coming in glory (30:1).

17. Contrary to common supposition, none of the versions say anything about any "multiplication" of loaves and fishes. The episode was later interpreted, within the synoptic tradition, both as a wonder and in sacramental terms.

18. See Hiers and Kennedy, "Bread and Fish."

19. Schweitzer's interpretation emphasizes the fact that Jesus himself, the one who is to be the Messiah, now gives them these sacramental pieces of bread and fish, just as at the Last Supper, *he* gives his disciples bread and wine. *Geschichte der Leben-Jesu-Forschung* (Tübingen: Mohr, 1951), pp. 421, 424–25.

20. Matt. 6:11. It also comports, of course, with the first petition: "Thy Kingdom come!" and with other fundamental words of hope and admonitions regarding the coming Kingdom, such as Matt. 6:33 = Luke 12:31; Luke 12:32; 18:1–8.

21. Matt. 11:16 = Luke 7:34.

22. See *HJKG*: 48–59. We do not know, of course, whether the saying, if authentic, was originally spoken in the present context. It does, however, imply a contrast with the ascetic way of life, and there is no reason to suppose that the tradition arbitrarily or mistakenly placed it in the context of sayings about John the Baptist.

23. Mark 2:18–22 and parallels.

24. Luke 13:25–29; cf. 14:12–24. See also Rom. 14:17, and below, footnote 59.

25. Mark 11:12–14. See R.H. Hiers, "Not the Season for Figs," *JBL* 87 (1968): 394–400.

26. See *HJKG*: 71–105.

27. Enoch 24:1–25:5. Cf. the abundant fruit and inexpressible fragrance of the Garden of Eden described in II Esdras 6:44. See also II Esdras 2:12, 18f.

28. II Bar. 29:5. See p. 82.

29. *Against Heresies*, V. 33:3. See p. 84. Cf. II Bar. 29:5.

30. See esp. Mark 4:30–32; Cf. Ezek. 17:22 ff., and also Ezek. 31:6–9; Dan. 4:12, 21. The preternatural tree described in the passages in Daniel was to provide food "for all."

31. See, e.g., Mark 10:23–31; Matt. 12:32. Kingdom of God and coming age appear to have the same meaning in these and all other synoptic contexts. Jesus more frequently referred to the Kingdom of God.

32. See Jeremias, *N.T. Theology*, p. 132, and Hiers, "Not the Season," pp. 397–98.

33. It is not clear whether Jesus was recognized as Messiah on this occasion by even his own followers. See *HJKG*: 77–82.

34. So also Rudolf Bultmann, *Jesus and the Word* (Scribner's, 1958), p. 29. See R.H. Hiers, "Purification of the Temple: Preparation for the Kingdom of God," *JBL* 90 (1971): 82–90.

35. Mark 14:25 = Matt. 26:29 = Luke 22:18. See *HJKG*: 96–97.

36. E.g., Exod. 3:8; Lev. 26:3–5; Num. 13:23; Deut. 8:7–10; Josh. 5:6.

37. Gen. 1:29; 2:8–9; see Isa. 51:3; Ezek. 36:35.

38. Gen. 31:54; Exod. 24:9–11; 1 Chron. 29:22.

39. Amos 9:13–14. These verses may have been added after the beginning of the Exile. See also Joel 3:18.

40. Isa. 65:17–25; 66:22. As to eating and drinking in this new earth, see Isa. 65:13, 21, 25; 66:12–14.

41. Gen. 49:10–12 implies that the coming king or Messiah will drink wine and milk, but says nothing about his eating or drinking with others, or about any "banquet." The idea that all would eat well in the promised land is inherent in its description as a land of "milk and honey" as well as fruit and other crops in abundance, e.g., Num. 13:23–27; Deut. 6:3, 10–11; 8:7–10; 11:8–15.

42. E.g., Ps. 65:9–13; Jer. 31:5, 12; Ezek. 34:27; 36:29–30, 35; 47:10–12; Joel 2:19, 22, 24–26; 3:18; Zech. 8:12.

43. See also II Esdras 7:75. Thus also Matt. 19:28.

44. E.g., I En. 10:18–19; 24:1–25; 25:4–5; 32:3ff.

45. See also Sib. Or. III: 746–50. Here the transformation of nature is set along with the transformation or redemption of the whole creation. All creatures will dwell together forever in the peaceable Kingdom of God (vv. 751–94). See also the saying attributed by Papias to Jesus, according to Irenaeus, quoted on p. 84.

46. II Bar. 29:5. See also I En. 10:18–19.

47. II Bar. 29:4. Cf. II Esdr. 6:49–52.

48. II En. 8:2. See also 8:1, 3–8; Apoc. of Moses 37:4; and II Esdras 7:123; 8:52. Str.–B. find the idea of a heavenly garden in a few places in rabbinic writings. See IV/2: 1131f., 1137–39.

49. II En. 8:5(A) also tells of springs sending forth honey, milk, oil, and wine.

50. See II Esdras 2:12f., 18, 35–38; 7:123. Some of these passages may reflect Christian editorial activity.

51. See p. 79.

52. Midrash Rabbah on Ex. 25:7f., Socino translation. For further such passages, see Str.–B. IV/2: 886–90, 948–54, 1131–33. Str.–B. observe that there is no lack of passages which speak of a real, i.e., bodily, eating and drinking (*ibid.*, p. 1132[1]).

53. See also Str. –B. IV/2: 886f.
54. See John F. Priest, "The Messiah and the Meal in IQSa," *JBL* 82 (1963): 95–100; see also his article, "Messianic Banquet," *IDB* Supplementary Volume (Abingdon: 1976): 591f.
55. See Bertil Gärtner, *The Temple and the Community in Qumran and the New Testament* (Cambridge Univ. Press, 1965), pp. 10–15.
56. Acts 1:6, 11; 2:16–21, 39–42, 46f.; 3:19–21.
57. Luke 24:30, 35, 41–43; John 21:9–14; Acts 10:41; Justin, *Dial.* 51:2.
58. Thus Paul speaks of dying and rising with Christ, and the new creation which is in part already actualized: see, e.g., Rom. 6:3–14; 7:4–6; 8:22–24; 2 Cor. 5:17. Paul was, of course, also oriented toward the future parousia, e.g.: 1 Cor. 6:3, 9f.; 7:29–31; 11:26; 13:8–13; 15:51–53; 16:22; Phil. 1:10; 3:20f.
59. Rom. 14:17. Paul's point here is that eating and drinking do not *per se* constitute the Kingdom of God, the distinctive marks of which are righteousness, peace, joy in the Holy Spirit, consideration for others, and faith. He probably meant that these characteristics are what should be important to those who aspire to the Kingdom, not what one eats or drinks. Cf. 1 Cor. 8:1–13; 10:14–31. In addition, Paul may have meant to oppose the enthusiastic and pretentious claim of some Christians who mistook their eating and drinking together to mean that they already were living in the Messianic age. Cf. 1 Cor. 4:8, 20.
60. Didachē 9:4; 10:5f.
61. Ep. Apost., 15–17. See, however, sect. 19, where it is said that in the place of rest (heaven) "there is neither eating nor drinking." This viewpoint may derive from Rom. 14:17. The place of rest and incorruptibility, like Paradise in II En. 8, is located above the earth or creation (Ep. Apost. 19). Paul, likewise, had expected that Christians would experience salvation with Christ "in the air" or "in heaven." 1 Thess. 4:17; Phil. 3:20. But cf. Irenaeus, *Against Heresies*, V, 33:1–3, quoted below and on p. 85.
62. For other references in Revelation to eating and drinking in the Messianic age, see 2:17; 7:16f.; and 19:9. Cf. 22:2.
63. Rev. 22:1f. Cf. Ezek. 47:12; II Esdras 2:18f. See also Rev. 22:14, 19.
64. Irenaeus, *Against Heresies* V, 33:3. Quoted from Cyril C. Richardson, ed., *Early Christian Fathers*, LCC vol. I (Westminster, 1953), pp. 394–95. Cf. Isa. 11:1–9. On the fruitful trees of Paradise, see also *Odes of Solomon* 11:12–24; for critical text and notes see J.H. Charlesworth, *The Odes of Solomon* (Oxford, 1973), pp. 52–59.
65. *Against Heresies* V, 33:1.
66. *Against Heresies* V, 33:2.
67. 1 Cor. 15:35–50.

68. Nevertheless, Wainwright finds that subsequent liturgies, particularly in Eastern Christianity, continued for several centuries to understand the eucharist in connection with its anticipated fulfillment in the future Kingdom of God. See his *Eucharist and Eschatology*, pp. 47–56.

Chapter VI

1. We do not, however, accept the commonly held but distorted understanding as to the latter category. See Preface, n. 10, and Chap. I, p. 10.

2. See Klaus Koch, *The Rediscovery of Apocalyptic*, SBT, 2d ser., no. 22 (London: SCM, 1972).

3. Nevertheless, many Christian interpreters who hold this view suggest that Jesus' Jewish contemporaries (if not all later Jews) are to be faulted for failing to recognize Jesus as "the Messiah."

4. See esp. the articles by William A. Beardslee and Theodore J. Weeden, Sr., in *JAAR* 47 (1979), no. one:57–72, 97–120.

5. E.g., Hermann Schuster, "Die konsequente Eschatologie in der Interpretation des neuen Testaments," ZNW 47 (1956): 22. "Is not the picture of Jesus thereby so changed in its essence that he ceases to be Lord of our faith?"

6. During the past several decades, N.T. scholars have shown considerable interest in form and redaction criticism and more recently, in structuralist analysis. Critics using these methods focus upon the tasks of tracing the history or development of tradition prior to its literary "fixation" (or composition), detecting theological or other interests on the part of the editors (or "redactors"), and defining the "structure" or organizational arrangement (or "plot") of a given writing by reference to various presumably universal literary or dramatic models. The result, functionally, is to turn attention away from the problematic questions associated with the character and significance of the historical Jesus, and toward such theologically less troublesome (and less consequential) questions as the understanding or intention of the churches or the evangelists.

7. E.g., the claim that Schweitzer depicted Jesus as a wild apocalyptic fanatic, or his "interim ethics" as a set of "rigid rules."

8. R.H. Hiers and D.L. Holland, "Introduction" to Johannes Weiss, *Jesus' Proclamation of the Kingdom of God* (Fortress, 1971), pp. 43–49.

9. E.F. Scott. See Chap. III in this volume, pp. 52, 54, 60.

10. Arthur C. Cochrane, *Eating and Drinking with Jesus* (Westminster, 1974), pp. 113–14.

11. Interpreters find Jesus' message of coming Judgment and his "interim ethics" morally as well as theologically problematic.

12. Only a few synoptic passages can be construed to mean that

Jesus thought the Kingdom of God present in some way. Those most often cited are Matt. 11:11–12, Matt. 12:28 = Luke 11:20, Luke 17:20–21, and some of the parables of growth. But see *KGST* chaps. 2–5, 7 and 9.

13. Thus also L.E. Keck, "The Historical Jesus and Christology," *Perkins Journal* 29 (1976): 19–25.

14. Albert Schweitzer, *The Quest of the Historical Jesus* (Macmillan, 1969), p. 398. This statement has misled more than one reader to conclude that Schweitzer meant that there never had been an historical Jesus. Schweitzer's point was that the non-eschatological Jesus depicted by rationalist and liberal interpreters never existed. The historical Jesus was the eschatological Jesus represented in the synoptic gospels.

Chapter VII

1. Some such premise is assumed, e.g., in A.C. Cochrane's syllogism: Jesus undoubtedly prophesied the coming of the Kingdom of God. The resurrection occurred. Therefore "the resurrection was the parousia." A.C. Cochrane, *Eating and Drinking with Jesus* (Westminster, 1974), p. 103.

2. Albert Schweitzer, *Out of My Life and Thought* (Mentor, 1953), p. 46.

3. Traditional Christianity has tended to overlook the fact that Paul, like Jesus, reportedly looked for the parousia in the near future. Paul expected it to occur in his own lifetime. See, e.g., 1 Thess. 4:15–17; Phil. 3:20.

4. New Testament scholars have recognized for the greater part of the past hundred years that the Fourth Gospel is best understood as the faith statement of a particular individual or community which was written down near the end of the first century A.D. Periodic efforts to discover historical tradition in the Fourth Gospel have not yielded any substantial results. The impetus for such efforts largely derives from interpreters' desire to find an historical Jesus more congruent with the faith-understanding of traditional Christianity than the Jesus portrayed in the synoptic gospels.

5. Johannes Weiss, *Jesus' Proclamation of the Kingdom of God* (Fortress, 1971), pp. 134–35.

6. Schweitzer referred especially to Jesus' ethic or religion of love, and to his ethic of self-devotion to others.

7. Often a particular Bible is made into a supposedly absolute authority, e.g., the King James or Schofield versions. The Jesus invoked, as we have seen, often is one made in the image of the interpreter's theology. This desire for absolute certainty or authority might be examined further in studies of the psychology of religion. But viewed from the standpoint of biblical faith and the "protestant principle," all

such attempts to locate final authority other than in God are expressions of mistrust and idolatry.

8. See Schweitzer's, M.D. thesis, *The Psychiatric Study of Jesus* (Beacon, 1948). Schweitzer found that the proponents of psychohistory whose work he examined were unaware of the results of the previous several decades of New Testament research, and thus innocently supposed that the Fourth Gospel provided direct historical evidence of Jesus' sayings and personality. Consequently, they enthusiastically pronounced him a megalomaniac (on the basis of the recurrent "I am" statements) or a schizophrenic (by reading, alternately, synoptic and Fourth Gospel traditions). These psychohistorians also had no understanding of the character and importance of eschatological beliefs in first century Judaism or Christianity, and so felt justified in questioning Jesus' sanity on the basis of their simple-minded assumption that anyone who thought the world about to end must have been deranged!

9. The writer of the Fourth Gospel did not hesitate to represent Jesus' behaviour in this fashion, e.g., John 11:1–44, esp. vv. 4–6, 14–15, 39–43.

10. The claim that Bible prophecies point to the end of history or "Second Coming" in our own time may also be little more than a technique for prompting conversions at revival meetings. See William D. Apel, "The Lost World of Billy Graham," *Review of Religious Research* 20 (1979): 138–149.

11. It is only in the Fourth Gospel that Jesus promises eternal life to those who believe in him. The synoptic Jesus never asks others to believe in himself, but he does call for their trust or belief in God.

12. In a letter to John Adams dated Oct. 12, 1813, Thomas Jefferson described Jesus' teaching as "the most sublime and benevolent code of morals which has ever been offered to man" (Thomas Jefferson, *The Life and Morals of Jesus of Nazareth* [Chicago: Manz Engraving Co., n.d.], p. 15). Others since, especially liberal Protestants, often have said much the same thing.

13. The instruction by the risen Jesus to baptize disciples of all nations (Matt. 28:19) is commonly thought to derive from the early church. See John Reumann, *Jesus in the Church's Gospels* (Fortress, 1968), pp. 316, 469, n. 54. Cf. John 3:22 and 4:1f.

14. The command to repeat the Lord's supper appears only in 1 Cor. 11:25.

15. The Fourth Gospel does not describe the last supper; however, it attributes to Jesus sayings about his body and blood which appear to presuppose readers' familiarity with the eucharist, e.g., John 6:53–58. Such sayings probably gave rise to Ignatius' description of the eucharist as the "medicine of immortality," and the later Catholic doctrine of transubstantiation.

16. "Pictures at an Exhibition: Reflections on Exegesis and Theology," *JAAR* 47 (1979):17.

17. The Gospels of John and Thomas are early instances of this pattern. Other early Christians, employing the epistle or letter format, ascribed their ideas and writings to various apostles, e.g., 1 and 2 Timothy, James, and 2 Peter.

18. See H. Richard Niebuhr's description of the ethics of henotheism or tribal faith in modern times, *Radical Monotheism and Western Culture* (Harper & Row, 1960), pp. 24–37. In contrast to those who cared only about members of their own ethnic group or class, Jesus called his hearers to concern for those beyond the pale: e.g., Matt. 5:46–48 (cf. John 13:34–35); Matt. 25:31–46; Luke 10:25–37, 16:19–31.

19. American culture has particularly tended to idolize "the individual." In part, this emphasis has served to excuse or justify pursuit of self-interest and denial of responsibility to and for others. See, e.g., the critiques by Reinhold Niebuhr, *The Children of Light and The Children of Darkness* (Scribner's, 1944), pp. 42–85, Robert Bellah, *The Broken Covenant* (Seabury, 1975).

20. The synoptic Jesus expected that the Kingdom of God would be established on earth, a transformed earth. See, e.g., Matt. 5:5; 6:10. Old Testament prophetic traditions are more explicit as to the character of life in the coming age, e.g.: swords would be beaten into ploughshares (Isa. 2:4), the wolf would dwell in peace with the lamb, and children would play with once deadly snakes (Isa. 11:6, 8).

21. See Perry Miller, *Errand into the Wilderness* (Harper & Row, 1964), esp. Chap. 1.

22. See H. Richard Niebuhr, *The Kingdom of God in America* (Harper & Row, 1959), pp. 128–132.

23. For example, where did the Kingdom of God go in the meantime, or what, if anything, might the partial presence of the Kingdom of God mean?

24. Though many of the 18th century French philosophes considered it a mark of their advanced state of enlightenment to dispense with all previous moral standards, modern culture was not original in its espousal of this doctrine. The editor of the book of Judges took note of the consequences that obtained when "everyman did what was right in his own eyes" (Judg. 17:6–21:25). The writer of Wisd. Sol. 1:16–2:24 also recognized the popularity of this sort of life style in his day, and discerned its attendant pretentions and cruelties.

25. Mark 10:45; 14:24; cf. Isa. 53:11.

26. See H. Richard Niebuhr, *Christ and Culture* (Harper, 1951), p. 22: "The ethics of Jesus does not seem to depend on his view of history any more than his view of history depends on his ethics; both are reflections of his faith in God."

27. E.g., Matt. 25:31–45; Mark 10:17–22; Luke 10:25–37.

28. Modern humanistic literary critics sometimes experience similar difficulty in recognizing the importance of religious beliefs, e.g., to 17th and 18th century writers. Likewise, modern psychohistorians who fail to recognize the central role of religious beliefs in the figures they attempt to "analyze" are tempted to account for everything in terms of theories derived from their own world view. See, e.g., Roland H. Bainton, "Psychiatry and History: An Examination of Erikson's *Young Man Luther*," in Roger A. Johnson, ed., *Psychohistory and Religion* (Fortress, 1977), pp. 19–56.

Index of Topics, Terms, and Biblical Names

Index of Post-Biblical Names

Index of Gospel Citations

DATE DUE

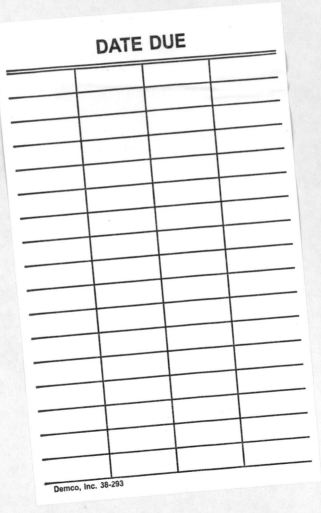

Demco, Inc. 38-293